MORE PRAISE FOR *FLUENT FOREVER*

"**Never before have I seen a language-learning method—or method for learning anything!—that synchs up so perfectly with our current scientific understanding of how memory works.** I now understand why my past attempts to learn other languages (Spanish, German, Latin) have left me with little more than a smattering of near-random vocabulary words, and I'm inspired to try again. *Fluent Forever* promises a fun, personalized learning regimen that is sure to wire a new tongue into your brain with speed and simplicity. And Wyner's sharp wit will keep you entertained along the way! **I've never been so excited to challenge my mind.**"

—Karen Schrock Simring, contributing editor at *Scientific American Mind*

"***Fluent Forever* is the book I wish I had had during my numerous failed attempts at learning different languages.** It's a refreshingly fun and engaging guide that shows you how to language hack your brain. Wyner's done all the hard work so that the reader can actually enjoy the process of becoming fluent in a language quickly!"

—Nelson Dellis, 2011 and 2012 USA Memory Champion

"*Fluent Forever* more than meets the daunting challenge of learning a new language by giving the reader a solid game plan based on how people *actually* learn and memorize information. **From the first chapter, I couldn't wait to get started using Wyner's techniques and tons of resources. His writing is engaging, smart, and conversational, making learning a real joy.** If you've ever wanted to become fluent in another language, do yourself a favor and start reading *Fluent Forever* now."

—Melanie Pinola, contributor writer for Lifehacker.com and author of *LinkedIn in 30 Minutes*

"**This is the book I'd use next time I want to learn a new language.** It employs an intelligent mix of the latest methods for learning a language on your own using the Web, apps, and voice-training tips in an accelerated time frame."

Kelly, senior maverick at *Wired* and author of *What Technology Wants*

"I know what you're thinking: *But learning a new language is soooo hard! The solution? Stop being a whiner and start reading Wyner.* **This book is a winner! Guaranteed to rewire your brain in as many languages as you'd like.**"

—Joel Saltzman, author of *Shake That Brain!: How to Create Winning Solutions and Have Fun While You're at It*

"**An excellent book** . . . Wyner writes in an engaging and accessible way, weaving in his personal language journey. His method, proven by his own achievements, is clear: focus on pronunciation, avoid translation, and use spaced repetition extensively. And he offers lots of specific techniques to make sure you'll never forget what you've learned. **I'd recommend this book to anyone who is serious—not just aspiring but really *serious*—about becoming fluent in a foreign language.**"

—Kevin Chen, cofounder of italki.com

"**Mash up the DNA of Steve Jobs and Aristotle and add training in engineering and opera, and you get Gabriel Wyner, whose ingeniously elegant system helps us knuckleheads learn not just foreign languages but, well, *everything*.** Autodidacts rejoice!"

—Jay Heinrichs, author of *Thank You for Arguing* and *Word Hero*

"Americans refuse to realize that all languages are foreign—yes, including English. It's time we learned how to speak like the rest of the world: in more ways than one. **This book is a hilarious toolbox that helps you get a head start.** Pick a foreign language (yes, including English) and *voilà: el futuro es tuyo.* **High-five to Gabriel Wyner!**"

—Ilan Stavans, author of *Dictionary Days: A Defining Passion*

Fluent Forever

HOW TO LEARN ANY LANGUAGE FAST

AND NEVER FORGET IT

GABRIEL WYNER

 HARMONY

BOOKS · NEW YORK

Copyright © 2014 by Gabriel Wyner

All rights reserved.

Published in the United States by Harmony Books, an imprint of the Crown Publishing Group, a division of Random House LLC, a Penguin Random House Company, New York.
www.crownpublishing.com

Harmony Books is a registered trademark, and the Circle colophon is a trademark of Random House LLC.

Library of Congress Cataloging-in-Publication Data is available upon request.

ISBN 978-0-385-34811-9
eBook ISBN 978-0-385-34810-2

Printed in the United States of America

Illustrations by Robert Bull
Cover design by Nupoor Gordon
Cover illustration: © Maydaymayday/Getty Images

20 19 18 17

First Edition

To the thrill of the journey

CONTENTS

3: Sound Play   54

4: Word Play and the Symphony of a Word   83

5: Sentence Play   108

6: The Language Game   143

The Toolbox

CHAPTER 1

Introduction: Stab, Stab, Stab

If you talk to a man in a language he understands, that goes to his head. If you talk to him in his language, that goes to his heart.

—Nelson Mandela

Americans who travel abroad for the first time are often shocked to discover that, despite all the progress that has been made in the last 30 years, many foreign people still speak in foreign languages.

—Dave Barry

Language learning is a sport. I say this as someone who is in no way qualified to speak about sports; I joined the fencing team in high school in order to get out of gym class. Still, stabbing friends with pointy metal objects resembles language learning more than you might think. Your goal in fencing is to stab people *automatically*. You spend time learning the names of the weapons and the rules of the game, and you drill the proper posture, every parry, riposte, and lunge. Finally, you play the game, hoping to reach that magical moment when you forget about the rules: Your arm moves of its own accord, you deftly parry your friend's sword, and you stab him squarely in the chest. Point!

We want to walk up to someone, open our mouths, forget the rules, and speak automatically. This goal can seem out of reach because languages seem hard, but they're not. There is no such thing as a "hard" language; any idiot can speak whatever language his parents spoke when he was a child. The real challenge lies in finding a path that conforms to the demands of a busy life.

In the midst of my own busy life as an opera singer, I needed to learn German, Italian, French, and Russian. Out of those experiences, I found the underpinnings for this book. My methods are the results of an obsessive need to tinker, research, and tinker again. My language-learning toolbox has, over time, turned into a well-oiled machine that transforms fixed amounts of daily time into noticeable, continuous improvement in my languages and in the languages of every person I've taught. In sharing it, I hope to enable you to visit the peculiar world of language learning. In the process, you'll better understand the inner workings of your mind and the minds of others. You'll learn to speak a new language, too.

BEGINNINGS

So far, my favorite moment of this crazy language-learning adventure took place in a Viennese subway station in 2012. I was returning home from a show when I saw a Russian colleague coming toward me. Our common language had always been German, and so, in that language, we greeted and caught up on the events of the past year. Then I dropped the bomb. "You know, I speak Russian now," I told her in Russian.

The expression on her face was priceless. Her jaw actually dropped, like in the cartoons. She stammered, "What? When? How?" as we launched into a long conversation in Russian about language learning, life, and the intersection between the two.

My first attempts to learn languages were significantly less jaw dropping. I went to Hebrew school for seven years. We sang songs, learned the alphabet, lit lots of candles, drank lots of grape juice, and didn't learn much of anything. Well, except the alphabet; I had that alphabet *nailed*.

In high school, I fell in love with my Russian teacher, Mrs. Nowakowsky. She was smart and pretty, she had a wacky Russian last name, and I did whatever she asked, whenever she asked. Five years later, I had learned a few phrases, memorized a few poems, and learned that alphabet quite well, thank you very much. By the end of it, I got the impression that something was seriously wrong. Why can I only remember alphabets? Why was everything else so *hard*?

Fast-forward to June of 2004, at the start of a German immersion program for opera singers in Vermont. At the time, I was an engineer with an oversized singing habit. This habit demanded that I learn basic German, French, and Italian, and I decided that jumping into the pool was the only way I'd ever succeed. Upon my arrival, I was to sign a paper pledging to use German as my only form of communication for seven weeks, under threat of expulsion without refund. At the time, this seemed unwise, as I didn't speak *a word of German*. I signed it anyway. Afterward, some advanced students approached me, smiled, and said, "Hallo." I stared at them blankly for a moment and replied, "Hallo." We shook hands.

Five insane weeks later, I sang my heart out in a German acting class, found a remote location on campus, and stealthily called my girlfriend. "I think I'm going to be an opera singer," I told her in whispered English. On that day, I decided to become fluent in the languages demanded by my new profession. I went back to Middlebury College in Vermont and took German again. This time, I reached fluency. I moved to Austria for my master's studies. While living in Europe in 2008, I went to Perugia, Italy, to learn Italian. Two years later, I became a cheater.

CHEATERS OCCASIONALLY PROSPER:
THE THREE KEYS TO LANGUAGE LEARNING

This book would not exist if I had not cheated on a French test. I'm not proud of it, but there it is. First, some background. The Middlebury Language Schools offer five levels of classes: absolute beginner, "false" beginner (people who have forgotten what they've learned), intermediate, advanced, and near fluent. At the time of the test, I was an absolute beginner in French, but I had already learned a Romance language, and I wanted to be with the "false" beginners. So, for my third stint at Middlebury, I cheated on the online placement test, using Google Translate and some grammar websites. Don't tell Middlebury.

A month later, I received my regrettable results. "Welcome and congratulations!" it began. "You have been placed in the intermediate level!" Shit. I had three months to learn a year's worth of French or look like an idiot at the entrance interview. These interviews are serious business. You sit in a room with a *real, live French person*, you chat for fifteen minutes about life, and you leave with a final class placement. You can't cheat; you can either speak French or make sad faces and wave your hands around like a second-rate Parisian mime.

As I was in the middle of completing master's degrees in opera and art song, the only free time I had was an hour on the subway every day and all day on Sundays. I frantically turned to the Internet to figure out how to learn a language faster. What I found was surprising: there are a number of incredibly powerful language-learning tools out there, but no single program put all of the new methods together.

I encountered three basic keys to language learning:
1. Learn pronunciation first.
2. Don't translate.
3. Use spaced repetition systems.

The first key, **learn pronunciation first**, came out of my music conservatory training (and is widely used by the military and the missionaries of the Mormon church). Singers learn the pronunciation of languages first because we need to sing in these languages long before we have the time to learn them. In the course of mastering the sounds of a language, our ears become attuned to those sounds, making vocabulary acquisition, listening comprehension, and speaking come much more quickly. While we're at it, we pick up a snazzy, accurate accent.

The second key, **don't translate**, was hidden within my experiences at the Middlebury Language Schools in Vermont. Not only can a beginning student skip translating, but it was an essential step in learning how to think in a foreign language. It made language learning *possible*. This was the fatal flaw in my earlier attempts to learn Hebrew and Russian: I was practicing translation instead of speaking. By throwing away English, I could spend my time building fluency instead of decoding sentences word by word.

The third key, **use spaced repetition systems** (SRSs), came from language blogs and software developers. SRSs are flash cards on steroids. Based upon your input, they create a custom study plan that drives information deep into your long-term memory. They supercharge memorization, and they have yet to reach mainstream use.

A growing number of language learners on the Internet were taking advantage of SRSs, but they were using them to memorize translations. Conversely, no-translation proponents like Middlebury and Berlitz were using comparatively antiquated study methods, failing to take advantage of the new computerized learning tools. Meanwhile, nobody but the classical singers and the Mormons seemed to care much about pronunciation.

I decided to use all of these methods at once. I used memorization software on my smartphone to get the French into my head, and I made sure that none of my flash cards had a word of English on them. I began making flash cards for the pronunciation rules, added a bunch of pictures for the nouns and some verbs, learned the verb conjugations, and then built up to simple French definitions of more abstract concepts. By June, in my hour a day on the subway, I had learned three thousand words and grammar concepts. When I arrived at Middlebury, I waited in a room for my entrance interview in French. This interview was meant to ensure that I hadn't done anything stupid, like cheat on my online placement test. It was the first time I had ever spoken French in my life. The teacher sat down and said, "*Bonjour,*" and I responded right back with the very first word that came into my brain: "*Bonjour.*"

So far, so good. As our conversation evolved, I was amazed to find that I knew all the words she was saying, and I knew all the words I needed to respond. I could think in French! It was halting, but it was French. I was stunned. Middlebury bumped me into the advanced class. In those seven weeks, I read ten books, wrote seventy pages' worth of essays, and my vocabulary grew to forty-five hundred words. By the beginning of August, I was fluent in French.

The Game Plan

What is fluency? Each of us will find a different answer to this question. The term is imprecise, and it means a little less every time someone writes another book, article, or spam email with a title like "U Can B FLUENT in 7 DAY5!1!" Still, we maintain an image of fluency in our minds: a summer afternoon in a Parisian café, casually chatting up the waitress without needing to worry about verb conjugations or missing words in our vocabularies. Beyond that café, we must decide individually how far we wish to go.

I would confidently describe myself as fluent in German. I've lived in Austria for six years and will happily discuss anything with anyone, but I certainly needed to dance around a few missing words to get out of a €200 fine for my rental car's broken gas cap. (Apparently, the word for "gas cap" is *Tankdeckel*, and the words for "I don't give a damn if I'm the first person to drive this car, the spring holding the gas cap closed was defective" start with *"Das ist mir völlig Wurst . . ."* and go on from there.) You'll have to determine for yourself whether your image of fluency includes political discussions with friends, attending poetry readings, working as a secret agent, or lecturing on quantum physics at the Sorbonne.

We struggle to reach *any* degree of fluency because there is *so* much to remember. The rulebook of the language game is too long. We go to classes that discuss the rulebook, we run drills about one rule or another, but we never get to play the game. On the off chance that we ever reach the end of a rulebook, we've forgotten most of the beginning already. Moreover, we've ignored the *other* book (the vocabulary book), full of thousands upon thousands of words that are just as hard to remember as the rules.

Forgetting is our greatest foe, and we need a plan to defeat it. What's the classic language-learning success story? A guy moves to Spain, falls in love with a Spanish girl, and spends every waking hour practicing the language until he is fluent within the year. This is the immersion experience, and it defeats forgetting with brute force. In large part, our proud, Spanish-speaking hero is successful because he never had any time to forget. Every day, he swims in an ocean of Spanish; how could he forget what he had learned? I learned German in this way, given an opportunity to leave my job, move to Vermont, and cut off all ties to the English-speaking world for two full summers. Immersion is a wonderful experience, but if you have steady work, a dog, a family, or a bank account in need of refilling, you can't readily drop everything and devote *that* much of your life to learning a language. We need a more practical way to get the right information into our heads and prevent it from leaking out of our ears.

I'm going to show you how to stop forgetting, so you can get to the actual game. And I'm going to show you what to remember, so that once you start playing the game, you're good at it. Along the way, we'll rewire your ears to hear new sounds, and rewire your tongue to master a new accent. We'll investigate the makeup of words, how grammar assembles those words into thoughts, and how to make those thoughts come out of your mouth without needing to waste time translating. We'll make the most of your limited time, investigating which words to learn first, how to use mnemonics to memorize abstract concepts faster, and how to improve your reading, writing, listening, and speaking skills as quickly and effectively as possible.

I want you to understand how to use the tools I've found along the way, but I also want you to understand *why* they work. Language learning is one of the most intensely personal journeys you can undertake.

You are going into your own mind and altering the way you *think*. If you're going to spend months or years working at that goal, you'll need to believe in these methods and make them your own. If you know how to approach the language game, you can beat it. I hope to show you the shortest path to that goal, so that you can forget the rules and start playing already.

After I learned German, I thought, "*Ach!* If I could just go back in time and tell myself a few things, I would have had a *much* easier time with this language!" I had precisely the same thought after Italian, French, Russian (which I finally learned in 2012), and Hungarian (2013's project). This book is my time machine. If I squint my eyes just right, then *you* are monolingual *me* from nine years ago, and I'm creating a time paradox by helping you avoid all of the pitfalls and potholes that led me to make my time machine in the first place. You know how it is.

HOW LONG DOES FLUENCY TAKE?

To estimate the time you'll need, we'll need to consider your fluency goals, the language(s) you already know, the language you're learning, and your daily time constraints. As I said earlier, there is no such thing as a hard language. There *are*, however, languages that will be harder for *you* to learn, because they aren't in the same family as the language(s) you already know. Japanese is difficult for English speakers to learn for the same reason that English is difficult for Japanese speakers; there are precious few words and grammatical concepts that overlap in both languages, not to mention the entirely different alphabets involved. In contrast, an English speaker learning French has much less work to do. English vocabulary is 28 percent French and 28 percent Latin. As soon as an English speaker learns proper French pronunciation, he already knows thousands of words.

The US Foreign Service Institute ranks languages by their approximate difficulty for native English speakers (see Appendix 2). In my experience, their estimates are spot-on. As they predicted, Russian (a level 2 language) took me nearly twice as much time as French (a level 1 language), and I suspect that Japanese (a level 3 language) will take me twice as much time as Russian. I reached a comfortable intermediate "I can think in French and use a monolingual dictionary" level in three months, working for an hour a day (plus weekend binges), and a similar level for Russian in six months at thirty to forty-five minutes a day (plus weekend binges). I then used seven to eight weeks of intensive immersion to bring both of those languages to advanced "comfortable in a cafe, comfortable chatting about whatever, somewhat uncomfortable describing car problems" levels. I've seen similar results with my students. Without an immersion program, I suspect advanced French would take five to eight months, working for thirty to forty-five minutes per day on your own. Level 2 languages like Russian and Hebrew should be twice that, and level 3 languages like Chinese, Arabic, Japanese, and Korean should take four times as long as French.

These harder languages do take time, but there's no reason you can't learn them. You've already met the only prerequisite: you're interested. Think about exercise for a moment. To succeed in an exercise routine, we need to enjoy it or we'll drop it. Most of us don't have six-pack abs or fit into a size 2 dress. I've certainly tried for the abs (I gave up on the size 2 dress long ago), but I never succeeded, because I rarely *enjoy* exercise. Those of us who *do*, succeed. Successful gym rats learn to find the joy (and endorphins) in grueling daily workouts. The rest of us can push ourselves into the gym with willpower, but if we don't find it enjoyable, we're unlikely to continue for the six to twenty-four months we need to see results. Fitness plans keep shrinking in time—30-Minute Fitness, the 10-Minute Solution, Ultimate Physical Fitness in 5 Minutes, the 3-Minute Workout—in an attempt to make something that's difficult seem more palatable. But no matter what, we're still going to be a sweaty, achy mess at the end of it, and getting ourselves fired up to do it every day is hard in the short term and harder in the long term.

As long as language learning is hard, we'll run into the same problems. Who enjoys drilling grammar and memorizing word lists? Even if I promise you Fluency in 30 Seconds a Day, you're going to have a hard time sticking to it if it's unpleasant.

We're going to drop the boring stuff and find something more exciting. The tools I've assembled here are effective. Much more important, they're fun to use. We enjoy learning; it's what addicts us to reading newspapers, books, and magazines and browsing websites like Lifehacker, Facebook, Reddit, and the *Huffington Post*. Every time we see a new factoid (e.g., "In AD 536, a dust cloud blotted out the sun over Europe and Asia for an entire year, causing famines that wiped out populations from Scandinavia to China. No one knows what caused it"), the pleasure centers of our brains burst into activity, and we click on the next link. In this book, we're going to addict ourselves to language learning. The discovery process for new words and grammar will be our new Facebook, the assembly process for new flash cards will be a series of quick arts-and-crafts projects, and the memorization process will be a fast-paced video game that's just challenging enough to keep us interested.

There's no coincidence here; we learn better when we're having fun, and in looking for the fastest ways to learn, I naturally ended up with the most enjoyable methods. My favorite thing about language learning is this: I can basically play video games as much as I like without suffering deep, existential regret afterward (e.g., "I can't *believe* I just wasted six hours of my life playing stupid games on Facebook"). I spend thirty to sixty minutes a day playing on my smartphone or watching TV. (The TV series *Lost* is *awesome* in Russian.) I get a language out of it, I feel productive, and I have fun. What's not to like?

Let's learn how to play.

DO THIS NOW: THE PATH FORWARD

An organizational note: over the course of this book, I'm going to introduce you to a *lot* of tools and resources. If you ever forget which one is which, you'll find them all in the Glossary of Tools and Terms at the end of this book, along with a brief explanation. With that said, let's get started.

I intend to teach you *how* to learn, rather than what to learn. We can't discuss every word, grammatical system, and pronunciation system that exists, so you'll need some additional resources specific to your language of choice. Speaking of which, you should probably begin by choosing a language to learn.

Choose Your Language

Choose a language based upon employment opportunities, difficulty, availability of resources, or number of speakers, but in the end, choose a language that you *like*. A reader on my website once asked me whether he should learn Russian or French. His relatives spoke Russian, he *loved* the culture, but he was worried about the difficulty. French seemed like a safe alternative.

Never settle for *safe* when you can have fun instead. Your language will become a constant companion, living in your head. If you *like* your language, then you'll have fun studying it, and when you have fun, you learn faster.

You have many resources at your disposal.

Language Books

Get yourself some books. Someone sat down and spent months (or years, heaven forbid) organizing the information you need, and you can have all of that effort in the palm of your hand for $15–$25. Thank you, Herr Gutenberg. In Appendix 1, I list my favorite picks for the top eleven languages you're most likely to be studying. If your language isn't there, go to my website, *Fluent-Forever.com*. I aim to have book recommendations for as many languages as people want to learn.

GET THESE NOW

A good grammar book will walk you through your language's grammar in a thoughtful, step-by-step manner.[1] On the way, it will introduce you to a thousand words or so, give you a bunch of examples and exercises, and provide you with an answer key. You will skip 90 percent of the exercises in the book, but having them around will save you a lot of time once we begin to learn grammar. If the book gives you "Englishy" pronunciation for each word (*Bonjour:* bawn-JURE, *Tschüss:* chewss), I give you permission to burn it and find a different one. Walking into a Parisian cafe and saying "bawn-JURE" is a good way to get ignored indefinitely by the waiter. If your new book comes with a CD, then so much the better.

There are two pitfalls here to avoid. First, avoid books systematically detailing every single solitary rule and detail and exception, all at once, in an uncontrollable torrent of grammatical despair. I used to love these books—until I tried learning from them. These are technical tomes that lay out the entire grammatical system of a language in giant flowcharts. They're lovely reference manuals but are very difficult to use in a step-by-step manner.

Second, be wary of most classroom books, especially those without an answer key. Books designed for classrooms are often sparse on explanations, because they expect that the teacher will be able to handle any confusion. You'll often have more luck with a self-study book.

A phrase book is a wonderful reference, as it's difficult to find handy phrases like "Am I under arrest?" and "Where are you taking me?" in a dictionary. Phrase books from the Lonely Planet company are cheap and come with a tiny, extremely practical dictionary in the back. We'll use *this* dictionary when we learn our first words, because it's a lot easier (and faster) to skim through than a real dictionary.

---

1. They'll do it, for the most part, in English. Yes, this breaks my no-English rule, but you know what they say about rules and breaking things.

We'll grudgingly allow "bawn-JURE" here but only because there are no phrase books without it.

CONSIDER THESE

A frequency dictionary typically contains the most important five thousand words of your target language, arranged in order of frequency. (The number one word in English, *the,* shows up once every twenty-five words.) These books are amazing, with lovingly picked examples and translations. They'll save you *tons* of time and they take so much work to compile that we should be throwing money and flowers at the feet of their authors. There are some online frequency lists, but they're not as good as the paper versions. Frequency dictionaries don't exist in every language yet, but if your language has one, you win. Get it.

 A pronunciation guide will walk you through the entire pronunciation system of your language, with the help of recordings and diagrams of your mouth and tongue. For many languages, you can find guidebooks with CDs devoted entirely to pronunciation. They're *wonderful* resources and well worth the purchase. In addition, I've made it my personal mission to develop computerized pronunciation trainers in as many languages as I can. These trainers can do a few neat things that textbooks can't, and we'll discuss them in depth in Chapter 3. You won't be able to find a guidebook or trainer in *every* language, but when they exist, they're extraordinarily helpful.

 You also want to find two dictionaries. It is up to you whether you find them online or in print. The first is a traditional **bilingual dictionary** (e.g., English-French/French-English), with accurate pronunciation listed for every word. Again, if you see "bawn-JURE," burn it. If you see funny symbols (e.g., [bɔ̃.ʒuʁ]), keep it. We'll make friends with the International Phonetic Alphabet in Chapter 3. The second is a **monolingual dictionary** (e.g., French-French), which has actual *definitions* (e.g., in French) rather than translations. You'll never see "bawn-JURE" in one of these, so don't worry about finding your lighter.

You may also want a **thematic vocabulary book**. These books arrange the words in your language by theme: words about cars, words for food, medical words, and so on. They're handy for customizing your vocabulary (we'll talk about them in detail in Chapter 6).

FOR THE INTERMEDIATES

If you've already spent some time studying your target language, adjust your shopping list as follows:

First, if you already have a grammar book, make sure that you actually *like* it and that it's sufficiently challenging. If not, get a new one that fits your level.

Second, if you don't have a phrase book, they're worth having. Even if you're already reading books in your target language, you might not know how to ask about business hours or rental car insurance. A phrase book will let you look up sentences for many day-to-day situations that don't show up in books.

Third, you probably don't have a frequency dictionary yet, and you'll use it much earlier than a beginner. Go get one.

Last, hold off on a pronunciation book or trainer until the end of Chapter 3. You'll have a better idea then as to whether you'll need one.

THE INTERNET

The Internet is filling up with free grammar guides, pronunciation guides, frequency lists, and dictionaries of all shapes and sizes. The quality varies drastically from site to site and changes daily. You *can* learn a language for free on the net, but you'll be able to do it faster if you combine the best Internet resources with well-written books. I list my favorite Internet resources on my website (*Fluent-Forever .com/language-resources*), and we'll be discussing the most important websites—Google Images and the new language exchange communities (e.g., Lang-8, italki, Verbling)—throughout this book.

TUTORS AND PROGRAMS

If you need faster results and have some funds to spare, you can speed up your learning with private tutors (who are *extremely* affordable at *italki.com*) or intensive programs at home and abroad. The fastest route to fluency is also the least convenient: intensive immersion programs will provide twenty-plus weekly hours of class time, ten to twenty weekly hours of homework, and a strict no-English policy. You'll leave with a comfortable proficiency in your language of choice in exchange for two months of your life and a wad of cash. Some of them have generous financial aid policies if you apply early enough, so they may be within your reach if you lack the funds but have the time.

LANGUAGE CLASSES

In this book, we're going to discuss the process of learning a language on your own, outside of the classroom. But if you're already enrolled in a class (or if there are some good affordable classes offered nearby), then be sure to check out Appendix 6: How to Use This Book with Your Classroom Language Course.

The Path Forward

In the coming pages, we will knock down language's challenges one by one. I'll introduce you to a memorization system that will allow you to remember thousands of facts effortlessly and permanently. Then we'll determine which facts to learn. I'll guide you step-by-step through your language's sounds, words, and grammar. Every step of the way, we'll use your memorization system to learn more rapidly. Finally, we'll develop your listening and reading comprehension, as we pave a path toward fluent speech.

Along the way, I'll show you all my favorite toys. I like finding ways to make life more efficient, even when *finding* a faster way to do something takes more time than simply doing it. Someday the month I spent memorizing a hundred composers' birth dates and death dates will pay off in time savings, but it hasn't quite yet.[2] When it comes to efficiency in language learning, I got lucky. I needed to learn four languages to fluency for my singing. Beyond these, I want to learn Yiddish, Hebrew, and Hungarian to speak with my relatives, and I'm *fascinated* by Japanese. With so many languages to learn, I could spend an *enormous* amount of time looking for efficiency and still justify the time expense. As a result, I have a chest full of neat tools and toys to play with. We'll begin with my favorite one: the Spaced Repetition System (SRS).

---

2. But every time I type out a recital program and don't have to look up a composer's dates (Johann Strauss Jr., 1825–1899!), I win back a little more time.

CHAPTER 2

Upload: Five Principles to End Forgetting

A man's real possession is his memory. In nothing else is he rich, in nothing else is he poor.

—Alexander Smith

A SCENE FROM THE MATRIX, *WARNER BROTHERS PICTURES,* 1999:

TANK smiles as he sits down in his operator's chair, flipping through several disks. He picks one, and puts it into his computer. NEO looks at the screen.

Neo: Jujitsu? I'm going to learn . . . jujitsu?

Smiling, TANK presses the Load button.
NEO's body jumps against the harness as his eyes clamp shut.
The monitors kick wildly as his heart pounds, adrenaline surges, and his brain sizzles.
An instant later his eyes snap open.

Neo: Holy sh*t!

TANK grins.

While we can't yet upload jujitsu directly into our brains, we *do* have technology that can help us learn faster. This technology derives its power from five principles of memory:

· Make memories more memorable.
· Maximize laziness.

- Don't review. Recall.
- Wait, wait! Don't tell me!
- Rewrite the past.

These principles will enable you to remember more in less time. Combined, they form a system that can insert thousands of words and grammar rules so deeply into your mind that you'll be able to recall them instantly. Most attractively, this system can take what little spare time you have and steadily turn it into a usable foreign language.

PRINCIPLE 1: MAKE MEMORIES MORE MEMORABLE

Qualsiasi dato diventa importante se è connesso a un altro.
Any fact becomes important when it's connected to another.

—Umberto Eco, *Foucault's Pendulum*

To learn to remember, we must learn about the nature and location of memory. Scientists working in the 1940s and '50s began their search for memory in the most obvious place: within the cells of our brains—our neurons. They cut out parts of rats' brains, trying to make them forget a maze, and found that it didn't matter what part of the brain they chose; the rats never forgot. In 1950, the researchers gave up, concluding that they had most definitely searched everywhere, and that memory must be somewhere else.

Researchers eventually turned their search for memories to the wiring *between* neurons rather than within the cells themselves. Each of the hundred billion neurons in our brains are, on average, connected to seven thousand other neurons, in a dense web of more than 150,000 kilometers of nerve fibers.[3] These interconnected webs are

---

3. This is a *ridiculous* number—it's more than enough nerve fiber to wrap around the earth three times. Our neurons can play the most extreme version of Six Degrees of Kevin Bacon ever devised: you can connect any neuron to any other in six jumps or less, and none of those neurons need to have anything to do with Kevin Bacon.

intricately involved in our memories, which is why scientists could never find the mazes in their rats. Each rat's maze was spread *throughout* its brain. Whenever the scientists cut out a piece, they damaged only a small portion of the involved connections. The more they removed, the longer it took the rats to remember, but they never forgot their mazes completely. The only way to remove the maze entirely was to remove the rat entirely.

These patterns of connections form in an elegantly simple, mechanical process: *neurons that fire together wire together*. Known as Hebb's Law, this principle helps explain how we remember *anything*. Take my first memory of cookies. I spent ten minutes waiting in front of the oven, bathed in radiating heat and the scent of butter, flour, and sugar. I waited until they came out of the oven and watched the steam rise up off of them as they cooled. When I could bear no more, my father gave me a glass of milk, I grabbed a cookie, and I learned empathy for my poor blue friend from *Sesame Street*. My neural network for cookies involves sight, smell, and taste. There are audio components— the sound of the word *cookie* and the sound of milk pouring into a glass. I remember my dad's face smiling as he bit into his own delicious cookie. This first cookie experience was a parade of sensations, which wired together into a tight web of neural connections. These connections enable me to return to my past whenever I encounter a new cookie. Faced with a familiar buttery scent, that old web of neurons reactivates; my brain plays back the same sights, sounds, emotions, and tastes, and I relive my childhood experience.

Compare this experience to a new one: your currently-forming memory of the word *mjöður*. There's not much of a parade here. It's not obvious how to pronounce it, and in a particularly obnoxious move, I'm not even telling you what it means. As a result, you're stuck looking at the structure of the word—it has two foreign letters sandwiched between four familiar ones—and not much else. Without Herculean efforts, you will forget *mjöður* by the end of this chapter, if not sooner.

Levels of Processing: The Great Mnemonic Filter

The divide that separates your new *mjöður* from my *cookie* is known as levels of processing, and it separates the memorable from the forgettable. My *cookie* is memorable because it contains *so* many connections. I can access cookie in a thousand different ways. I will remember *cookies* if I read about them, hear about them, see them, smell them, or taste them. The word is unforgettable.

We need to make your *mjöður* just as unforgettable, and we will do it by adding four types of connections: structure, sound, concept, and personal connection. These are the four levels of processing. They were identified in the 1970s by psychologists who created a curious questionnaire with four types of questions and gave it to college students:

- **Structure:** How many capital letters are in the word BEAR?
- **Sound:** Does APPLE rhyme with Snapple?
- **Concept:** Is TOOL another word for "instrument"?
- **Personal Connection:** Do you like PIZZA?

After the questionnaire, they gave the students a surprise memory test, asking which words from the test they still remembered. Their memories were dramatically influenced by the question types: students remembered six PIZZAs for every BEAR. The magic of these questions lies in a peculiar mental trick. To count the capital letters in BEAR, you don't need to think about brown furry animals, and so you don't. You've activated the shallowest level of processing—structure—and moved on. On the other hand, you activate regions *throughout* your brain to determine whether you like PIZZA. You automatically utilize structure to figure out what word you're looking at. At the same time, you'll tend to hear the word *pizza* echoing within your skull as you imagine a hot disk of cheesy goodness. Finally, you'll access memories of pizzas past to determine whether you enjoy pizza or just haven't met the right one yet. In a fraction of a second, a simple question—*Do you like PIZZA?*—can simultaneously activate all four levels of processing. These four levels will fire together, wire together, and form a robust memory that is six times easier to remember than that BEAR you've already forgotten.

The four levels of processing are more than a biological quirk; they act as a filter, protecting us from information overload. We live in a sea of information, surrounded by a dizzying amount of input from TV, the Internet, books, social interactions, and the events of our lives. Your brain uses levels of processing to judge which input is important and which should be thrown out. You don't want to be thinking about the number of letters in the word *tiger* when one is chasing after you, nor do you want to be assaulted by vivid memories of cows when you buy milk. To keep you sane, your brain consistently works at the shallowest level of processing needed to get the job done. At the grocery store, you are simply looking for the words *chocolate milk,* or perhaps even *Organic Wholesome Happy Cow Chocolate Milk.* This is pattern matching, and your brain uses structure to quickly weed through hundreds or thousands of ingredient lists and food labels. Thankfully, you forget nearly every one of these lists and labels by the time you reach your milk. If you didn't, your encyclopedic knowledge of supermarket brand names would make you a terrible bore at parties. In more stimulating circumstances, such as that tiger in hot pursuit, your brain has a vested interest in memory. In such a case, should you survive, you'll likely remember *not* to climb into the tiger enclosure at the zoo. In this way, levels of processing act as our great mental filter, keeping us alive and tolerable at parties.

This filter is one of the reasons why foreign words are difficult to remember. Your brain is just doing its job; how should it know that you want to remember *mjöður* but not *disodium phosphate* (an emulsifier in your chocolate milk)?

How to Remember a Foreign Word Forever

To create a robust memory for a word like *mjöður,* you'll need all four levels of processing. The shallowest level, structure, allows you to recognize patterns of letters and determine whether a word is long, short,

and written in English or in Japanese. Your brain is recognizing structure when you unscramble *odctor* into *doctor*. This level is essential for
reading, but it involves too little of your brain to contribute much to
memory. Almost none of the students in the levels of processing study
remembered counting the capital letters in BEAR. Words like *mjöður*
are difficult to remember because you *can't* get any deeper than structure until you know how to deal with odd letters like *ö* and *ð*.

Your first task in language learning is to reach the next level:
sound. Sound connects structure to your ears and your mouth and allows you to speak. You'll start by learning the sounds of your language
and which letters make those sounds, because if you begin with sound,
you'll have a much easier time remembering words. Our college students remembered twice as many APPLEs (which do, in fact, rhyme
with Snapple) as they did BEARs (which has *four* capital letters). Sound
is the land of rote memorization. We take a name, like Edward, or a
pair of words, like *cat–gato*, and we repeat them, continuously activating the parts of our brain that connect structure to sound. Our *mjöður*
is very roughly pronounced "MEW-ther," and the more accurately we
learn its pronunciation, the better we'll remember it.[4] Eventually, our
mjöður will be as memorable as a familiar name like Edward. This is
better than structure, but it still isn't good enough for our needs. After
all, many of us don't remember names very well, because our brains
are filtering them out as quickly as they arrive.

We need a way to get through this filter, and we'll find it at the third
level of processing: concepts. Our college students remembered twice
as many TOOLs (synonym for *instruments*) as APPLEs (Snapples).
Concepts can be broken down into two groups: abstract and concrete.
We'll begin with the abstract. If I tell you that my birthday is in June,
you probably won't immediately see images of birthday cakes and party

---

4. Earlier I told you to burn books that contained "Englishy" pronunciation like "bawn-
JURE." Now I'm resorting to Englishy pronunciation myself, with a terribly inaccurate
"MEW-ther." I'm going to do this a lot, because I don't think you want me to explain pro-
nunciation in every language. Sorry. Please don't burn this book.

hats. You don't need to, and as we've discussed, our brains work at the shallowest level required. It's efficient, and it saves us a lot of work and distraction. Still, the date of my birthday is a meaningful, if abstract, concept. This makes it deeper and more memorable than pure sounds, which is why you'll have an easier time remembering that my birthday is in June than you'll have remembering that the Basque word for "birthday" is *urtebetetze*.

Deeper still than abstract concepts are concrete, multisensory concepts. If I tell you that my upcoming birthday party will take place in a paintball arena, after which we'll eat a cookies-and-cream ice-cream cake and then spend the rest of the evening in a swimming pool, you'll tend to remember those details much better than you'll remember the month of the event. We prioritize and store concrete concepts because they engage more of our brains, not because they're necessarily any more important than other information. In this case, it is less important that you know the details about my birthday than that you know when and where to show up.

Given this phenomenon, how do we make a strange, foreign word like *mjöður* memorable? The word itself is not the problem. We are not bad at remembering words when they are tied to concrete, multisensory experiences. If I tell you that my email password is *mjöður*, you probably (hopefully?) won't remember it, because you're processing it on a sound and structural level. But if we're in a bar together, and I hand you a flaming drink with a dead snake in it, and tell you, "This—*mjöður*! You—drink!" you won't have any trouble remembering that word. We have no problem naming things; nouns comprise the vast majority of the 450,000 entries in *Webster's Third International Dictionary*.[5] It's when those names aren't tied to concrete concepts that we run

---

5. How much of a majority? No one knows precisely. While we can analyze specific texts with precision (nonfiction texts are approximately 80 percent nouns), we run into problems when counting words more generally. Words turn out to be extraordinarily slippery creatures when you attempt to count or classify them. Is *bear* a noun, a verb, or both? Should we count *bear* separately from *bears*? Answering these questions is sometimes more an art than a science.

into trouble with our memories. Our goal, and one of the core goals of this book, is to make foreign words like *mjöður* more concrete and meaningful.

Breaking Through the Filter: The Power of Images and Personal Connections

Earlier in this chapter, we encountered a translated word pair: *cat–gato*. As we discussed, standard study practice involves repeating *gato* and *cat* until they form a sound connection. This is too shallow to remember easily, but it's also beside the point; when you read *gato*, you don't want to think the word *cat*; you want to think *this*:

We'll get better results if we skip the English word and use an image instead.

We recall images *much* better than words, because we automatically think conceptually when we see an image. Image-recall studies have repeatedly demonstrated that our visual memory is phenomenal. Memory researchers in the 1960s subjected college students to one of the most terrifyingly-named memory tests ever invented: the Two-Alternative Forced-Choice Test. In it, college students were shown 612 magazine ads (*possibly* tied to chairs with their eyes held open) and then asked to identify the old pictures when shown a new mixture of images. The students correctly picked the old images *98.5 percent of the time*. Unsatisfied, the researchers repeated their tests with more images, trying to determine what college students will put up with for low pay and free food. There doesn't seem to be a limit. Students were willing to sit in dark rooms for five consecutive days, watching ten thousand images in a row. After the study, these students accurately identified 83 percent of the images. Our capacity for visual memory is extraordinary; we only need to learn how to take advantage of it.

Since we need to learn words, not pictures, we will use combinations of words *and* pictures. Such combinations work even better than pictures alone. This effect even applies to totally unrelated images: you will remember an abstract drawing with the sentence "Apples are delicious" better than that drawing alone. Faced with an incomprehensible image and an unrelated word, your brain struggles to find meaning, even if there isn't any. In the process, it automatically moves the word out of the *disodium phosphate* trash can and into *cookie* territory. As a result, you'll remember.

We can go one step deeper than pictures by taking advantage of the last level, *personal connection*. You will remember a concept with a personal connection 50 percent more easily than a concept without one, which is why our college students remembered 50 percent more PIZZAs (*Yes, we like them*) than TOOLs (*Yes, they are synonymous with instruments*). This is not to say that concepts alone are ineffective. If you connect *gato* to a picture of some cute cat, you will have an easy time remembering that word. But if, in addition, you can connect *gato* with a memory of your own childhood cat, that word will become practically unforgettable.

How do we use this in practice? A new foreign word is like a new friend's name. Our new friend could be a person, a cat, or a drink; the memory burden in each case is the same. Let's make a new friend's name memorable using levels of processing.

Our new friend is named Edward. Simply by thinking "Edward," we have already reached the second level of processing—sound. If we want to go deeper, into concept territory, we would search for a concrete image for the name Edward, such as the movie character Edward Scissorhands. If we spent a moment imagining our new friend with a pair of scissors for hands, we would have an easy time remembering his name later. This strategy is used by competitive memorizers (yes, there are competitive memorizers) to quickly memorize people's names, and we'll discuss it in depth in Chapters 4 and 5.

But we're not done yet. We'll do even better if we can find a personal connection with his name. Perhaps you still remember watching *Edward Scissorhands* in a theater, perhaps your brother is named Edward, or perhaps you too have hands made of scissors. As you imagine your new friend interacting with Edward-related images and Edward-related personal memories, you are activating broader and broader networks in your brain. The next time you see Edward, this parade of images and memories will come rushing back, and you'll be hard pressed to forget his name. This gives you valuable social points, which are sometimes redeemable for wine, cheese, and board game nights.

This thought process can take creativity, but you can learn to do it quickly and easily. For a concrete word like *gato*, you can find an appropriate image on Google Images (*images.google.com*) within seconds. If you simply ask yourself, "When's the last time I saw a *gato*?" you will add a personal connection and cement your memory of the word. Easy.

For an abstract word like *economía* (economy), our job is still very simple. When we search Google Images, we'll find thousands of pictures of money, piggy banks, stock market charts, and politicians. By choosing *any* of these images, we'll force ourselves to think concretely and conceptually. As a result, the word will become much easier to remember. If we ask ourselves whether the *economía* has affected our lives, we'll get the personal connection we need to remember that word forever.

In this book, we're going to learn vocabulary in two main stages: we'll build a foundation of easy, concrete words, and then we'll use that foundation to learn abstract words. Throughout, we'll use levels of processing to make foreign words memorable.

KEY POINTS

- Your brain is a sophisticated filter, which makes irrelevant information forgettable and meaningful information memorable. Foreign words tend to fall into the "forgettable" category, because they sound odd, they don't seem particularly meaningful, and they don't have any connection to your own life experiences.
- You can get around this filter and make foreign words memorable by doing three things:
    - Learn the sound system of your language
    - Bind those sounds to images
    - Bind those images to your past experiences

PRINCIPLE 2: MAXIMIZE LAZINESS

I've heard that hard work never killed anyone, but I say why take the chance?

—Ronald Reagan

Forgetting is a formidable opponent. We owe our present understanding of forgetting to Hermann Ebbinghaus, a German psychologist who spent years of his life memorizing lists of nonsense syllables (*Guf Ril Zhik Nish Mip Poff*). He recorded the speed of forgetting by comparing the time it took him to learn and then later relearn one of his lists. His "forgetting curve" is a triumph of experimental psychology, tenacity, and masochism:

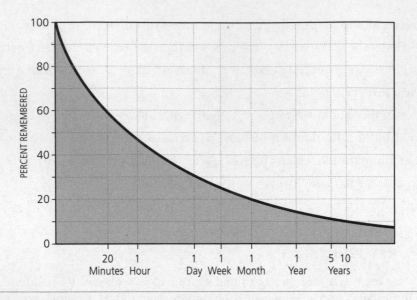

THE FORGETTING CURVE

The curve reveals how rapidly we forget and what remains once we've forgotten. The right side of his curve is encouraging: even years later, Ebbinghaus could expect old random gobbledygook to take him measurably less time to learn than new random gobbledygook. Once he learned something, a trace of it remained within him forever. Unfortunately, the left side is a disaster: our memories rush out of our ears like water through a net. The net stays damp, but if we're trying to keep something substantial in it—like telephone numbers, the names of people we've just met, or new foreign words—we can expect to remember a paltry 30 percent the following day.

How can we do better? Our instinct is to work harder; it's what gets us through school tests and social occasions. When we meet our new friend Edward, we generally remember his name with rote repetition; we repeat his name to ourselves until we remember. If we *need* to remember—perhaps Edward is our new boss—then we can repeat his name continuously until we're sick of it. If we do this extra work, we'll remember his name significantly better . . . for a few weeks.

Extra repetition is known as overlearning, and it doesn't help

> ### *One Metronome, Four Years, Six Million Repetitions*
>
> Hermann Ebbinghaus's 1885 study has been referred to as "the most brilliant single investigation in the history of experimental psychology." He sat alone in a room with a ticking metronome, repeating lists of nonsense syllables more than six million times, pushing himself to the point of "exhaustion, headache and other symptoms" in order to measure the speed of memorization and the speed of forgetting. It was the first data-driven study of the human mind, and I suspect it made him a *blast* at social events.

long-term memory *at all*. Can you remember a single fact from the last school test you crammed for? Can you even remember the test itself? If we're going to invest our time in a language, we want to remember for months, years, or decades. If we can't achieve this goal by working *harder*, then we'll do it by working *as little as possible*.

KEY POINTS

- Rote repetition is boring, and it doesn't work for long-term memorization.
- Take the lazy route instead: study a concept until you can repeat it once without looking and then stop. After all, *lazy* is just another word for "efficient."

Principle 3: Don't Review. Recall.

In school we learn things then take the test,
In everyday life we take the test then we learn things.

—Admon Israel

Suppose I made you an offer. I'll give you $20 for every word you can remember from a list of Spanish words. The test is in a week, and you have two options: (1) you can study the list for ten minutes, or (2) you can study the list for five minutes and then trade it for a blank sheet of paper and a pencil. If you choose the second option, you can write down whatever you still remember, and then you have to give the sheet back.

Here are results from a similarly worded experiment. In it, students either read a text twice or read it once and wrote down what they remembered. They then took a final test five minutes, two days, or one week later. Notice how studying twice (i.e., overlearning) helps for a few minutes and then screws you in the long run. Oddly enough, a blank sheet of paper will help you *much* more than additional study time. You'll remember 35 percent more in a week.[6]

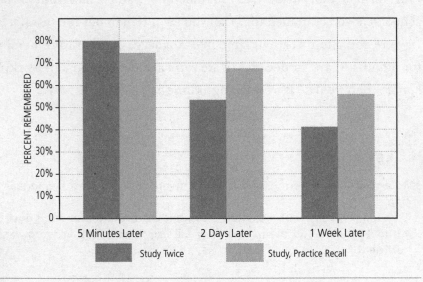

TWO DIFFERENT STUDY SCHEMES (STUDY TWICE VS. STUDY + TEST)
RECALL RESULTS AFTER FIVE MINUTES, TWO DAYS, OR ONE WEEK

Try this one: after reading through your Spanish word list, you can:

A. Get five more minutes with your word list.

B. Get a blank sheet of paper and test yourself.

C. Get three blank sheets of paper and test yourself three times.

---

6. Additional studies show a 5:1 benefit for testing over studying, meaning that five minutes of testing is worth twenty-five minutes of studying.

Here are your final recall results, one week later:

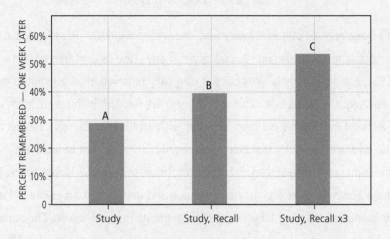

**THREE DIFFERENT STUDY STRATEGIES
RECALL RESULTS, ONE WEEK LATER**

Madness. How can taking an *identical* test three times in a row produce such a large effect? Odd as it is, this follows rules of common sense.
When you study by reading through a list multiple times, you're practicing reading, not recall. If you want to get better at recalling something, you should practice *recalling* it. Our blank sheet of paper, which
could be replaced by a stack of flash cards, a multiple choice test, or
simply trying to remember to yourself, is precisely the type of practice
we need. It improves our ability to recall by tapping into one of the most
fascinating facets of our minds—the interplay of memory and emotion.

Deep within our brains, a seahorse and a nut are engaged in an
intricate chemical dance that allows us to decide what is important
and what is forgettable. The seahorse-shaped structure is known as
the hippocampus, and it acts as a mental switchboard, connecting
distant regions of the brain and creating a map of those connections.
You access this map in order to recall any recent memory.[7] The con-

---

7. Note that when I refer to "memory," I'm referring to *declarative* memory—the memory of
facts and events. *Nondeclarative memory*—memory of habits, skills, and so on—seems to be
located elsewhere. People with a damaged hippocampus will lose their ability to form any
new declarative memories, but they're still able to learn and improve at skills (like drawing)
even if they can't recall learning how to do them.

The Curious Case of H.M.

The hippocampus's role in memory was discovered relatively recently, in one of the most famous case reports in neuropsychology—the case of Henry Molaison. In 1953, Molaison had his hippocampus surgically removed in an attempt to cure his epilepsy. His illness was cured, but the surgery left him with severe amnesia. He retained most of his old memories, but without his hippocampus, he lost his ability to store new ones. Molaison could recall his distant past because the map of those memories had spread throughout his brain. In losing his hippocampus, he lost the ability to make and access *new* maps and thereby lost his ability to form new memories. His story later became the inspiration for *Memento*, Christopher Nolan's film about a man with anterograde amnesia in search of his wife's killer.

nected neurons reactivate, and you relive your past experience. Over the course of months and years, these networked neurons lose their dependency on the hippocampus's map and take on an independent, Bohemian lifestyle in the outermost layers of the brain.

The hippocampus's nut-shaped dance partner is the amygdala, and it tells the hippocampus what to keep and what to throw out. It does this by translating our emotions into chemicals, causing our adrenal glands to send out bursts of memory-enhancing hormones according to the situation. If we encounter emotionally arousing input—"Look, a tiger! Ow, my arm!"—then the amygdala will strengthen that memory. If not—"Look, a pencil. I'm hungry"—then it won't. This leaves us with a healthy fear of tigers and a healthy disregard for pencils as food items.

Coupled with the nearby reward centers in the brain, the amygdala provides the mechanism behind our magical blank sheet of paper. Our emotions are reflexive creatures. They respond to our environment whether we want them to or not. While we can try to trick our brains into getting excited over a list of Spanish words, our brains know better. Unless learning that *el dentista* means "the dentist" in Spanish gives you goose bumps, your amygdala will not give those memories much of a boost. *El dentista* is just not as important as *el tigre*. You can try to inject amphetamine directly into your amygdala, which *will* work, but that may prove to be more trouble than it's worth.

Our blank page, however, changes everything. At the moment where your performance is judged, your brain realizes that it had better get its act in gear. As a result, every memory you recall gets a squirt of memory-boosting chemicals. Those memories are reactivated, your amygdala calls for hormones, your hippocampus maps out the involved networks, and your neurons wire tightly together. Every time you succeed at recalling, the reward centers in your brain release a chemical reward—dopamine—into your hippocampus, further encouraging long-term memory storage. Your blank sheet of paper has created a drug-fueled memory party in your brain. Your boring word list never stood a chance.

KEY POINTS

- Acts of recall set off an intricate chemical dance in your brain that boosts memory retention.
- To maximize efficiency, spend most of your time recalling rather than reviewing.
- You'll accomplish this goal by creating flash cards that test your ability to recall a given word, pronunciation, or grammatical construction. Coupled with images and personal connections, these cards will form the foundation of a powerful memorization system.

PRINCIPLE 4: WAIT, WAIT! DON'T TELL ME!

If it's hard to remember, it'll be difficult to forget.

—Arnold Schwarzenegger

We've all gone through situations in school and work in which we're supposed to memorize something, but rarely does someone tell us how to do it. This is not without good reason. There is *no such thing* as "memorizing." We can think, we can repeat, we can recall, and we can imagine, but we aren't built to memorize. Rather, our brains are designed to think and automatically hold on to what's important. While running away from our friendly neighborhood tiger, we don't think, "You need to remember this! Tigers are bad! Don't forget! They're bad!" We simply run away, and our brain remembers for us. The closest mental action that we have to memorizing is practicing recall ("What was that guy's name?"). Now we need to investigate precisely what effective recall *feels* like.

Try to recall the foreign words that have shown up so far in this book. You'll remember some words immediately—perhaps the words from the previous section: *el tigre, el dentista*. If you keep looking, you'll find a few more in relatively easy reach—perhaps *gato* is still lurking about. Last, hiding in the murky fog of your brain, a few words may reluctantly emerge.[8] If we were to track your ability to remember each of these words, we would see a curious result. By next week, you're most likely to forget the words you knew *best*—those words that you remembered immediately. You're 20 percent more likely to retain the words that took a little more time. But the words that took the most effort to recall—those you had all but forgotten—will etch themselves deeply into your consciousness. You're 75 percent more likely to remember them in the future, and if they spent a few moments just out of reach at the tip of your tongue, then you're *twice* as likely to remember them.

What's going on here? Let's look at the most extreme example, a word that dances on the tip of your tongue before you finally recall it. A word like this is an incomplete memory. You have access to fragments of the word, but you can't see the whole picture yet. You can recall that it

---

8. I've used *urtebetetze* (birthday), *Tankdeckel* (gas cap), *Das ist mir völlig Wurst* (I don't give a damn), *economía* (economy), *bonjour* (hello/good day), *tschüss* (bye!), and *hallo* (hello). *Mjöður* is the Icelandic word for "mead." It's not actually a flaming drink, but you can put a dead snake in it if you like.

starts with the letter *s*, or that it's something like a poem or a monologue, or that it sounds like *solipsist* or *solitaire*, but you need time to reach the word *soliloquy*. More often than not, in these situations, we recall accurate information. Our word *does* start with the letter *s*. Our brains fly into a wild, almost desperate search for the missing piece of our minds, frantically generating *S* words and throwing them out when they don't match what we're looking for. Your amygdala treats these searches as matters of life and death, for surely if you don't remember the actor who played Matt Damon's therapist in *Good Will Hunting*, you will leap out of the nearest window.[9] You experience such relief at finally finding your goal that the word becomes nearly impossible to forget.

How do we take advantage of this? Do we even want to? Tricking our brains into a permanent, desperate chase after missing words sounds stressful. Doing this a hundred times a day sounds like a recipe for early heart failure. Fortunately, we don't need to be stressed to remember; we just need to be interested. We will get bored if we spend our days incessantly asking ourselves whether we still remember our friend Edward's name. It's too easy, it's tedious, and it doesn't work very well. If we wait longer—until we're *just about to forget*—then remembering Edward's name becomes a stimulating challenge. We're aiming for the point where a dash of difficulty will provide just the right amount of spice and keep the game interesting. If we can find it, we'll get twice as much benefit for our time, and we'll have much more fun in the process.

KEY POINTS

- Memory tests are most effective when they're *challenging.* The closer you get to forgetting a word, the more ingrained it will become when you finally remember it.
- If you can consistently test yourself *right before* you forget, you'll *double* the effectiveness of every test.

---

9. It was Robin Williams.

PRINCIPLE 5: REWRITE THE PAST

The difference between false memories and true ones is the same as for jewels: it is always the false ones that look the most real, the most brilliant.

—Salvador Dalí

I remember waking up one day with a symphony in my head. I had dreamt that I was sitting at my desk, composing, and I woke up with the results intact. Beaming with pride, I ran to my brother. "Listen to this," I said, and began humming a few bars. "Isn't that awesome? I composed it in my sleep!" "No, you didn't," my brother replied. "It's from the Superman movie. We saw it last week."

As we discussed earlier, a memory is just a web of connections: disparate neurons fire together, wire together, and become more likely to fire together in the future. In my dream, I remembered the Superman theme at the same time as I envisioned myself composing. My brain reflexively connected the two into a convincing new memory—a *false* memory—and I went and embarrassed myself in front of my brother. This happens to all of us, and it's a result of the way we store memories.

In a 2011 memory study, researchers showed two groups of college students a vivid, imagery-laden advertisement for a new, fake brand of popcorn: Orville Redenbacher's Gourmet Fresh. Afterward, they thanked the first group and sent them home. Then they gave the second group samples of fresh popcorn. One week later, they brought both groups back and asked them about their impressions. Here's where it gets creepy: *both* groups vividly remembered trying the popcorn, even though one group never had. They all thought it was delicious.

When we remember, we don't just access our memories; we rewrite them. Prompted by the popcorn advertisement, these college students remembered movie nights at home, the smell of corn and butter, the crunch in their mouths, and the salt on their lips. In the midst of reliving these experiences, they saw images of other people enjoying popcorn in bags marked "Orville Redenbacher's Gourmet

Fresh," and their memories changed. The network of neurons from past movie nights activated at the same time as they saw the brand's logo. Because *neurons that fire together wire together*, their brains stored these new connections as if they had always been there.

Our "single" memories are amalgamations of every recall experience we've ever had. When I remind you of the word *gato*, you probably recall the little image of a cat from earlier in the chapter. But as that image floats around in your head, you can't store it just as it was. You are a different person now, with different information in your head and a different section of this book in front of you. Perhaps you've changed rooms, or your emotional state, or perhaps you now have a cat in your lap. You have a wholly new set of neurons involved in this *gato* experience compared with your last one. As a result, your new *gato* memory will join the new connections from your present to the old reactivated connections from your past. In that single act of recall, your *gato* network has doubled in size.

This rewriting process is the engine behind long-term memorization. Every act of recall imbues old memories with a trace of your present-day self. This trace gives those memories additional connections: new images, emotions, sounds, and word associations that make your old memory easier to recall. Once you've rewritten these memories enough times, they become unforgettable.

Feedback to the Rescue

Of course, you must *remember* a memory before you can rewrite it. You will remember "American Express: Don't leave home without it" to your dying day because American Express has spent millions of dollars making its ads memorable. Every time you see a new American Express ad, the vivid images and sounds are rewritten into your memory of their all-important slogan. You would forget their slogan between each commercial cycle if they eliminated the famous actors and imagery-laden travel scenarios from their ads. If this happened, the crucial rewriting process would never occur. "Don't leave home without it" would become just another forgotten advertisement, rather than one of the most successful ad campaigns in history. In practicing recall, we are striving to continuously rewrite our memories. We create a memory for *gato*, and we build upon that memory with every recall until it is as unforgettable as an ad slogan.

But what happens when we *can't* remember? Surely we won't be able to remember *everything* we learn, particularly if we're trying to wait as long as possible between practice sessions. The day may come when we try to remember *gato* and draw a blank instead. We've forgotten the word, and in this scenario, it will *stay* forgotten. Like Ebbinghaus's gobbledygook, we'll be able to learn it faster in the future, but we won't get any benefit from our practice. We need a way to restore our forgotten memories, and we'll find it in *immediate feedback*.

Feedback is a simple concept with dramatic results. If we encounter our *gato* flash card and get stumped, then we can simply look at the back side of the card and see a picture of a cat. We have just given ourselves immediate feedback, and as a result, one of two things happens. If our memory of *gato* has vanished, then we start over. We form a new, "original" experience at the moment we got stumped and looked at the answer. This is not as good as remembering our *actual* original experience, but it's still very effective. Our brains are primed and ready to create a new memory. As we search our memories for *gato*-related images and associations, we build a wide network of neural connections. We may remember that *gato* is a type of animal but can't remember which one. If we encounter an image of a cat while these connections are still active, our completed network will burst into activity, the reward centers of our brains will activate, and we'll have a new, deep, and memorable experience to build upon.

Alternatively, we may still have access to our original memory of *gato*. This memory will burst into life—"Oh, yeah!"—at the moment we see that picture of a cat. In this scenario, we'll relive our memory, our new experience will join it, and the memory will be rewritten with new connections. Thanks to a simple act of immediate feedback, we've re-gained our rewrite. Feedback allows us to resuscitate forgotten memories and get the most out of our practice sessions.

KEY POINTS

- Every time you successfully recall a memory, you revisit and rewrite earlier experiences, adding bits and pieces of your present self to your past memories.
- You'll make the best use of your time when practicing recall if your earlier experiences are as memorable as possible. You can accomplish this by connecting sounds, images, and personal connections to every word you learn.
- When you *do* forget, use immediate feedback to bring back your forgotten memories.

TIMING IS EVERYTHING: THE END OF FORGETTING

μέτρα φυλάσσεσθαι· καιρὸς δ᾽ ἐπὶ πᾶσιν ἄριστος.
Observe due measure, for right timing is in all things the most important factor.

—Hesiod

How do we combine the five principles? We want our original memories to be as deep and multisensory as possible (1: Make memories more memorable). We want to study as little as possible (2: Maximize laziness), and practice recall as much as possible (3: Don't review. Recall). We want our recall practice to be challenging but not too hard (4: Wait, wait! Don't tell me!). Last, when we practice, we want to nearly forget those original experiences but not forget them completely. When we *do* forget, we want immediate feedback to put us back on track (5: Rewrite the past).

If we could predict exactly how long we could remember each thing we learn, we would be able to work miracles with our minds. We would have an alarm that went off right before we forgot where we left our car keys, and life would be a wonderful paradise free of forgetting.

Unfortunately, our memories are too messy. They make unpredictable connections to everything we experience or imagine. They lose pieces of our past and gain pieces of our present. Any mention of a car, a lock, or even a word that rhymes with *key* can enhance or suppress our key-related memories. I can't count the number of times that I've memorized some word, only to have some new, similar-sounding word come along and screw everything up months later. We can't accurately predict when we will forget a single memory.

However, we *can* make predictions about a *group* of memories. Take a gaggle of college students and teach them obscure trivia, like "Who invented snow golf?" Then let them practice recall once, and test them six months later.[10] Depending upon the timing of that single practice session, you'll see quite different results:

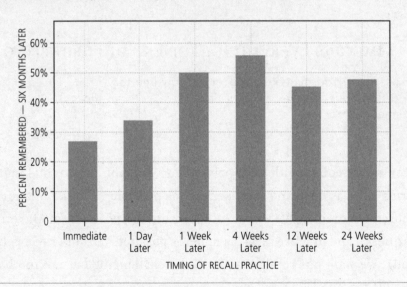

TEST RESULTS SIX MONTHS AFTER LEARNING TRIVIA, WAITING FOR AN INTERVAL, AND THEN PRACTICING RECALL ONE TIME

For students trying to remember something for *six months*, the immediate practice session (which produced a 27 percent final score) is not

---

10. It was Rudyard Kipling, who couldn't bear to wait until spring for his favorite pastime. While writing *The Jungle Book* in rural Vermont, he painted his golf balls red, put tin cans on the snow, and went to town.

bad at all. But as the delay increases to twenty-eight days, the students' scores double. This pattern appears in numerous studies, although the ideal delay changes depending upon the final test date. There is a complex balance between the advantages of *nearly* forgetting and the disadvantages of *actually* forgetting, and it breaks our forgetting curve in half:[11]

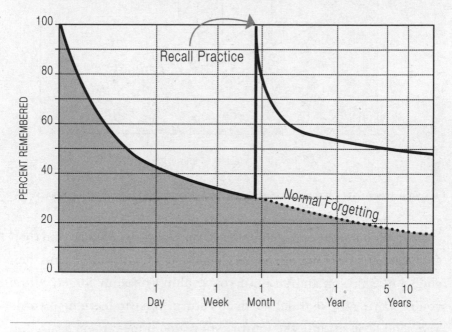

YOUR NEW FORGETTING CURVE (EFFECTS OF A PRACTICE SESSION ON DAY 28)

That single practice session has made the difference between forgetting nearly everything and remembering quite a bit. Here's the final leap: if immediate recall practice is good, and delayed practice is better, and if one session is good and many sessions are better, what happens if you delay your recall practice many times?

---

11. The magic number turns out to be 10–20 percent of the final test delay, so if their test was a year later, we would see the best results at a delay of fifty-six days. It is as if our brains know that something we encounter once a week will be important in five to ten weeks, but something we only encounter once a year will be important in five to ten years.

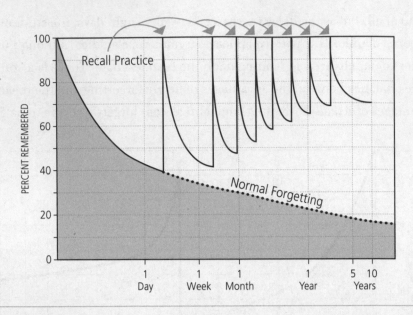

YOUR *NEW*, NEW FORGETTING CURVE (MULTIPLE, DELAYED PRACTICE SESSIONS WITH FEEDBACK)

We've found the end of forgetting. You learn a word today and then shelve it for a while. When it comes back, you'll try to recall it, and then shelve it again, on and on until you couldn't possibly forget. While you're waiting for your old words to return, you can learn new words and send *them* off into the future, where you'll meet them again and work them into your long-term memory. At least until you can upload jujitsu directly into your brain, this is the most efficient way to memorize large amounts of information permanently.

In Search of the Perfect Interval

You want to remember as much as possible now, later, and *much* later. To choose how often to practice, you have to balance efficiency and comfort. In general, you're not studying for a single test with a specific date, so you can't pick an optimal interval and run with it. For the extreme long term, you'll get the best efficiency if you wait *years* between practice sessions, but that won't help you in the short term at all. Moreover, your practice sessions would be extremely frustrating. After such a long delay, you'd have forgotten almost everything. On the other hand, if you practiced all the time, you'd be able to remember almost everything, but your old words would come back so often that they would bury you in hours of daily work.

The thread between these two goals—remembering now and remembering later—starts small and grows rapidly. You'll begin with short intervals (two to four days) between practice sessions. Every time you successfully remember, you'll increase the interval (e.g., nine days, three weeks, two months, six months, etc.), quickly reaching intervals of *years*. This keeps your sessions challenging enough to continuously drive facts into your long-term memory. If you forget a word, you'll start again with short intervals and work your way back to long ones until that word sticks, too. This pattern keeps you working on your weakest memories while maintaining and deepening your strongest memories. Because well-remembered words eventually disappear into the far off future, regular practice creates an equilibrium between old and new. You'll spend a fixed amount of time every day learning new words, remembering the words from last week, and occasionally meeting old friends from months or years back. By doing this, you'll spend most of your time successfully recalling words you've almost forgotten and building foundations for new words at a rapid, steady clip.

Playing with timing in this way is known as spaced repetition, and it's extraordinarily efficient. In a four-month period, practicing for 30 minutes a day, you can expect to learn and retain 3600 flash cards with 90 to 95 percent accuracy. These flash cards can teach you an alphabet, vocabulary, grammar, and even pronunciation. And they can do it without becoming tedious, because they're always challenging enough to remain interesting and fun. Spaced repetition is a godsend to memory intensive tasks like language learning. It's a pity that it wasn't a subject back in school, when I had a lot more to remember.

At its most basic level, a Spaced Repetition System (SRS) is a to-do list that changes according to your performance. If you can remember that *pollo* means "chicken" after a two-month delay, then your SRS will automatically wait four to six months before putting *pollo* back on your to-do list. If you're having trouble remembering that *ropa* means "clothing" for more than two weeks, your SRS will put *ropa* on your list more frequently until it sticks for good.

What does this look like in practice? SRSs come in two main flavors: on paper or on computer. The computerized versions will perform all scheduling on their own. Every time you access your computerized SRS, it will automatically teach you twenty to thirty new cards and quiz you on the hundred or so cards you're about to forget. Your job is to tell your SRS whether or not you remember a particular card, and your SRS's job is to build a daily, customized to-do list based upon your input. This list is designed to help you memorize as efficiently as possible, so that you can spend your time learning instead of micromanaging.

A paper SRS accomplishes the same feat using a flash card file box, a carefully designed schedule, and a few simple instructions. It's basically a simple board game. The game contains seven levels, which correspond to seven labeled sections in your file box (i.e., level 1, level 2, etc.). Every card starts on level 1, and advances to the next level whenever you remember it. If you forget, the card falls all the way back to level 1. Whenever a card gets past level 7, it has won its place in your long-term memory.

Every time you play with your paper SRS, you'll consult your schedule and review the levels of the day (e.g., December 9: Review levels 4, 2, and 1). This is your daily to-do list, and it adapts to your performance because of the way your cards gain and lose levels. By following the rules of the game (see Appendix 3), you create a primitive, paper computer program. This program is just as effective and fun as a computerized SRS and is satisfying in an "I did this by myself" sort of way. At the end of this chapter, we'll compare paper and computerized SRSs in depth, so you don't have to make up your mind just yet.

DIY Deck Building

This is not Rosetta Stone. You can't just download a deck of flash cards for your SRS and magically learn a language. Why not? Flash cards are fantastic at reminding you about your original experiences, but

---

The Power of the Creative Process

Have you ever studied for a test by writing out a summary of your notes? It worked fairly well, didn't it? When you create something, it becomes a part of you. If, instead, you simply copied someone else's notes, you wouldn't benefit nearly as much. When you try to memorize someone else's work, you are fighting an uphill battle with your brain's filters. Even though *gato* = [picture of a cat] is much easier to remember than *gato–cat*, it still isn't stimulating enough to store permanently, because *someone else* chose it, not you. In contrast, when *gato* is a cat that *you* chose, then that choice allows you to sidestep your mental filters. As a result, you'll have a much easier time remembering.

---

they're not particularly good at creating memories in the first place. If you read someone else's *gato* flash card, you probably won't spontaneously think of your childhood cat or of the numerous *Shrek: Puss in Boots* (*Gato con Botas*) images that show up on a Google Images search for the word. There's no movie, no sound, and no story. Under these circumstances, you'll be hard-pressed to form a deep, multisensory memory while you're busily studying on the way to work. This isn't the SRS's fault; it's in the nature of the language game.

One of the reasons why language programs and classes fail is that no one can *give* you a language; you have to take it for yourself. You are rewiring your own brain. To succeed, you need to actively participate. Each word in your language needs to become your word, each grammar rule your grammar rule. Programs like Rosetta Stone can provide decent original experiences for words like *ball* and *elephant*, but eventually, you need to deal with words like *economic situation*. Abstract words like these require complex, personal connections if you're ever going to use them comfortably while speaking. You have to make those connections for yourself, because no one else can tell you how the current *situación económica* has affected *you*.

You also need to retain the connections you've made, even when you're busy learning new words. This is a lot to do at once, so you might as well use the best tools for the job. Until someone puts a USB port into the back of our skulls, our most effective weapon against forgetting is spaced repetition. And since we need deep, memorable experiences to get the most out of spaced repetition, we might as well get them in the process of making our flash cards.

The card construction process is one of the most fun and satisfying ways to learn a language. Content in the knowledge that every detail will become a permanent memory, you become the architect of your own mind. What breed of dog will you think about when you wish to remember the word *dog*? Which examples will you choose to form your verb conjugations? What vocabulary is most useful for your own life?

Making these decisions forms an exciting part of the learning process and, ultimately, *takes very little time*. After getting used to your SRS, you can add new cards in a matter of seconds. For most nouns, you can simply type the word once, search for a picture on Google Images, and copy (or draw) it onto your card. This can take less than fifteen seconds. Imagery for more complicated ideas will, of course, take more time to identify—a process that itself gives you the connections you need to make a word your own.

I sincerely wish I could sell my personal flash card decks. If their usefulness were transferable, I'd make a lot of money and help a lot of people. Instead, I give them away for free on my website with the disclaimer that *no one* has successfully used them to learn a language. Of the few thousand people who have downloaded them, no one has tried to refute that claim, so I feel confident stating here that my personal decks are *useless* to anyone but myself. Use them at your own peril.

Frustration and the Fate of Your Smartphone

For a moment, let's consider what happens when someone (not *you*, of course) tries to use one of my decks. At some point, he'll run into my card for *dog* and see a golden retriever puppy. Now, I have had the fleeting, fifteen-second experience of searching for this image on the Internet, seeing many different dogs of many different ages and breeds, and choosing this golden retriever. In those few seconds of searching, I learned what this word means and chose a pleasant reminder for this learning experience. However, anyone else will have to answer a number of questions and have nothing to base their answers upon. Does this word refer to the breed of dog? Its age? Its color? In using a non-personalized deck, this instant of confusion will be recorded along with the memory, and the meaning of the word will be uncertain.

On its own, uncertainty is not a *terrible* thing; a great deal of uncertainty is often involved in learning a language in a foreign country. The problem with uncertainty in your flash cards is that it makes your daily reviews more difficult, which translates to added time and added forgetting (which also adds time). The original experience that you'll remember with every review will become "WHAT does this MEAN? I don't have TIME for this $#*@!" which can quickly become frustrating.

This last point is the deadly one. As soon as your daily reviews become frustrating, it gets harder and harder to sit down and do them. You may be able to force yourself to stick with it for a few weeks, but you need longer than that to see major results. This becomes a vicious cycle, because frustration impedes your ability to remember, which puts the frustrating cards in front of you more often, which eventually causes you to throw your smartphone out of the nearest window.

All of this is unnecessary. The learning process for a new word takes very little time, and it's time well spent. If you take just a moment to figure out how to remind yourself of the meaning of a word, you can retain that word forever. This point was nicely summed up by Damien Elmes, the creator of my favorite SRS program, Anki: "Creating your own deck is the most effective way to learn a complex subject. Subjects like languages and the sciences can't be understood simply by memorizing facts—they require explanation and context to learn effectively. Furthermore, inputting the information yourself forces you to decide what the key points are and leads to a better understanding." I'd add that the card creation process is a lot of fun, too. You get to spend time by yourself and for yourself, learning, discovering, and creating.

Once you've done this, your daily reviews become enjoyable, because most of your time is spent saying to yourself, "Holy sh*t! I can't *believe* I still remember that! I am a rock star!" It's a daily self-esteem booster that *happens* to teach you a language at the same time, and it's an easy habit to form and maintain. We like habits; they make the difference between comfortably chatting with the Parisian waitress and awkwardly asking for the English menu.

KEY POINTS

- Spaced repetition systems (SRSs) are flash cards on steroids. They supercharge memorization by automatically monitoring your progress and using that information to design a daily, customized to-do list of new words to learn and old words to review.

DO THIS NOW: LEARN TO USE A SPACED REPETITION SYSTEM (SRS)

We have found a way to defeat forgetting. Now we must decide what to remember. In the next four chapters, I'll show you precisely what to learn and how to learn it.

We'll begin with the sounds and alphabet of your language. This will give you the structure you need to remember new words easily. To accomplish this, I'll show you old and new tools that can quickly rewire your ears, and we'll use spaced repetition to rapidly memorize example words for every important letter combination (e.g., *gn* as in *gnocchi*). In short order, you will master the sounds of your language.

Armed with your language's sounds, you can begin to tackle words. I will show you a list of the 625 most frequent concrete nouns, verbs, and adjectives. These words are easy to visualize, which makes them easy to remember. We will insert them into your SRS with a combination of pictures, personal connections, and sounds. In turn, your SRS will quickly insert those words into your long-term memory. In the process, you'll construct a foundation upon which you can build the rest of your grammar and vocabulary.

Finally, I will show you how to use Google Images to find illustrated stories for every word and grammatical concept in your language. You'll use these stories to make effective, memorable flash cards for your SRS. Before long, your grammar will become a reflex, and you won't need to worry about it. Every new word will reinforce that grammatical reflex, and every new piece of grammar will reinforce your words. Your language will build itself to fluency, and you'll come along for the ride.

Before we begin, you have a choice to make. There are two main types of SRSs: paper-based and computer-based. Choose your SRS and learn to use it. Then look at your daily schedule and determine how much time you have available. We'll use that information to create a language-learning habit.

Choose Your Spaced Repetition System

The most popular SRSs are computer-based, and my absolute favorite is Anki. First released in 2008, Anki is free, easy to use, and runs on every operating system and smartphone.[12] It syncs between devices (so you can study at home on your computer and then continue on your smartphone on the train to work), and it can handle images and sound files. You tell it how many new flash cards you want to learn every day, and it handles the rest. In roughly thirty minutes per day, you can learn thirty new cards and maintain all of your old cards. Scale up or down as needed to fit your schedule and tolerance for LCD screens.

---

12. Anki is free in all cases but one: if you want to be able to study *off-line* on an iPhone or iPad, then you'll have to fork out a fair bit of money for the app. If you have a reliable Internet connection on your iPhone or iPad, then the app is unnecessary (although I wholeheartedly recommend it). The Android app is free.

If you prefer working with your hands, you can create an SRS with physical flash cards. Named after an Austrian science journalist writing in the 1970s, the Leitner box is just a particularly clever way to use a flash card file box, some dividers, and a calendar. In the original version, your box is divided into four sections. You review section 1 every day, section 2 every two days, section 3 every three days, and so on. When you successfully remember a card—*gato* = [cute picture of a cat]—it moves into the next section. If you forget, it moves back into section 1. This acts like a gauntlet for words; any flash cards that can get all the way to the last section have won their way into your long-term memory. The original system uses shorter intervals than we need (one/two/three/four days as opposed to weeks/months), but we can fix that by adding a few more dividers and changing the schedule around. You'll find detailed instructions and an appropriate schedule for a Leitner box in Appendix 3, along with download links for Anki.

Not sure whether or not to use a Leitner box? When you use physical flash cards, you benefit from an involved, hands-on arts and crafts experience with each of your cards. This is a *wonderful* learning experience that will make your cards much easier to remember, and you lose this experience when you move to a computer. Still, computerized SRSs have a number of advantages over physical flash cards, so don't make your decision just yet.

First things first. You can't make paper flash cards talk. You'll be learning pronunciation before you learn vocabulary, and it's much easier to learn pronunciation when your flash cards can talk to you. If you use physical flash cards, you'll need to set aside time to listen to recordings of your words, and you'll need to become *very* comfortable with a phonetic alphabet (**a fənɛtɪk ælfəbɛt**). This won't take you a long time, but it is work, and now you can't say I didn't warn you ahead of time.

Second, it is extraordinarily easy to get pictures from Google Images into computerized flash cards, and pictures are the most effective way to remember large amounts of information. Even if you use physical flash cards, and even if you're a *terrible* artist, you should be drawing pictures for every word you encounter. Your visual memory is too helpful to ignore, and as long as *you* can tell your cat stick figure from your dog stick figure, you'll still reap the benefits.

Third, the process of *finding* images for computerized flash cards is one of the most powerful learning experiences you could ever hope for. Again, your brain sucks in images like a sponge. Just a few seconds browsing through twenty dog images will create a powerful, lasting memory. Even if you're using physical flash cards, don't pass up the opportunity to learn your words through Google Images. We'll cover this process in depth in Chapter 4.

Last, you'll be making two cards for many words: a comprehension card (*bear = ?*), and a production card (*big, furry animal, likes to eat honey = ?*). Making duplicate cards on a computer is easy; doing it by hand can get tedious. If it's too tedious, skip the production cards. You may get enough of a memory bump from the arts and craftiness of physical flash cards to spare yourself the need for them, and if you're having trouble keeping a word in memory, then you can always make the production card later.

Go to Appendix 3 and pick your poison. If you choose to use a Leitner box, then you have some supplies to pick up and a calendar to fill in. If you go for Anki, then download it, install it, and follow the video tutorials until you understand how to use it.

Time Commitments and Your Language Habit

Take a moment to plan out your budding language habit. You will have two customizable time commitments: creating your flash cards and reviewing those flash cards. Your flash card reviews should be regular; ideally, you're looking for a slot in your schedule that you can maintain on a daily basis. If you can connect your review time to another regularly recurring event in your life (e.g., breakfast or your daily commute), you'll have an easier time establishing a new language habit.

While daily reviews are best, *any* regular routine will naturally adapt to your schedule. If you skip weekends, for example, you'll have more reviews on Mondays. But since you're only learning for five days a week, you'll have fewer reviews than someone practicing daily, so it will stay manageable.

Start with a small number of new cards (fifteen to thirty) per day; you can always decide later if you want to go crazy with your flash cards. As mentioned earlier, you can learn thirty new cards per day and maintain your old cards in exchange for thirty minutes a day. If you go overboard with learning new cards, they *will* come back later, whether you have time for them or not. In the middle of my Russian adventures, I spent a summer learning sixty new cards per day (it took me around an hour a day). After the summer, when I had significantly less time, those cards showed up for *months* in my daily reviews. I eventually got through them, but if I had *begun* learning Russian in that way, I may have run away screaming. Learn new cards at a rate that you know you can maintain.

Do note that we're talking about learning thirty new *cards* per day, rather than thirty new *words*. Over the next few chapters, I'm going to show you how to break sounds, words, and grammar into their smallest, easiest-to-remember bits. You'll memorize each bit individually. As a result, some words may involve a small handful of cards. This may sound like more work ("I have to memorize *four* flash cards for a single Chinese character?"), but as you'll see, it's going to make your life *much* easier. SRSs give you the ability to retain *everything* you throw into them. As long as you can review a little bit each day, there's no end to what you can jam into your head, and as long as your cards are simple and easy to remember, you'll be able to learn them quickly and easily.

There's one more time commitment—card creation—and it can be much more sporadic than card reviews. I tend to go on card creation binges once a month, sitting for absurd numbers of hours in front of my computer and making hundreds upon hundreds of cards in a week-

---

A Tip for Missed Days

When dealing with a bloated re-view pile, continue learning two to three new words per day. It will spice things up a bit without adding much to your time commit-ment.

---

end. I get obsessive when I'm having fun. You may prefer a more moderate approach. You'll find that it's a nice way to spend a long Sunday afternoon, and if your schedule demands something more regular, then twenty minutes every day should do the trick.

If you miss a day (and you will oc-casionally), then it's not the end of the world. The only difficulty is that your reviews will pile up whether you want them to or not. Remember, your SRS is just a fancy to-do list. If your SRS believes that you're about to forget the word *pollo*, then that flash card will land in your to-do list even while you're vacationing in Hawaii. Once you get back from your vacation, you may have a long list waiting for you. At that point, you should complete those reviews first. They'll give you the best payback for your time, and they'll get you back on track with your language habit. Cut back on learning new cards, and spend a few days working at your reviews until they're back to normal levels.

Once you find a convenient time to review, your routine will trans-form into a habit on its own. These habits form easily for the same rea-sons that SRSs work so well. All of those hormones that help you store information tend to *feel good*. As a result, you'll find your hands auto-matically reaching for your flash cards as soon as you sit down on the train. Let's get you some flash cards, so you can get started already.

For the Intermediates

You're going to be relying upon your SRS just as much as the beginners. Choose your system and get familiar with how it works. Then look at your schedule and figure out where your language studies will fit in.

CHAPTER 3

Sound Play

L'accent est l'âme du discours, il lui donne le sentiment et la verité.
Accent is the soul of language; it gives language its feeling and truth.

—Jean-Jacques Rousseau, *Émile*

We are now the knights who say, "Ekki ekki ekki FIKANG! Zoop boing brn zroyen!"

—The knights who until recently said, "Ni!," *Monty Python and the Holy Grail*

We've spent two chapters pontificating about learning and memory, and admittedly, we haven't gotten much *done*. You haven't learned any useful words, and I'm about to tell you *not* to open your grammar book. Instead, we're going to venture off into the land of sound. We'll discuss many reasons why, but the most important is this: when you're not sure about the way your language sounds, you're stuck learning *two* languages instead of just one.

In an ideal world, the written language and the spoken language walk together, hand in hand. They share words freely among themselves, help each other through tough spots, and generally have a good time together. You come along, hang out, and soon enough, the three of you are good buddies. Written language gives you some good book recommendations, you have dinner over at spoken language's house, and the three of you have a blast. What's not to love? The two languages have a new companion, and you're getting to know them at breakneck speed, because you can chat about what you've read, and you can read about what you've heard.

All of this goes to crap if we don't start with pronunciation, because we get stuck with a bunch of broken words.

We encounter a broken word whenever we *think* a word is pronounced one way, but it's *actually* pronounced a different way. These words can't be shared between the written language and the spoken language, and as a result, they break up our little circle of friends.

You may have encountered broken words in English. I certainly have; I spent the majority of my life convinced that the word *scheme* was pronounced "sheem." I read about color *sheems*, pyramid *sheems*, and the *sheeming* con men who ran them. Unfortunately, *sheem* had a friend named *skeam*. *Skeam* seemed quite similar in meaning and usage to *sheem*, but I never seemed to see both words in the same place, so I never knew when to use which word. I avoided using either of them whenever possible. I only discovered the true identity of *skeam* in the middle of college, when I finally decided to Google both words and figure out the real differences between them and instead discovered that my two words were in fact *one* word and one pronunciation mistake.

My two *schemes* lived in a crevice they had hewn between my spoken language and my written language. This crevice was, thankfully, small. I only rarely fell in and became confused, because schemes are not everyday occurrences. But imagine, for a moment, how difficult it would be if your entire language were dotted with *schemes*, *skeams*, and *sheems* lurking behind every corner. You would never be sure of the precise meaning and usage of *any* of these words, and as a result, you'd have a terribly difficult time using or remembering them.

In English, you're unlikely to fall into the broken word trap many times. You're surrounded by conversations, books, movies, and television shows that will inevitably catch the wackiest of pronunciation mistakes. In a foreign language, you're not so lucky. At the end of my French immersion program, I sat in a classroom with seven advanced French students, discussing philosophy. We had recently read *Huis Clos* by Sartre, and we were comparing Sartre's ideas with those of Descartes. It may have been the most esoteric, highbrow conversation I've ever had, and it was in *French*, of all things. One of my colleagues raised her hand and pointed out that there was *another* philosopher we should be discussing.

His name was Dess-CART-eez.

My colleague had been caught by a broken word, but this time, her language was *full* of them. French is notorious for its quirky spelling. The vast majority of French's final consonants are thrown away: *beaux* is pronounced "bo," and *vous* is pronounced "vu." Oddities like these emerge in nearly every language: in English, phrases like "I'm going to go" are gradually replaced with "I'm gonna go," which may eventually turn into "I gonn' go." These changes occur more quickly in the spoken language than in the written language, so each language eventually splits in half. French is, accordingly, two languages: the written language of *Descartes* and the spoken language of *Dekart*.

In the ideal world we discussed earlier, you and these two languages will grow together and support each other. When you read a book, new words and bits of grammar find their way into your conversations. In those conversations, you'll hear *new* words, which will find their way into your writing. Every time you encounter new input, it improves your understanding and fluency in every aspect of your language.

This process only works if you can successfully connect the words you *read* to the words you *hear*. My colleague had read about Dess-CART-eez from books, and she had heard about Dekart in discussions. Because she hadn't internalized French's drop-the-final-consonants rule, she was struggling to keep track of broken words with similar names, very similar beliefs, and the exact same professions. By the end of our discussion, she learned about her mistake, but what about the hundreds or thousands of words that we *hadn't* discussed? Which broken *desserts*, *budgets*, and *terrains* were still hiding in the shadows, armed with their silent final consonants, and waiting for their opportunity to cause confusion?

The better you internalize good pronunciation habits in the beginning, the less time you'll waste hunting down broken words. If you can build a gut instinct about pronunciation, then every new word you read will automatically find its way into your ears and your mouth, and every word you hear will bolster your reading comprehension. You'll understand more, you'll learn faster, and you'll spare yourself the hunt for broken words. Along the way, you'll have an easier time memorizing, you'll make better impressions upon native speakers, and you'll speak more confidently when you're ready.

How can you do this quickly? If you spend two months poring over spelling rules and vowel charts before learning a single word, you're probably going to get bored. You need a path through pronunciation that quickly teaches you the basics and then reinforces and develops your pronunciation instincts while you're busy learning the rest of the language. In this chapter, I'll break down the three main challenges you're up against: ear training, mouth training, and eye training. We'll cover the differences between them, the methods you'll use to beat them, and the rewards you'll find when you do.

Train Your Ears, Rewire Your Brain

At the edge of the North Sea, a German coastguard officer waits at his radio.
"*Kshht* Mayday! Mayday! Hello, can you hear us? We are sinking!"
"Ja, hallo! Zis is ze German coastguard!"
"We are sinking! We are sinking!"
"OK. Vat are you sinkink *about*?"

—Berlitz advertisement

Babies get a lot of credit in the language-learning world. They have a seemingly superhuman ability to hear the differences between *every* sound in *every* language, and there are quite a lot of sounds to hear. The world's languages contain roughly 800 phonemes (six hundred consonants and two hundred vowels). Most languages choose around 40 of these to form their words, although the range is quite broad—there's a neat language called Rotokas in Papua New Guinea with only 11 phonemes, and Taa, spoken in Botswana, uses up to 112 (plus four tones!).

Some of these phonemes are totally foreign to an English speaker's ear—the click languages of Africa can sound bizarre—but most phonemes are subtle variations on familiar sounds. There are at least ten *t*'s that occur in the world's languages, and English speakers rarely hear the differences among *any* of them. Two different *t*'s allow you to hear the difference between "my cat Stan" and "my cat's tan." Unless you frequent cat tanning salons, this distinction isn't particularly important in English. If, on the other hand, you were learning Korean, you would find that *t* as in *tan* and *t* as in *Stan* are two entirely different letters, which form entirely different words.

> ### Three Korean T's
>
> Korean has *three* consonants that could be mistaken for a *t*: ㅌ as in *tan*, ㄸ as in *Stan*, and ㄷ, which sounds something like a cross between a *t* and a *d*.

You can't easily hear the distinctions between the ten *t*'s because you've learned to ignore them. Back when you were a baby, you could hear *all* of them. This made your world a very confusing place. You were surrounded by babbling adults, each of whom had slightly different ways of saying their vowels and consonants. Your ears rang with the sounds of *hundreds* of different consonants and vowels, and you lay within this chaos, searching for order.

You began to find this order between six months and one year of age. The best data we have on this process come from studies of Americans and the Japanese. By using brain scans, researchers can see whether an individual can hear the difference between any two sounds. An American adult listening to a monotonous "rock . . . rock . . . rock . . .

rock . . . lock" will show a sudden spike in brain activity when "lock" breaks the monotony, but a Japanese adult won't show any change whatsoever. A Japanese baby, however, has no trouble whatsoever recognizing the two sounds, an ability that gradually vanishes between six and twelve months of age.

What happens at this critical juncture? The baby's brain is collecting statistics. There is a smooth line that connects the letters *r* and *l*, and a consonant can fall *anywhere* on that line. In an American household, a typical baby will hear hundreds of slightly different consonants that tend to fall into two large piles along this line: sounds that are mostly *r*-like, and sounds that are mostly *l*-like. If you record a typical day in an American baby's life and count up those sounds, you'll see this:

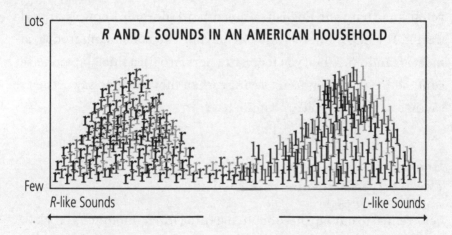

We tend to think of *r* and *l* as two distinct sounds, but they are not. Each consonant is a *group* of sounds that are roughly similar. We create these groups according to the sound environment in which we're raised. Because we don't hear many sounds halfway between *r* and *l*, we (rightly) decide that those babbling adults are all using variations of *two* consonants instead of *hundreds*. A baby in a Japanese household may hear many of the same sounds, but most of these sounds fall directly in the middle of the *r–l* spectrum:

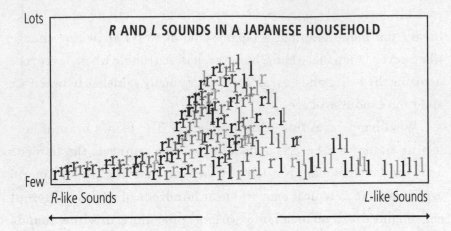

They (rightly) group *all* of these sounds together into a conso-nant halfway between *r* and *l*. This consonant—the Japanese *r*—doesn't sound quite like *r*, and it doesn't sound quite like *l*. If you listen to it, you'll find that your English-attuned brain doesn't know what to do with it. It will get filtered into one of your two consonant groups, al-most at random. When you listen to a person with a thick Japanese ac-cent, notice this: they aren't saying *r* when they mean to say *l*. They're saying a consonant you can't quite hear.

Hearing the Unhearable:
The Magic of Minimal Pair Testing

Let's return to our Japanese adult, listening to a monotonous "rock . . . rock . . . rock . . . rock . . ." in a brain scanner. As was discussed, he won't show any neural response if we surreptitiously sneak in a "lock." What wasn't yet discussed is how terrifying this is for language learn-ing. It is not that he misinterprets what he hears; he literally *cannot* hear the difference between these two sounds. As far as his brain is concerned, the words *rock* and *lock* might as well be spelled the same. In learning English, he is fighting his own brain. How can he possibly hope to succeed?

The most promising research in this field comes from a collection

---

The Elusive Japanese R

The Japanese *r* (found in words like *origami, rāmen,* and *tempura*) actually sounds like a combination of *r, l,* and *d,* with a little more *r* than anything else. It's a terribly difficult consonant to nail down for an American. I've spent a good half hour repeating after a recording of the word *rāmen* to prepare for one of my pronunciation demo videos, and I still can't hear the damn thing or produce it well. Fortunately, Japanese speakers never misinterpreted me when ordering *biru* (beer) in Japan. How could they? There's no such thing as *bilu* in Japanese.

---

of studies performed at Stanford and Carnegie Mellon. Researchers took a group of Japanese adults, gave them a small wad of cash, head-phones, and a computer and told them to sit in a room and listen to recordings of the words *rock* and *lock.* Their job was to press a button labeled "Rock" when they heard "rock" and to press a button labeled "Lock" when they heard "lock." Understandably, their performance was terrible. Even after practicing, it remained terrible. So far, so bad.

Here comes the magic: another group of participants was placed in the same situation, only this time their computer screens provided immediate feedback after each button press. For every correct guess, they saw a green checkmark. For every incorrect guess, they saw a red X. Suddenly, they began to learn. After 3 twenty-minute sessions, they had successfully rewired their brains. On later brain scans, they showed a *marked* response in the "rock . . . rock . . . rock . . . lock . . ." tests. They had learned to hear the unhearable.

We can take this research and use it for our own needs. *Rock* and *lock* are classic members of a special group of words known as minimal pairs. These are pairs of words that differ by only one sound, and every language is full of them. I've tortured quite a few of my Austrian En-glish students on the differences between minimal pairs like *thinking* and *sinking,* SUS-*pect* and sus-*PECT,* and *niece* and *knees.* These pairs get right to the heart of the hearing problem in a language, and practicing them with feedback provides the best way to train our ears and rewire our brains.

You'll be able to find the essential minimal pairs in your language at the beginning of many grammar books with CDs (and *definitely* throughout all pronunciation books), and I'm making it a personal mission to provide minimal pair tests on my website in as many languages as I can find (*Fluent-Forever.com/chapter3*). These tests are as basic as they get—they play a recording ("lock") and then ask you what word you heard ("rock" or "lock"?)—but what they lack in panache they make up for in results. I used them to learn the (obnoxiously difficult) sounds of Hungarian in twenty minutes a day for ten days. They're also a lot of fun; you can feel your ears changing with each repetition.

The Benefits of Ear Training: Pattern Recognition and Pattern Breaking

When you use minimal pair testing at the *beginning* of your language journey, you'll learn much faster in the long run. You'll have an easier time remembering new words, because they no longer sound foreign. You'll also understand native speakers better, because your ears are in sync with their speech. Instead of wasting your time correcting bad pronunciation habits, you'll be able to spend your time consuming language at breakneck speed.

How does ear training cause all of this to happen? You've given yourself the ability to recognize individual sounds, but that's not the end of the story. Because you've spent time *focusing* on those sounds, you'll be aware of the subtle changes that occur when you string those sounds together. This gives you two superpowers: you can hear sound rules, and you can hear when those rules are broken.

Sound rules connect spelling to sound and sound to sound. They tell you which sounds can be combined ("sticks" is okay in English) and which can't ("svickz" is not). Languages are full of complex sound rules, and we're very good at picking them up *if we can hear them*. You can observe this with kids. There's a neat linguistic test that researchers like to perform on five-year-olds. They show them a weird bird drawing and proclaim, "This is a wug!"

A WUG

Then they show the kids two of them and say, "Now there are two of them! There are two . . ." and the kids gleefully exclaim, "Wugz!"

This all seems simple and pleasant enough, but keep in mind that these kids are performing an *extraordinarily complex* operation. Somehow, deep within their cute little heads, they know that the plural of this *entirely new word* sounds like "z," whereas the plural of a different new word, like *heef,* sounds like "s" (and the plural of *tass* sounds like "iz"). These rules are nothing to sniff at, and they're different in every language (German kids say *"Vaks,"* not "wugz"). If your ears are sensitive to each new sound in your language, you will *notice* when there's a strange sound rule afoot, and every time you notice it, you'll get closer to internalizing it.

Your second superpower allows you to notice when words break those rules. In English, we have lots of pronunciation rules: a *k* is always pronounced like "k" (as in *kick*), except when it's not (*knife*). The nice thing about rules and exceptions is that even when they're as maddeningly complex as English (and lucky for you, they are nearly *always* simpler in other languages), they never create new sounds. There is *no* word in English that doesn't reuse the forty-one or forty-two sounds of the English language. This is the case in every language.

If you can hear all of the sounds in your language, then you might get surprised by the *spelling* of a word but never by the sound of a word. This helps you learn faster because your memory doesn't need to struggle to store some indescribable new sound. If a word like *mjöður* is just a combination of six familiar sounds, then it's no longer particularly foreign, and it won't be any harder to remember than an unusual but understandable name like Lakira.

Because of this, you'll be able to memorize the pronunciation of new words accurately, which will allow you to recognize them when they're spoken by a native speaker. Poof—you've just given your listening comprehension a massive boost from the start. If you have better listening comprehension, you'll gain more vocabulary and grammar every time you hear someone speak your language. Poof—you've just boosted your vocabulary and grammar knowledge for the rest of your life. You gain all this at the expense of a few hours of minimal pair study. Now if we can learn to *produce* those sounds, we're in business.

KEY POINTS

- Your brain is hardwired to ignore the differences between foreign sounds. To rewire it, listen to minimal pairs in your target language—similar sounding words like *niece* and *knees*—and test yourself until your brain adapts to hear these new sounds.
- By practicing in this way, you'll be better equipped to recognize words when they're spoken, and you'll have an easier time memorizing them on your own.

TRAIN YOUR MOUTH, GET THE GIRL[13]

Nobody cares how much you know, until they know how much you care.
—Theodore Roosevelt

I was recently asked the following: "If I had four hours to prepare for a date with a Cambodian supermodel, what would be the best use of my

---

13. Or boy.

time?" Here's my answer: learn to say one phrase—*any* phrase—really well. Sit on YouTube or Wikipedia for a few hours, look at pictures of mouth positions, and mimic recordings until you can sound like a native speaker for three seconds. It will Blow. Her. Mind.

An accurate accent is powerful because it is the ultimate gesture of empathy. It connects you to another person's culture in a way that words never can, because you have bent your *body* as well as your mind to match that person's culture. Anyone can learn "bawn-JURE" in a few seconds. To learn how *bonjour* fits into your companion's mouth and tongue; to learn how to manipulate the muscles, the folds, and even the texture of your throat and lips to match your companion's— *this* is an unmistakable, undeniable, and irresistible gesture of care.

To be fair, a good accent can occasionally get you in a bit of trouble. A few years ago, I went to Japan and learned a few simple Japanese phrases. I remember walking up to a lady and asking where to find the nearest department store. Her eyes opened wide, surprised by the tall lanky white guy addressing her with a half-decent Japanese accent. Then she exploded into a rapid-fire, paragraph-long answer to my question. I winced, put up my hands, and blabbered something in Japanese on the order of "Japanese! I! No! A little! A little little! Is!" She stopped, laughed a bit, and pointed to the left. All in all, I think developing a good accent is worth the effort, even if it makes people think you know more than you do.

The alternative—a thick, non-native accent—will get you in much more trouble. Paris has a particularly bad reputation on this front; as rumor has it, a momentary "bawn-JURE" will spoil your meal in any restaurant.[14] But you will see this *everywhere*. People with strong foreign accents are frequently treated as less adept at the language (and less intelligent as a person) than they are.

And even if this is unfair, it is understandable. It's uncomfortable to speak with someone when you aren't sure what they're saying

---

14. This reputation may be unfair nowadays. I haven't heard of anyone going to Paris recently who has seen any *particularly* rude behavior.

or whether they understand you. To try to relieve this discomfort, you may start speaking louder, using simpler words, switching to their language (if you can), or avoiding the person altogether. My father inexplicably develops an exaggerated Spanish accent whenever he orders Chinese food: "I LIKE-A CHEEKON FRY RICE-O PLEASE-O." We all go a little nuts when we don't feel understood.

This phenomenon can screw up your language learning. You currently speak the most common language on earth. If you're trying to speak French and French people prefer to speak to you in English, you won't get the language exposure you need.

Train Your Mouth

Let's figure out how to develop a good accent. I've frequently heard that it's impossible to perfect an accent after the age of twelve. But this *can't* be true; actors and singers do it all the time, and we're not any smarter or better than the rest of humanity. We just care about pronunciation—we have to; no one will pay us for *bad* German—so we take the time to do it right: we start early, and we gain an awareness of what's going on in our mouths when we speak.

Half of a good accent is simply a matter of timing. Singers learn pronunciation *first*, and as a result, we don't have to fight years of bad habits. We learn to parrot words accurately before we have any idea what they mean, so that we can get onto a stage without embarrassing ourselves. You should do the same. If you wait until later to work on your accent, you will have butchered every word in your vocabulary hundreds (or thousands) of times. This is where myths like the twelve-year cap on accent learning come from; it's hard to unlearn bad habits. If, instead, you work on your accent early, then you will tend to pronounce all of your new words correctly. With every new word you learn, you'll reinforce good pronunciation habits, and those habits will last you a lifetime.

If you've *already* studied a language, you may have some deeply ingrained bad habits. Your road will be longer, but there's hope for you yet. First the bad news: your old habits are not going to vanish; they're carved permanently into some crevice of your brain. We'll build new habits in the crevice next door. Once you've trained your ears and mouth to produce the sounds of your language correctly, your job will be to learn each new word with your fancy new accent. Eventually, you will find two voices in your head—an old, crummy one, and a new, awesome one. As you consistently and consciously choose to use your new voice for new words, you'll strengthen your good habits until they become more familiar and comfortable than your bad habits. A few "bawn-JUREs" may slip through occasionally, but overall, you'll have the snazzy accent that gets you that Cambodian supermodel you were clambering after.

So how do you learn to pronounce new sounds? What do the actors and singers know that everyone else doesn't? It's not all that complex. We simply know that the sounds we make are created by the movements of muscles in our mouths. We pick up an awareness of the everyday movements of our tongues and lips, and we combine them in a few new ways. For example, when you say "oo" as in "Boo!" your lips form a circle. If you keep your lips in that same circle while you try to say "ee" as in "see," you'll make a funny sound. This is a new vowel, which you'll find at the end of French words like *fondue*. If you practice it a little, you'll be able to act like a pretentious jerk at parties. ("Sorry, *what* did you eat? Fawn-Dew? Perhaps you meant Fon*due*? Oh, *now* I understand!")

To master your own mouth, you'll need information. You need to know what your mouth is actually *doing* whenever you open it. This information can be hard to access, because it's hidden in relatively impenetrable linguistic jargon. Terms like *voiceless epiglottal fricative* aren't particularly inspiring, and so most people are forced to rely upon terrible, confusing descriptions: "It's kind of like 'ch,' like when a Scottish person says 'Loch,' only it's farther back in the throat, kind of like gargling, only even deeper." I've made a series of

YouTube videos to help you get the pronunciation information you need (*Fluent-Forever.com/chapter3*). Watch them. They take thirty-five minutes, and at the end, you'll understand how your mouth does what it does.

In those videos, I go over a tremendously valuable tool known as the International Phonetic Alphabet (IPA). It was created, naturally, by the French, who needed some way to deal with the fact that four of the five letters in *haies* (hedges) were silent (it's pronounced "eh"). The phonetic alphabet they developed does two awesome things: it turns languages into easily readable sounds, and it tells you exactly how to make each of those sounds. In English, there are ten ways to spell the "oo" sound in the word *too*. In IPA, there is *only one, always*: *u*.

Ridiculous English Spelling: food, dude, flu, flew, fruit, blue, to, shoe, move, tomb, group, through

Awesome IPA Spelling: **fud, dud, flu, flu, fɹut, blu, tu, ʃu, muv, tum, grup, θɹu**

Every IPA letter is not only a sound but also a set of instructions on how to make that sound. This is super useful. When I began Hungarian, I looked up the sounds of that language on Wikipedia. Hungarian has a few odd sounds, including ɟ͡ʝ, which is basically our *j* as in *jar* if you keep the front of your tongue touching your bottom teeth. I've never spoken to a Hungarian about this, and no one has ever told me to put my tongue in that weird position. The IPA symbols *themselves* spell it out for me, and they can do it for you, too.

There are two barriers in the way: the IPA is usually full of nasty technical jargon and it uses weird-looking symbols. I can't get rid of the symbols—English uses twenty-six letters for forty-two sounds; a phonetic alphabet *needs* extra symbols—but I can show you a way around the jargon. In general, you only need three pieces of information to make any sound: you need to know what to do with your tongue, with your lips, and with your vocal cords, and there aren't *that* many options. Your vocal cords go on and off. That's it—it's the only difference between "ssss" and "zzzz." When you're speaking vowels, your lips are basically rounded like "oo" or not. That's all. The rest of the IPA focuses upon the location and behavior of your tongue.

In Appendix 4, I give you an IPA decoder chart. Any time you come across some weird sound you don't understand, you can load up the Wikipedia article for your language (e.g., "IPA for Spanish" or "IPA for Swahili") and compare it to the chart. The chart will tell you what to do with your tongue, your lips, and your vocal cords. You can use this chart as a universal decoder device that translates a word like *mjöður* into a series of tongue, lip, and vocal cord positions. Coupled with your newly trained ears, you'll have a much easier time mimicking each new sound in your language.

Back-Chaining: How to Get Ridiculous Words into Your Mouth

So you've dutifully learned each of your sounds, you fling open your textbook, and run face first into a German word like *Höchstgeschwin-digkeitsbegrenzung* (speed limit). Now what? Each of the sounds isn't particularly hard, but how do you get your tongue to jump through so many hoops in a row?

Go backward. Say the *end* of the word, and then add one letter at a time until you can say the whole thing. Let's try the Russian word for "flinch" (as in "I *flinch* whenever I see this word"), *vzdrognu*. It manages to string together four consonants in a row before reaching its first vowel. Ick. We'll go backward. While you might have trouble saying "*vzdrognu*," you *can* say "*nu*." Now you can add a letter and practice saying "*gnu*." Once that's comfortable, keep building up, one letter at a time:

o . . . gnu . . . ognu

r . . . ognu . . . rognu

d . . . rognu . . . drognu

z . . . drognu . . . zdrognu (this one's tricky; buzz like a bee—"zzzzz"— and then say "drognu." Zdrognu!)

v . . . zdrognu . . . vzdrognu (same story: "vvvvvzzzzzz-drognu." Say that ten times fast.)

Tongue Tricks

Back-chaining is, incidentally, the cheat code for tongue twisters. You can use it to combine words in the same way you would use it for letters. For a real challenge, enjoy this Czech classic: *Strč prst skrz krk* (which means, naturally, "Stick your finger through your throat").

This is called back-chaining, and it's an old singer trick that can work tongue-related miracles. You're using muscle memory to trick your tongue into doing things it wasn't able to do before. While your tongue can't handle eight new movements at once, it *can* handle a single new combination of two familiar sounds. If you split long, difficult words into small, easy chunks, you'll find that your tongue is capable of remarkable acrobatic feats.

You may wonder why we're going backward. After all, we *could* start with "*v*" and progress to "*vz*," "*vzd*," "*vzdr*," and so on. Indeed you can, but in my experience, it doesn't work as well. By going backward,

KEY POINTS

- Impressions matter, and your accent makes your first impression in any language. A good accent can make the difference between a conversation that starts in French and ends in English, and a full conversation in French.
- Improve your accent by learning the raw ingredients—the tongue, lip, and vocal cord positions—of every new sound you need. You can find that information in the International Phonetic Alphabet (IPA).
- If you run into difficult combinations of sounds, back-chain them together until your tongue performs automatically.

you practice the end of the word *every* time you add a letter. This makes it easier and easier to finish the word correctly and automatically. Because of this, you only need to focus your attention for a brief moment at the very beginning (*H . . .*), and you can let your tongue go on autopilot for the rest of the word (*. . . öchstgeschwindigkeitsbegrenzung!*). By making the *end* of a word as easy and familiar as possible, you'll never get lost on the way there.

TRAIN YOUR EYES, SEE THE PATTERNS

I have a spelling checker,
It came with my PC.
It plane lee marks four my revue
Miss steaks aye can knot sea.

Eye ran this poem threw it,
Your sure reel glad two no.
Its vary polished in it's weigh.
My checker tolled me sew . . .

—Jerrold H. Zar, "Candidate for a Pullet Surprise" (excerpt)

You know how to train your ears to hear new sounds, and you know how to train your mouth to produce them. But how do you know which sounds to produce? Somehow, you have to connect the writing system of your language to your mouth and ears.

Now wait a second. What if you only want to speak? Kids learn languages without first learning to read. Why can't adults?

We *can*, but it's time consuming and expensive. Kids learn languages by listening and watching adults for *thousands upon thousands of hours*. Adults do this for free for their own kids, but those same adults will tend to charge *you* a lot of money.

The written word, on the other hand, is plentiful and free. Even if you never intend to read a book in French, you can get a thousand illustrated examples of every word in your language from Google Images. This is too good a resource to ignore. The problem with written resources is the danger of broken words—our Dekart and Descartes—and this is the problem we must overcome.

This challenge is different in every language, because every language shows a different degree of correspondence between its spelling and pronunciation. English is one of the worst offenders when it comes to our spelling system—it is legendary for its wackiness—but even English operates under (a large set of) dependable rules, which is why you can predict the pronunciation of fake words like *ghight*, *phime*, and *moughtation.* Even in Chinese, a language where single characters refer to whole words rather than sounds, you'll find that the characters often contain pronunciation hints, a feature that allows Chinese native speakers (and advanced Chinese students) to predict the pronunciation of new characters. Every language has its patterns, and we make our job much easier if we can get those patterns into our heads.

This task can be a piece of cake if we know what we're doing. We're very good at internalizing patterns—even a five-year-old knows that dogs are *dogz* and cats are *cats.* There is only one prerequisite to learning a new pattern: we need to *notice* it when it passes by.

We can do this in many ways—we could listen to recordings of every new word we read, for example—but the *best* way to do this involves a phonetic alphabet. This is not to say that recordings aren't helpful. I think they're great (necessary, even)! It's just that sometimes we need

---

Sound Clues in Chinese

More than 80 percent of Chinese words contain phonetic clues. For example, the character 沐—*mù*—(to wash oneself) contains a little character for a tree—木—which is also pronounced "mù." As you get a feel for the basic Chinese characters, you'll be able to guess at the pronunciation of a new character reasonably well—you might guess "pang" when the word is actually *bang.* Chinese characters also can hint at their own meaning: 木—*mù* (wood/tree), 森—*sēn* (forest). It's a *really* neat writing system.

to be told what we're hearing before we can truly hear it. We've already encountered one good phonetic alphabet—the IPA—but the particular alphabet is less important than the information it conveys. Hell, you can use "bawn-JURE" if you know *exactly* what that would sound like in a French person's mouth.[15] We're looking for a way to *see* what we're hearing and, equally important, what we're *not* hearing.

Our eyes are a powerful source of input. If we aren't careful, they can trick our ears into a state of inattention, and inattention can prevent us from learning the patterns we need. I once showed a friend one of my digital flash cards for French. It had a picture of a cat with the word *chat* underneath, and it played a recording of the word.

"Shah," said the recording (the *t* is silent).

"Shot," repeated my friend.

"No, it's *shah*," I corrected.

"Oh. Okay," he replied. "Shaht."

I run into this problem a lot with my English students. It's *terribly* difficult to get a student to say "lissen" when he sees a word like *listen*. This problem vanishes as soon as I teach them a phonetic alphabet. No one pronounces the t in "listen" when they're reading lɪsn.

When I learn a language, I tend to use a combination of recordings and a phonetic alphabet, at least until the little French man in my head starts sounding *very* French. Then I stop with the recordings and rely on my phonetic alphabet. If my language is *very* friendly, phonetically speaking, I'll phase out my phonetic alphabet once I'm feeling (over) confident about my pronunciation.

Do you *need* to learn a new phonetic alphabet? Not really, especially if your language has relatively simple and strict spelling rules, like Spanish or Hungarian. You can rely upon recordings instead. But even for those languages, a phonetic alphabet can make your job easier in two ways: it helps you to see and hear whenever a sound rule shows up—when you're reading *wugs* but saying "wugz"—and it

---

15. But seriously, don't use "bawn-JURE." Bleh.

gives you one more way to look at the same information. Because of the quirky nature of memory, this makes your task *easier*. By learning more, you'll work less.

More Is Less: The Learning Paradox

On the surface, it seems you have a lot to do. You're building connections between your ears, your mouth, spelling, and a phonetic alphabet. I promised you an easy, fast learning method and have given you a giant pile of new things to learn. Instead of *rue*, pronounced "rew" (street), I'm giving you this:

r

Spellings in French: Just r

Symbol in IPA: Upside-down R: ʁ

Tongue position (from Appendix 4): Back of tongue touches your uvula, a little bit behind "k."

Type of consonant (from Appendix 4): Trill. You let your uvula flap up and down rapidly against your tongue.

Vocal cords (from Appendix 4): Buzzing

ue

Symbol in IPA: y

Tongue position (from Appendix 4): Tongue up and forward, like "ee"

Lips (from Appendix 4): In a circle, like "oo"

We haven't even gotten to the "street" part. What the hell?

I'm doing this on purpose, and here's why: the more you can learn about something, the easier time you'll have mastering it, and the less time you'll need over the long term. If you're trying to make the "foreign" sounds of your new language familiar, then your *easiest, shortest* path is to learn *as much as you possibly can* about those sounds.

This phenomenon shows up in every subject. As a kid, I loved math. It had this neat quality, because everything was connected. You memorize that 3×4 is 12, and then you learn that 4×3 is also 12, and eventually you start realizing that you can switch the order of *any* two numbers you're multiplying. You see that 3×4 and 4×3 are examples of something much larger—some abstract, floating pattern known as *multiplication*—and every new example helps you hold more of that giant floating pattern in your head. That pattern changes and becomes more subtle and nuanced with every little fact you learn. Soon you begin to see the connections between multiplication and division, and multiplication and exponents, and multiplication and fractions. Eventually, your giant floating pattern of multiplication becomes part of a *bigger* floating pattern—a universe of *math*.

As long as I could connect every new thing I learned to this universe, I had an easy time with math. And I noticed that classmates who had problems with math weren't struggling with *math*; they were struggling with *connections*. They were trying to memorize equations, but no one had successfully shown them how those equations connect with everything they had already learned. They were doomed.

At some point along their path, their interconnected math universe had shattered into fragments, and they were trying to learn each piece in isolation—an extremely difficult proposition. Who could possibly remember the formula for the volume of a hexagonal prism? How could you make yourself care enough to actually remember?

It was so much *easier* if you could see how all the pieces interrelated—how multiplication connected with the area of rectangles, how the area of rectangles connected with triangles and trapezoids, and how the volume of prisms connected back with multiplication. I didn't have to memorize formulae; they were just examples of something much, much larger.

Math can be hard for the same reason that languages can be hard.

At some point, you miss a connection, and if no one goes back, takes you by the hand, and shows you that connection, then you're suddenly doomed to memorize crappy formulae.

We know why this is so; we've already discussed the nature of memory. Every time we can connect two memories, we strengthen *both* of them—*neurons that fire together wire together*. If you learn that the *è* in French's *mère* (mother) sounds like "eh," you've built one connection. If you then learn that the *ai* in *lait* (milk) is also pronounced "eh," you've built *three* connections: "eh" connects with *lait*, "eh" connects with *mère*, and *lait* connects with *mère*. These three connections are much easier to remember than your original *è* = "eh." By adding more pieces to learn, you're making your job much easier. You're learning faster, which means *less* work over time.

Naturally, there are limits. There is an art to building memories; it takes balance. You could spend *days* learning trivia about "eh," and it won't necessarily help you learn French. On the other hand, if you skipped it, and I simply told you to learn a bunch of French words, you'd be back in math class, memorizing formulae. How can you determine where more is less and where more is just more?

The key is *relevance*. If *you* see something as useful, then it's worth learning. If not, then not. In Appendix 4, I give you a decoder for the entire IPA, but if your favorite textbook or dictionary doesn't use IPA symbols, then don't memorize IPA symbols (just use them for a reference).[16] If you know how to pronounce "ee" already (and you do), then you don't need to worry about the location of your tongue. On the other hand, if a sound seems foreign and difficult, then go nuts. Learn everything. Learn its spellings, its behavior in your mouth, its relationship to the other sounds you already know. See how your textbook or dictionary notates it. Find some example words. Do whatever you can; the more you do, the less work it will be. It's magic.

---

16. To be fair, my decoder is missing a *few* pieces from the IPA, but you probably don't need the African clicks.

KEY POINTS

- Every language contains a pattern of connections between its spelling and its sounds. If you can internalize that pattern and make it automatic, you'll save yourself a great deal of work.
- The easiest way to internalize those patterns is to use your SRS. Create flash cards to memorize every spelling pattern you need.
- In the process, approach foreign sounds and complex patterns from as many angles as you can—from their spellings to their sounds, even down to the individual mouth positions used for each sound. You're taking advantage of one of the stranger quirks of learning: the more bits and pieces you learn, the less work it takes to learn them.

DO THIS NOW: LEARN YOUR LANGUAGE'S SOUND SYSTEM

It doesn't necessarily take much time to learn a language's sound system. If you're learning a language like Spanish, you can listen to a few recordings, look at a few example words of each spelling in your language, and move on to vocabulary. If you're learning Arabic, you have a bit more work to do.

But *work* is too strong a word. I find that working with sound is deeply satisfying and fun, and I don't believe that's just because I'm a singer. I think it's the other way around. Sound is the way we connect our thoughts to our bodies. We see an eagle in the sky, we turn to a companion, and our tongue flies up and forward, our lips fly open, and our vocal cords engage. "Eagle!" To paraphrase Rousseau, when we learn an accent, we are taking on the soul of that language. This isn't work; it's communion.

Let's get communing. In the back of this book, you'll find The Gallery (page 177). There you'll learn how to make pronunciation flash cards, but the extent to which you'll use them (or *whether* you'll use them at all) depends upon which path you choose.

There are two basic paths through pronunciation: the standard

route and the off-road route. The standard route uses published resources: either a grammar book with a CD or a special book/CD combo
dedicated exclusively to pronunciation. If your grammar book comes
with recordings, it likely contains a series of pronunciation lessons
scattered through the book. Ignore all the vocabulary and grammar
in your book and jump to each pronunciation section. There, listen to
and mimic the recordings and then move on to the next pronunciation lesson until you're done. If your grammar book is text only, then
consider buying a dedicated pronunciation book with CD and working
through it from cover to cover. If you need help remembering a given
sound or spelling, then you can pick and choose whichever flash cards
you need from the Gallery.

The off-road route takes the tools we've found—minimal pair
tests for ear training, the IPA for mouth instructions, and our SRS
for getting it all into our heads—and builds a pronunciation trainer
out of them. These trainers test your ears until you can hear your new
language's sounds, connect those sounds to the spelling patterns in
your language, and dump that information into your head through
your SRS.

I've tried to make your job easier by doing as much of the grunt
work as possible; I'm creating trainers as fast as I can in as many languages as I can. If I've done one for your language, then grab it. These
trainers are cheaper than a pronunciation guidebook, and they should
do a much better (and faster) job than the standard route. If you use
these, you won't need to make *any* flash cards now; just download
them, install them, and within a few weeks, you'll have pronunciation
mastered.

If I haven't done your language (or if you prefer to do things yourself), then jump to the First Gallery (page 191). There I'll show you how
to make your own pronunciation trainer in a few hours. You'll use a
combination of resources.

Resources

Pronunciation resources are a mixed bag. Some textbooks begin with a detailed chapter devoted to the alphabet, spelling, and sounds, with CDs brimming with individual phonemes, minimal pairs, example words, and example sentences. Other textbooks give you a passing overview ("Some French vowels are nasal") and move on. Here's what's at your fingertips:

FREE RESOURCES

ESSENTIAL TOOL!—*Forvo.com* (FREE RECORDINGS OF WORDS): First things first. Get acquainted with *Forvo.com*. Free, native-speaker recordings of more than 2 million words in three hundred languages. Once you start making flash cards, Forvo will become your best friend. If you're using Anki, put recordings from Forvo into your flash cards. If you're using a Leitner box, go through your vocabulary list at least once a week, read your newest words aloud, play their recordings on Forvo, and if you didn't sound the same, repeat until you do. Once you're consistently accurate with your pronunciation, you can stop double-checking, but until then, stick with it. There's no reason to become fluent in a badly pronounced language, because *no one will speak it with you*.

A Hint for Rhinospike

Your request for a recording will be done more quickly if you record something in English for someone else. It's how they encourage people to record.

Rhinospike.com (FREE RECORDINGS OF SENTENCES): Rhinospike is a handy website for native-speaker recordings. You submit a text and someone will record it for you, usually within twenty-four to forty-eight hours. If your textbook has a list of minimal pairs but doesn't come with a recording of those words, you can get someone on Rhinospike to record those words for you. It's also a lovely place to get recordings of full sentences with intonation, so if your textbook has some example sentences, put them up on Rhinospike as well.

ESSENTIAL TOOL!—MY PRONUNCIATION YOUTUBE SERIES (*Fluent-Forever.com/ chapter3*): Go watch these. They take you on a tour of your mouth and the IPA. They make pronunciation understandable, and they give you access to one of the most powerful pronunciation tools available, the IPA.

ESSENTIAL TOOL!—WIKIPEDIA'S IPA FOR SPANISH, IPA FOR FRENCH, AND SO ON is a tool I mentioned earlier. You can copy all of its example words for each sound, and you can use it with Appendix 4 to get mouth instructions for any weird sound in your target language.

ONLINE DICTIONARIES (*Wiktionary.org*): Wiktionary is turning into a great resource for many languages, with pronunciation entries in IPA for many words.

ONLINE DICTIONARIES (OTHERS): Each language has several online dictionaries, some of which are *excellent*. I have the best ones linked on my website. Digital dictionaries with pronunciation information are extremely handy if you're using Anki; you can put in your word, copy the pronunciation information, and paste it directly onto your flash cards in seconds.

YOUTUBE contains resources of mixed and undependable quality, but I've found it particularly helpful when it comes to questions like "How do I roll my Spanish *r*?" You're not necessarily listening to experts, but you *are* often listening to native speakers who have good tips.

THE FOREIGN SERVICE INSTITUTE (*fsi-language-courses.org*) has forty-one languages' worth of free, public-domain textbooks online, most of which come with MP3s, and about half of which start with a detailed pronunciation section, complete with minimal pair tests, spelling rules, and the works. These courses are old and some of them are *extraordinarily* boring, but many contain excellent recordings. If you can stay awake through them, you'll get all the information you need.

PAID RESOURCES

MY PRONUNCIATION TRAINERS (*Fluent-Forever.com/chapter3*) provide you with minimal pair tests, spelling rules, example words, and enough vocabulary to ingrain the sounds and spelling patterns of your new language in your head. They run on Anki, and over the course of using them, you'll get a sense for how Anki works (and you'll be ready to make your own flash cards).

ITALKI.COM can get you in touch with native speakers, who will talk with you or train you for *very* small amounts of money or in exchange for an equal amount of time speaking in English. You can spend an hour going through words with them and asking them to correct your pronunciation, which can help immensely.

A GOOD PRONUNCIATION GUIDEBOOK will come with a CD, provide diagrams of your mouth and tongue, and walk you through the entire pronunciation system of your language. The best of these will include minimal pair tests. These books don't exist in every language, but they're extraordinarily helpful when they do.

AN *EXCEPTIONALLY* GOOD TEXTBOOK/CD COMBO will start with a good pronunciation guidebook and provide you with everything you need.

A GOOD DICTIONARY will give you a guide to its phonetic alphabet, which may range from a couple occasional marks to full-blown IPA (or full-blown *something-random-the-publisher-decided-upon*) and may even begin with a good discussion of the spelling rules. If you buy a physical dictionary with clear pronunciation information, then you can use it to easily browse for example words when you're making your first flash cards.

For the Intermediates

Some intermediate language learners get lucky. They studied with teachers who stressed excellent pronunciation habits and, as such, built a solid foundation. They have no trouble hearing the sounds of their target language, they have good pronunciation, and they've built an intuitive sense of the connections between sound and spelling. Others aren't so lucky.

You'll need to do an honest assessment of your abilities. Then you can pick and choose the tools that you need. If you have trouble hearing the differences between similar sounds in your language (say, the difference between *roux* and *rue* in French), then you should use minimal pair testing to help. Use one of my pronunciation trainers; it's what they're there for.

If you can hear the sounds, but you have trouble producing them, then play around in Appendix 4 or get a tutor on *italki.com* to coach you on pronunciation until you get a feel for your target language's sounds in your mouth.

If you can't quite remember which spellings make which sounds, then just use the flash cards in the First Gallery (page 191).

Any effort you put in now will speed up your progress for the rest of your journey. It'll also ensure that native speakers actually *speak* to you instead of switching to English at the earliest opportunity.

CHAPTER 4

Word Play and the Symphony of a Word

Das Aussprechen eines Wortes ist gleichsam ein Anschlagen einer Taste auf dem Vorstellungsklavier.
Uttering a word is like striking a note on the keyboard of the imagination.
— Ludwig Wittgenstein

Boy, those French! They have a different word for everything.
— Steve Martin

On the surface, words are simple. We point to a fuzzy animal and name it. *Dog.* And so a word begins.

But this is just a fragment of the story. In the last chapter, we learned how to hear a language's sounds, but we haven't yet learned to hear its music. And we need to, because we're aiming for *fluency.* We want to speak our minds without thinking about grammar or translations, and the key to this ability lies beneath the surface of every word. There, if we learn how to listen, we will hear a quiet symphony.

In this chapter, you'll find the tools you need to hear this symphony. These tools will teach you what the French think of when they picture *déjeuner* (lunch) and give you the bare grammatical necessities to talk about *déjeuner* when you're ready. We'll discuss which words to learn first and how to learn them easily. You'll learn how to skip translating and *think* in a new language from the very beginning.

So what's hiding beneath the surface of our words?

A word in your brain contains within it every neural pattern it's ever connected. Your "dog" contains a fragment of every dog you have ever seen, heard, or read about. It's shaped by thousands of experiences that you and I have never shared, and yet we can talk about "dog" and our brains light up in mostly the same way.

Words are, after all, our communal brain. As a group, we point at things and say corresponding words until our minds and brains tune to each other—an orchestra of minds so immense that the violist in Los Angeles can't possibly hear the violinist in Pennsylvania, and yet here we are, playing in perfect harmony and perfect rhythm all the same. It is an impossible thing, a word.

And it's not as if the chords we play are simple; they contain thousands of notes, connecting sound and spelling to meaning and grammar. The grammar provides the lowest notes: You and I would *never* talk about "an dog" or "dog," as we might talk about "an elephant" or "beer." This is the grammar of a dog, and it vibrates in our skulls—a throbbing, sustained tone from the cello section.

Sound and spelling are playing too, naturally. They're probably in the woodwinds, and they tell us to write *d-o-g-s* and say "dawgz" without a second's thought as to why.

Meaning serves as the melody, and it is no simple ditty; it's a cacophony of images, stories, and associated words. I can point to a little yappy ball of fur and say "dog," and you will agree. "Yes," you will say. "That *is* a dog." I can then point to a giant Great Dane and say "dog," and you will *still* agree. I can even say things like "In a remarkable display of *dogged* determination, he won the race," and you will still understand, even in the absence of actual dogs in our story.

Beyond twenty or so *dog* definitions, there is a multitude of kindred words. When "dog" enters your brain, a thousand of these words spring to the ready and ten thousand unrelated words recoil in retreat. A dog *barks*, but it doesn't yell or shout. You can pursue someone doggedly, but you usually don't doggedly eat a sandwich, even if it's a very large sandwich. Words go together automatically, and you instinctively know which ones fit and which ones don't.

All of these pieces—the bits of grammar, the sounds, the spellings, the meanings and the connected words—are contained within the immense symphony known as "dog." And the moment I tell you that *sobaka* is the Russian word for "dog," that whole symphony collapses into a single, out-of-tune horn solo. *Bwaaaap.*

Russian Dogs Are Not Your Friends

You can speak fluently because your words fit together automatically. When you think "dog," you instantly gain access to the thousand words that might come next in your story. Your dog might yip, or bark, or save Timmy from the well. You have multilayered instincts built into your "dog," and you lose those instincts the moment you translate that word into another language.

Why? Because translations strip the music out of words.

Our "dog" symphony only exists in English; *no one else* can hear it. When I was in Russian school, we watched a movie where the protagonist got drunk, forgot his shotgun, and got eaten by *sobakas*. Seriously. In English, dogs are man's best friend. In Russian, *sobakas* leave behind empty, tooth-marked boots.

I've told you that *sobaka* is the Russian word for "dog," but it's not quite true. Even if a Chihuahua and a Great Dane *are* types of *sobaka*, we're still missing the rest of the orchestra. Where's the grammar, the pronunciation, or the spelling? Where are the alternate meanings of the word? You'll never hear about displays of *sobaka*-ed determination. Where are the kindred words that bring *sobaka* to life in your mind and mouth?

Let's learn to hear the symphony in our new words. Because once you can hear it, you'll never want to hear translation—that out-of-tune horn player—again.

Where to Begin: We Don't Talk Much About Apricots

Some people have a way with words, and other people . . . oh, uh, not have way.

—Steve Martin

You can't learn the music in your words before you know which words to learn. How can you know where to start?

Not all words are created equal; we use certain words far more often than others. English has at least a quarter of a million words. But if you only knew the top *hundred* words in English, you'd recognize half of everything you read. We get a *lot* of mileage out of our most frequent words.

To be fair, many of these words are so-called function words—old standbys like *be* and *of, in,* and *on*—and they behave differently in every language, so you can't start with them. You'll need a few nouns before you can put something "in" them or "on" them. Still, even if you set function words aside for a moment, you'll find a small group of useful, simple words that you use *all the time*.

These words are an excellent place to start a language, because you'll see them everywhere. They'll let you work more efficiently, because you're not wasting your time with rare words. You're *seventy-nine* times more likely to talk about your mother than your niece. Why not learn *mother* first and *niece* later?

Grammar books and language classes don't follow this principle, in part because it's easy to plan lessons around themes like "family" and "fruit." As a result, you'll find *niece* and *mother* in the exact same place in your grammar book, regardless of their relative utility. In language classes, you'll learn words for apricots and peaches when your time would be much better spent learning about laptops, medicine, and energy. These are the words of our lives. Why not learn them first?

Enter the word frequency list. Researchers take a giant mass of text—millions of words from TV scripts, novels, newspapers, the Internet, news broadcasts, academic papers, and magazines—and jam it all into a computer. The computer counts the words and spits out *gold*: the words of a language in order of their importance.

It's an extraordinary tool. With only a thousand words, you'll recognize nearly 75 percent of what you read. With two thousand, you'll hit 80 percent. As you might expect, you'll run into diminishing returns after a while, but these frequency lists provide an incredible foundation for your language.

In practice, they're also extremely weird. You gain an ability to talk about complex topics before you can do the "simple" language tasks found in textbooks. I showed up to a Russian immersion program with the top thousand words in my head. In the entrance exam, I responded to two essay questions:

> *Question 1: "You have a party. What will you buy? Make a shopping list."*

> *Question 2: "Should teacher salaries scale according to the performance of their students?"*

My answer to the first question was fairly embarrassing. I didn't have the right vocabulary for a shopping list. I wrote something like "I will buy meat! Lots of meat. Chicken, beef, and pork! Delicious! All types of meat. And . . . beer! Vodka! Also, many bottles of wine! Oh yes, in addition, we shall have bread with cheese!" Ick.

My answer to the second question was a four-page-long rant about governmental policy in the United States and the media's effect upon societal opinion. They placed me in the advanced class. Within a few weeks, I picked up the vocabulary I was missing. My shopping lists are significantly longer now.

Frequency lists aren't the end-all of vocabulary study—eventually, you may *want* to talk about your niece and her love of apricots—but they're an ideal place to start. We've already covered the basics of pronunciation, and you can learn many of these words without using a shred of English; Russian dogs may not be our best friends, but they do *look* the same. As such, you can learn these words with pictures alone.

So how shall we begin?

The most frequent words aren't the same in every language; you won't need *Republican* to learn Russian, and *collective Soviet farming community* doesn't show up in Spanish very often. Each language has its own frequency list (the best frequency dictionaries are published by Routledge), and they are *fascinating*, both because of the words they include and the words they *don't*.

Unfortunately, these lists can be cumbersome. At least in the beginning, you're looking for words that are easy to visualize—words like *bus* and *mother*. You could find them in your language's frequency list, but you'd have to root through hundreds of function words like *the* and abstract words like *society*. This can get tedious, which is why I'm giving you a shortcut.

Despite the differences between languages, there *is* a fair amount of overlap in every language's most frequent words. We'll use that overlap to save us time. In Appendix 5, you'll find a list of 625 words (in English) to start with. These words are practical, easy to visualize, and quick to translate—words like *dog, school, car,* and *city*. I'll show you how to turn them into flash cards and put them into your SRS with pictures (and without their English translations).

Because your flash cards won't have any English on them, you'll learn to see a dog and *immediately* think about the corresponding word in your target language. There's no pesky translation step to get in the way, and that will provide you with substantial rewards. First, you'll solidify the pronunciation foundation you built in the previous chapter. With every word you learn, you'll become increasingly familiar with the sound and spelling system of your language. As a result, you'll find that your words become easier and easier to remember.

Second, you'll also get used to connecting sounds to images and concepts. You're learning to absorb words into your vocabulary, just as you did as a kid. Back then, you asked your parents about new words: "What's that?" "A skunk." "Oh." And once you asked, you never forgot.

Now you're going to have the tools to find this information yourself. What's more, because of your SRS, you'll learn your words faster than a kid can, and you'll be literate from the very beginning.

Third, you'll often learn key prefixes and suffixes without even trying—your language's equivalents of the -*er* in *teacher*, or the -*tion* in *train station*—which will make future words with the same prefixes and suffixes easier to remember.

Finally, when you get to grammar and abstract vocabulary, you'll already know most of the words you need. This makes the rest of your new language much easier to learn. It's easy to manage a sentence like "My dog chased a cat up a tree" when you already know *dogs, cats, chasing*, and *trees*. You'll know the players and actions in your stories, and grammar will simply tell you who's chasing whom.

KEY POINTS

- You use certain words much more frequently than others. Learn those first.
- In Appendix 5, I give you a list of 625 simple, common words. These words are easy to visualize, and so you can learn them with pictures instead of translations. This will give you the foundation you need to easily learn abstract words and grammar in the next two chapters.

GAMES WITH WORDS

We are never more fully alive, more completely ourselves, or more deeply engrossed in anything, than when we are at play.

—Charles Schaefer

We have two goals in this chapter: we need to hear the music in our words, and we need to *remember* it when we do. In Chapter 2, we talked about our mental filters, and how they save us from information over-

> ## Use Small Dictionaries
>
> Lonely Planet Phrasebooks and glossaries at the end of grammar books are great resources, because they only contain the most basic words. A big dictionary might give you ten synonyms for "house." You only need one right now, and you'll find it easily in your glossary or phrase book.

load. To learn vocabulary efficiently, we'll need to overcome those filters, by creating memorable, interesting experiences with our words.

You can accomplish these goals through a series of quick games, which you'll play whenever you learn new words. The first will show you what your words really mean, and the second will connect that meaning to your own life. Here, fun is serious business. If you get bored, your mental filters will turn on, and all of your precious work will leak out of your ears. So take a moment to have fun; it's much more efficient.

To create a deep, multisensory memory for a word, you'll need to combine several ingredients: spelling, sound, meaning, and personal connection.

We've discussed spelling and sound in the previous chapter, and you'll reinforce that knowledge with every word you learn. You can look up the spelling of each of your words in a dictionary or the glossary section of a grammar book, and you can usually find pronunciation information in the same place, supplemented by recordings at *Forvo.com*.

Next comes meaning.

Game 1—The Spot the Differences Game: Finding Meaning through Google Images

In the beginning of this chapter, we talked about the limitations of translation—how translation strips words of their music. We're going to put the music back by playing with the greatest illustrated book ever written: Google Images.

Google Images is Google's search engine for pictures. You may have used it already. You go to *images.google.com*, type in "smiling man with an iguana," and poof, you have two hundred thousand images of iguanas and men. Hooray. If you were so inclined, you could take these images, pull out a dictionary, and make some flash cards for *la iguana* (iguana), *el hombre* (man), and *sonreír* (to smile). This is a fine use of time but not extremely interesting. You can do better, by searching for your words *in your target language.*

Hidden beneath Google Images' colorful exterior is a treasure trove: every image comes with a caption, and those captions exist in 130 languages. You can search for some obscure word—*aiguillage* (French for "railroad switch")—and get 160,000 examples of the word in context, along with more pictures of railroad switches than you know what to do with. It's an effectively unlimited source of tiny, illustrated stories about every word you need to learn.[17]

> ## Google Images as a Storybook
>
> To find stories in Google Images, search for a word and scroll all the way down to the bottom of the page. There you'll see the link Switch to Basic Version. Every image will now show up with its corresponding caption.

These images come from websites in your target language, and so they can tell you *precisely* how a word is used. The Russian word *devushka* means "girl." Simple enough. But Google Images will tell you a much more nuanced (and weird) story. Nearly every *devushka* on Google Images is a close-up chest shot of an eighteen-year-old girl in a bikini. You look at this, and you think "Hm!" And this "Hm!" is exactly what we're after. It's the moment you realize that Russian words aren't just funny-sounding English words; they're *Russian* words, and Russian words wear less clothing than you might expect (especially given the cold climate).

These "Hm!" moments get seared into your brain because they're

17. Google occasionally shuts down some of its services (in fact, *35 percent* of Google's offerings eventually disappear, for reasons ranging from lack of profits to lack of users). Should this happen to Google Images' Basic Version, I'll post some alternative options at Fluent-Forever.com/GoogleImages.

interesting. While you might be a bit disturbed by the sexual overtones in *devushka*, you'll certainly *remember* them. When you research a word using Google Images, you're playing the Spot the Differences game; you're looking for the difference between what you *expect* to see, and what you *actually* see. The game is a lot of fun; the Internet is full of weird, funny pictures in all sorts of languages. What's a *German* grand-mother look like? What's a *Hindi* cake? Take ten to twenty seconds to play (and then move on to the next word—before you get sucked in for an hour!)

You'll store your memories of this game into your flash cards. Every time you encounter a "Hm!" moment, you've gone through a rich, multisensory experience with a new word. You'll want your flash cards to bring those experiences back. You'll choose one or two images that you found particularly telling—perhaps one of the grandmoth-ers that seemed *especially* German—and you'll put them in your flash cards. If you're drawing your pictures by hand, then you can create a reminder however you choose. I suspect stick figure *devushkas* wear stick bikinis.

Game 2—The Memory Game: Boosting Meaning Through Personal Connection

Images by themselves are very powerful. Somewhere in your head, you store every image you see. In the process of searching for your images, you create a unique, memorable experience for every word in your vo-cabulary, and your flash cards will serve as reminders of your personal Spot the Differences game. Because you've chosen (or drawn) your *own* images, you'll be able to differentiate between words with easily conflated images like *girl, woman, daughter, mother, granddaughter*, and *grandmother*.

You can make your word memories even more distinct by adding a personal connection. You're playing the Memory game: What's your *grand-mère's* (grandmother's) name? Which *chat* (cat) comes to your mind first? You're looking for *any* memory that you can connect with your new word. If you can find one, you've just made your word 50 percent more memorable. Even if you can't, the process of *searching* for a memory gives you a major boost. I've tried to find a connection to the number *harminckettő* (thirty-two) in Hungarian. I can't. It's the worst number ever. I don't think I've ever said "thirty-two" in English. Now, whenever I see *harminckettő*, my first thought is "Oh, that's thirty-two, the worst number ever." Mission accomplished.

To play the Memory game, you'll spend a few seconds looking for any memory about your word that comes to mind. It could be your childhood cat or your friend's T-shirt. Try to keep the *new* word in mind rather than the translation. You'll make some weird English-French hybrid sentence like "The last time I saw my *grand-mère* (grandmother) was last weekend." Don't worry about the lack of French grammar; no one can hear you. As you make your flash cards, you'll write down a little reminder of this memory—the city you were in last weekend, the name of a friend you were with, and so on.

Later, when you review your flash cards, you'll play the same game. You'll see a cat, scan your memory for anything that connects, and if you get stumped, you'll find a helpful reminder on the back of your flash card. These connections aren't your main focus—you want to see a cat and think *chat*—but they can make your job easier, by making your

KEY POINTS

- You can make your words more memorable in two ways:
    - By investigating the stories they tell
    - By connecting those stories to your own life

- When you create flash cards, use the best storytelling tool ever invented: Google Images.
- Then spend a moment to find a link between each word and your own experiences.

chats and *grand-mères* more relevant to your own life and therefore much more memorable.

The Gender of a Turnip

I don't want to talk grammar. I want to talk like a lady in a flower shop.
—Eliza Doolittle to Henry Higgins (*Pygmalion*, George Bernard Shaw)

At this point, you're doing pretty well. You've taken the spelling and pronunciation of a word and connected it to a pageful of imagery. You've played Spot the Differences and chosen your favorite image or two, and you've played the Memory game and connected your word with a personal experience. You've built a multisensory memory into your new word, and you have a flash card or two that will remind you about all of these experiences at precisely the moment when you need it. Your little orchestra is starting to play, and it sounds pretty good.

Are you done? *Maybe.* You're still missing your cello section—grammar—but you might not need it just yet. Whether you need a little grammar *now* or *later* depends upon what language you're learning. I'll explain.

In English, we treat most of our nouns equally. We can take a sentence—"I bought a dog"—and swap in a different noun—"I bought a *cat*"—without screwing up the grammar. Unfortunately, this doesn't work in many languages. Other languages' *cats* can fall into a different grammatical group than their *dogs*. This was once the case in English; a thousand years ago, we talked about *án docga* (a dog) and *ánu catte* (a cat), and woe be unto you if you forgot the *u* in *ánu*. Eventually, we got sloppy with our grammar and forgot the grammatical differences between dogs and cats, but many languages didn't. In any of these languages, you need to memorize each noun's grammatical group in order to build a sentence successfully. This is known as *grammatical gender*, and it's a pain in the neck.

Modern English still contains a similar sort of madness.

"Why, oh why," my English students ask, "can't we buy *a milk*?"

I know this one. "Because milk is *uncountable*," I respond. "You might want a gallon or a cup, a drop or a swimming pool."

"But then why can't we tell you *an information*?" they retort. "You could have one information to say."

This is true. Germans frequently talk about *an information* or *informations* without causing confusion. I try imagery: "In English, information is . . . metaphorical. We think of information like a big ocean, and we take out a bit and tell it to each other."

"And a luggage? A luggage is metaphorical, too?"

The real question my students are asking is "Why doesn't grammar make *sense*?"

And the answer is illuminating: grammar is a mirror to ourselves. It is a living history of our desire to make sense of our words. In English, we're currently turning *sneaked* into *snuck*. To many ears, *snuck* seems to "sound better," but that's not why we're doing it. We're doing it because it makes two nonsensical verbs—*stuck* and *struck*—seem a little less nonsensical. We did this to *catched* several hundred years ago, putting it into a group with *taught*, *bought*, and *thought*, and we'll probably turn "dragged" into "drug" before the next century is up. We like to have groups of words that follow patterns, even when those patterns—our irregular verbs, in this case—don't really make sense.

Does Your New Language Use Gender?

Probably. Gender was a prominent feature of Proto-Indo-European, a language spoken in the fourth millennium BCE by a nomadic tribe living in southwestern Russia. Their language gave birth to most of the languages spoken in Europe, the Americas, Russia, and the Indian Subcontinent. There are three *billion* native speakers of languages in the Proto-Indo-European family, so there's a good chance you're learning one of these languages, and therefore need to learn gender. If you're not sure, check here: *TinyURL.com/wikigender*.

And so, it's not surprising that we create nonsensical groups for our nouns, too, like uncountable (*luggage*) and countable (*bags*), or that the Germans have feminine (German *turnips*), masculine (German *cheese*), and neuter (German *maidens*). These are two sides of the same coin; we just love making groups, sensible or not.

Sooner or later, you're going to encounter nonsensical groups like these. If you're studying a Germanic, Romantic, Slavic, Semitic, or Indian language, you need to deal with this *now*. Each of your words has a *gender*, and these genders don't make any sense. To quote Mark Twain:

> Gretchen: Wilhelm, where is the turnip?
> Wilhelm: She has gone to the kitchen.
> Gretchen: Where is the accomplished and beautiful English maiden?
> Wilhelm: It has gone to the opera.
>
> —Mark Twain, "The Awful German Language"

Unfortunately, in any of the languages with genders, you have to know a word's gender before you can do *anything* with it, which is why your grammar book starts with a long tirade about gender in the first or second chapter. Your book will either tell you that you "just have to memorize it" or give you a pile of rules with a list of exceptions that you "just have to memorize." The book is right. You *do* need to memorize it. But there's an easy way to do this, and I'll show you how in our next game.

If your language doesn't have gender—if you're studying one of the languages of Eastern Asia, the Philippines, or Turkey—then you can breathe easy for now. But don't worry; you'll find your own uses for our mnemonic game soon enough.

Game 3—The Mnemonic Imagery Game: How to Memorize Nonsensical Bits of Grammar

To continue with the German genders: a tree is male, its buds are female, its leaves are neuter; horses are sexless, dogs are male, cats are female, —Tom-cats included, of course; a person's mouth, neck, bosom, elbows, fingers, nails, feet, and body are of the male sex, and his head is male or neuter according to the word selected to signify it, and *not* according to the sex of the individual who wears it, —for in Germany all the women wear either male heads or sexless ones; a person's nose, lips, shoulders, breast, hands, and toes are of the female sex; and his hair, ears, eyes, chin, legs, knees, heart, and conscience haven't any sex at all. The inventor of the language probably got what he knew about a conscience from hearsay.

—Mark Twain, "The Awful German Language"

Welcome to the Mnemonic Imagery game. In the next few pages, you're going to memorize the genders of twelve of Twain's troublesome nouns. You'll do it quickly, you'll do it easily, and you'll even have fun. Let's go.

Tree—masculine, *Tree bud*—feminine, *Leaf*—neuter, *Horse*—neuter, *Dog*—masculine, *Cat*—feminine, *Mouth*—masculine, *Neck*—masculine, *Hand*—feminine, *Nose*—feminine, *Knee*—neuter, and *Heart*—neuter.

You might be able to memorize these by rote repetition, but not for more than a few minutes. We'll try something a bit more interesting (and long lasting) instead. I want you to imagine all of the masculine nouns exploding. Your tree? Kaboom, splinters of wood everywhere. A branch gets embedded in the wall behind you. Dog chunks splatter all over the ceiling and floors. You wipe bits of fur and gore from your forehead. Make your images as vivid as you can stomach.

Feminine nouns should catch fire. Your nose spews fire out of it like a dragon, a flaming cat sets fire to your bedroom. Feel the heat of each image; the more senses you can involve, the better.

Neuter items should shatter like glass. Jagged, brown-red, sparkling shards of horse spread across the floor, as does your broken heart (sniff). Take a moment to imagine the remaining images yourself: an exploding mouth and neck (masculine), a burning hand and tree bud (feminine), a shattering leaf and knee (neuter).

No, really. Go back and do this. It shouldn't take you more than a minute. I'll wait.

See how many of these images stick. We'll even mix up the order to be tricky: tree, leaf, horse, dog, cat, mouth, neck, hand, nose, heart, knee, tree bud.

Not so bad, eh? Depending upon how vivid your images were, you may have remembered all of them, and if you missed a few, you'd get better with practice. Mnemonic images work for reasons you might already surmise: we're *really good* at remembering images, particularly when those images are violent, sexual, funny, or any combination of the three. While "gender" can conjure up some images—you can probably imagine a male dog—it falls flat on others (a neuter knee—meh). Vivid, action-packed verbs are much more memorable.

To play the Mnemonic Image game in your language, you'll need to come up with images for the nonsensical grammatical groups in your new language. Since we're restricting ourselves to noun genders for the moment, then you'll need two to three particularly vivid verbs (these combine well with nouns).

Later, when you're making your flash cards, you can use mnemonic imagery as needed. If *a man* is masculine in your target language, you probably don't need imagery for that word. But if you're making a flash card for *a maiden* (neuter), then take a few seconds to shatter her into a thousand maidenly pieces. Make your images as vivid and multisensory as you can. If you do, you'll have an easy time recalling each word's gender whenever you review, and if you get stumped, you can create a new image then and there. After a few hundred words, you'll begin to do this automatically with every new word, and gender will cease being a problem from then on.

As you learn more, you'll find that this tool can come in handy *everywhere*. Any time you encounter some frustrating group of irregularities you "just have to memorize," you can create a mnemonic image. You can even make images for spelling—if *ch* is for *chat* (cat), then that cat can ride on top of your *cheval* (horse). We'll cover more advanced uses in chapter 5. (I use this game for all sorts of nasty things: verb conjugations, prepositions, noun cases, and irregular plurals, to name a few.) Until then, make a few images and try it out. It's a fun tool, and it makes light work of one of the hardest aspects of language learning.

KEY POINTS

- Many languages assign a nonsensical grammatical gender to each of their nouns, which is a standard source of trouble for language learners.
- If your language has grammatical gender, you can memorize it easily if you assign each gender a particularly vivid action and then imagine each of your nouns performing that action.

Do This Now: Learn Your First 625 Words, Music and All

You're about to learn a lot of words very quickly. You'll play some games, make some flash cards, and within a month or two, you can expect to have a 625-word vocabulary. But you'll have much more than the ability to name some objects. You'll have a foundation.

In this stage, you're learning to connect sounds and spellings to meaningful words. This is a huge leap past what we've all done in language classes. You're learning to associate a new word—*gato*—to images, feelings, and sounds of cats found throughout your memories. Rather than translating your *gatos* into *cats*, you're learning to put music into your words. This is no small feat; you're beginning to *think* in your new language, and this skill will follow you for the rest of your journey.

You're going to learn this skill by studying flash cards in your SRS, but the key moments occur in the beginning, when you *create* those flash cards. In those moments, you're taking new words and connecting them to as many images, thoughts, and memories as you can find. You are creating the core connections that will underlie your language, and of equal importance, you're having a good (and therefore, memorable) time in the process. Your flash cards are just a practical souvenir of that experience. You'll only use them to deepen memories you've already formed.

We'll talk about the nitty-gritty of flash card creation in the Gallery (page 177). You can turn to that section when you're ready to actually make your cards. Here we'll talk about the connections we're building—the sounds, images, spellings, and memories in each word—and how to build those connections as quickly as possible.

The Connections: Sound, Spelling, Meaning, Personal Connection (and Gender)

We've already discussed sound and spelling in the previous chapter. These are the special pieces of a word that allow us to imagine an image—a unicorn, for example—and send that image to another person. They're the basic substance of each word, and as you learn your words, this substance will become more familiar and easier to remember.

Next comes *meaning*. You'll want to discover what your words *actually* mean, rather than what their translations *seem* to mean. What do Russian *devushkas* (girls) wear, and what do the French eat for *déjeuner* (lunch)? You'll want to build new, meaningful associations into every word you learn.

Finally, you'll want *personal connections*. While your new words may not line up perfectly with their English translations, they *will* line up with your own experiences. We've all met *devushkas* and eaten *déjeuner*. We need to bring out these memories and remember when they happened, how we felt, what we heard, and what we saw.

If your language uses *gender*, you'll want that mixed into your words, too. Right from the beginning, your masculine nouns should be *different* from your feminine nouns, and you can create those differences with vivid mnemonic imagery.

Every one of these connections will make your words easier to remember and easier to use in the future. Any flash cards you create will be a dim reminder of the colorful mass of memories you assemble.

When you review them, they'll bring back a fragment of those memories, and your brain will supply the rest in a sudden rush of color, feeling, and music. Then you'll move on to the next card.

It's an intense, unforgettable experience.

Resources

TRANSLATIONS (SPELLING): Appendix 5 is a list of 625 English words that show up frequently in every language: *dog, car, city,* and so on. You'll want to find translations for all of these words in your target language. You could use Google Translate, but you'll usually get a lot of weird, messed-up translations. Machine translation isn't that good, especially when you're translating lists of words, rather than sentences.

If you use a standard dictionary, you may find too *many* results; you don't need ten synonyms for *house*. Here's your chance to use that pocket phrase book you bought. Phrase books are quick to peruse, and they'll give you the most frequently used translations for each word. If you don't have one, you might be able to get the same results from the glossary section of your grammar book.

Alternatively, if you're studying a relatively common language, you can probably find a professional translation of the 625 words on my website. Go to *Fluent-Forever.com/Appendix5*.

SOUND: You'll find recordings of your words at *Forvo.com*. Listen to them, particularly in the beginning, when your connections between sound and spelling are still wobbly. You'll have an easier time understanding what you hear if you also use phonetic transcriptions of your words. You *may* find these in your glossary, but if not, you'll find them in your favorite dictionary and/or *Wiktionary.org*.

MEANING: Find your word in Google Images. You have a couple options here, the first of which is easy to use (and great), and the second of which takes a bit of initial setup (but is *awesome*. Use number two!):

Option 1 (Basic Version): When you go directly to *images.google.com*, you can find pictures, but you won't see the best part—the captions. Let's turn them on.

- Step 1: Search for a word (any word). Here we'll search for *cheval* (horse).
- Step 2: Scroll *all* the way down to the bottom of the page.
- Step 3: There you'll see the link *Switch to Basic Version*. Click it.
- Step 4: Bookmark this page, so you don't have to do steps 1–3 every time.

Alternatively, just go to *TinyURL.com/basicimage*, and bookmark *that* page.

You'll see a wonderful page with twenty images and captions that look like this:

Chevalworld.com
Cheval dans la neige.

Option 2 (Basic Version, Automatically Translated): These captions are great, but they're all in your new language, and you don't speak that language yet. What if all of those little captions were machine translated into English? You can stick this page into Google Translate. Now, instead of twenty captioned images in French, you'll see this:

The translations aren't always great, but when you see twenty of them with pictures, you get a *very* clear sense of each word's meaning. I can't imagine a better resource than this for investigating words. You'll find a guide on my website to setting this up (it takes a few minutes to get it working) at *Fluent-Forever.com/chapter4*.

We're breaking one of my cardinal rules here—no translation, but that's okay; you won't remember those translations for long. While your first exposure to *cheval* might be in English, your *second* exposure won't be. When you step from Google Images to your flash cards, you'll wipe out every trace of English (and leave the images). In time, you'll forget the original English sentences, and remember only the pictures and the stories they told about your *cheval*.

Throughout this book, we're going to use translation whenever it can save you time without screwing up your fluency. If you need the French word for "sandpaper," there's no harm in looking it up in a dictionary (it's *papier de verre*), and your only 100 percent French option involves hours cruising through French Wikipedia, hoping that someday you'll wander into *papier de verre* by clicking the right sequence of links. To determine when translation will help you and when it will hurt you, you can use this rule of thumb: *if you put it on your flash cards, it's not in English*. As long as you follow that rule, you'll be okay.

Let's get back to Google Images.

Occasionally, you'll run into difficulties in finding a decent picture for a word. Suppose you were learning the French word *jolie* (pretty, cute). If you search for it on Google Images, you'll find a hundred million pictures, but the first seventy-eight million are all Angelina Jolie. (Be thankful you didn't want "a smith"; Will Smith has five *billion* photos online.)

When you run into problems, you have two options. If you're *sure* you know what your word means (perhaps you can't find a good picture, but you've seen a few clear sentences with the word), then you can search for a suitable picture in English. You'll be able to find something "cute" within a few seconds (or if you're drawing your pictures, then you can come up with your own "cute"). If you *can't* tell what your word means (perhaps the sentences and pictures you've found don't seem to make any sense), then skip it. The word you're investigating may be more complex and multifaceted than you can handle right now, and there are plenty of other words to learn. Move on.

A word of warning: Google Images can be addictive; at least for now, don't spend all day on one word. Limit yourself to twenty seconds per word (*maybe* thirty, if you must). Once you have some grammar under your belt, then you can really delve into Russian memes and the like, but for now, you have some vocabulary to learn!

PERSONAL CONNECTIONS: I can't give you your personal connections, but I can give you questions to help spur your memories. Use them whenever you have trouble finding a good memory for a new word. When you do, ask yourself about your *new* word rather than its English translation. Instead of asking about the last time you saw your *mother*, ask about the last time you saw your *mère*. Even when the words sound almost the same (timid/*timide*), you'll create more useful connections when you mentally hear those words in the accent of your new language:

Concrete Nouns: When's the last time I saw my *mère* (mother)?

Concrete Nouns: When's the first time I encountered a *moto* (motorcycle)?

Abstract Nouns: How has the *économie* (economy) affected me?

Adjectives: Am I *timide* (timid)? If not, do I know someone
who is?

Adjectives: What do I own that's *rouge* (red)?

Verbs: Do I like to *courir* (run)? Do I know someone else
who does?

Answer one of these questions and write down a little reminder
for yourself on the back of your flash cards. You might write the name
of your *timide* niece, the city where you first rode a *moto*, or a sad face
(*I seriously don't like to* courir). These reminders should be short and
enigmatic—"Sally"—so when you review them, they prompt a moment
of "Sally? . . . Oh yeah, Sally has a skirt like that."

Whenever possible, stick to names of people and places—they
don't violate our no-English rule—but if an errant English word or two
like *last Christmas* creeps in, the language police probably won't catch
you. Just don't make it a habit.

GENDER (IF NECESSARY): If you're not sure whether your language uses
gender, check Wikipedia (*en.wikipedia.org/wiki/List_of_languages_by_
type_of_grammatical_gender*). If it does, open your grammar book, find
the introductory discussion on gender, and read it. You'll learn how
many genders there are and whether your language has any predictable
patterns (perhaps nearly all feminine words end in *a*).

You'll also discover whether there's a standard way to indicate the
gender of each word. German words, for example, are usually listed
with their definite article, so instead of *dog, cat,* and *horse,* you'll always
see *the dog, the cat,* and *the horse: der Hund* (the [masculine] dog), *die
Katze* (the [feminine] cat), and *das Pferd* (the [neuter] horse). You'll
find the gender of each word in your glossary or dictionary.

Create a mnemonic image for each gender you need. They can
be *anything.* I like to use relatively violent verbs for noun genders;

my nouns rarely survive shattering, exploding, melting, burning, or cracking. Sexual verbs are classic choices. To quote Joshua Foer in *Moonwalking with Einstein:*

> When forming images, it helps to have a dirty mind. Evolution has programmed our brains to find two things particularly interesting, and therefore memorable: jokes and sex—and especially, it seems, jokes about sex . . . . Even memory treatises from comparatively prudish eras make this point. Peter of Ravenna, author of the most famous memory textbook of the fifteenth century, first asks the pardon of chaste and religious men before revealing "a secret which I have (through modesty) long remained silent about: if you wish to remember quickly, dispose the images of the most beautiful virgins into memory places; the memory is marvelously excited by images of women."

But you may get tired of watching every flower, nose, shopping bag, and tennis ball in your path furiously fornicating in some particular manner. You might prefer *swing dancing* flowers and noses or *singing* shopping bags. It's your call.

Be aware that you'll need to get creative when it comes to abstract nouns. *A burning tennis ball* may prove easier to imagine than *a burning year,* but both are possible (and a *burning* year is still much easier to remember than a *masculine* year).

We're ready. Turn to Appendix 5, get your word list ready, and then start creating flash cards. You'll find flash card designs in the Gallery on page 177.

For the Intermediates

You probably know many of the words in Appendix 5. You don't need to learn them twice, although if your language has grammatical gender, you may want to relearn any words whose genders you're unsure about.

Go through the 625 list and separate the words into three categories:

1.   Words you know: You immediately recall the word, you know how to pronounce it, you know its gender, and you don't need to waste time relearning it.

2.   Words you kind of know: If you looked them up in a dictionary, you'd think, "Oh yeah!" Perhaps you've forgotten precisely how to pronounce them, their gender or their spelling, but they definitely seem pretty familiar.

3.   New words: You *might* have learned them at some point, but they don't seem familiar at all.

Skip all the words in category 1. You don't need to spend time with them. For words in category 2, use the Refresher Track in the Gallery (page 177). It will help you dust off your old memories without taking too much of your time. For words in category 3, follow the instructions in the Gallery as if you were a beginner. You'll use the Normal Track or Intensive Track, depending upon your needs and the trickiness of your target language.

CHAPTER 5

Sentence Play

First you learn the instrument, then you learn the music, then you forget all that s**t and just play.

—Charlie Parker

Yᴏu've learned to play with simple words, and simple words are the makings of simple stories. *SLEEP EAT WORK EAT WORK EAT SLEEP* is a common story in *any* language, and you don't need an ounce of grammar to tell it. If you added some dramatic pauses, a glass of wine, and a good French accent (*dormir . . . manger . . . travailler . . .*), you could probably be mistaken for a French philosopher or poet in the right setting.

But there's more to language than simple stories, and few people will tolerate "You hamburger give! I hamburger eat! You fast give!" for very long.

Enter grammar.

In this chapter, you'll learn how to use grammar to spin magic with your words. You'll discover how to reawaken the instincts that taught you grammar as a child, with the help of the sentences and stories in your grammar book. You'll learn to break down the most complex of grammatical constructions into easy-to-learn pieces, and memorize those pieces using your SRS. And you'll begin to tell stories of your own. With the help of new online tools that can connect you with native speakers, you'll convert those stories into a custom, self-run language class that provides all the instruction you need without wasting a second of your time.

At the end of this journey, you will possess the ability to think in a new language and weave stories in a completely new way. It's a thrilling process.

THE POWER OF INPUT: YOUR LANGUAGE MACHINE

Le génie n'est que l'enfance retrouvée à volonté.
Genius is nothing more nor less than childhood recaptured at will.
    —Charles Baudelaire, *The Painter of Modern Life and Other Essays*

You may not realize it, but there is a little machine hiding within your brain. It runs off of sentences it hears, absorbs their patterns, and after a little while, spits out perfectly grammatical language without a

---

The Two Grammars

There are two sorts of grammar that we encounter in our lives: the spoken grammar we acquire as kids, and the written grammar we learn in school. Most people think of the latter when they hear the word *grammar:* school days devoted to the proper use of the comma, the removal of prepositions from the ends of our sentences, or the roles of *your* and *you're* and *which* and *that.* Many of these rules can be frustrating because they're based upon a great deal of academic nonsense. Our ban on prepositions at the end of sentences, for example, is a recent import from *Latin,* of all places. The ban snuck into our language when a group of London publishers released a series of competing style manuals and somehow convinced the populace that those rules had always been features of "proper" English. The written language is, in fact, our first foreign language—a dialect of our native tongue that each of us learns with varying degrees of success.

moment's effort or thought. When you were a child, you used this machine to learn your native language, and you'll use it again to learn a new one. Let's figure out how it works.

Children are ridiculously good at learning grammar. They're so good that, by the age of six, they can reliably create sentences that they've never heard before in their lives, and each of these sentences is a grammatical masterpiece. You can test this yourself, if you have access to some kids and some puppets. Show any group of three-to-five-year-old, English-speaking kids a monster puppet, and tell them that this monster likes to eat mud. They will tell you that your puppet is a *mud-eater*. If you show them a different puppet that eats mice, they'll call it a *mice-eater*. But if your puppet likes to eat rats, they'll *never* call it a *rats-eater*; they'll say *rat-eater*.

There's a subtle grammar rule operating here, where nouns with irregular plurals (*mouse–mice*) form compound nouns using their plural forms (*mice-infested*), and nouns with regular plurals (*rat–rats*) form compounds using their singular forms (*rat-infested*). This is the sort of annoying, esoteric rule that gives my English students nightmares, and yet every illiterate, English-speaking kid learns it perfectly.

So how do they do this? Clearly, they're learning English from their family and friends, but they're not just copying what they hear. In all likelihood, they've *never* heard of rat-eaters or English's rules about the formation of compound nouns, and yet these words cause them no trouble at all. Somehow, they've absorbed language input from their surroundings and turned it into something much bigger. They've picked up a kind of perfect, automatic grammar that lets them create entirely new words and sentences.

Comprehensible Input

Let's get a bit more precise. Kids don't learn their language from just *any* kind of language input. The only input that seems to matter is input that kids can *understand.* In linguistic circles, this is known as *comprehensible input.* The basic idea is this: kids need to understand the gist of what they hear in order to learn a language from it.

If you wave a cookie in front of a toddler's face and say, "Do you want a cookie?" she is not going to have any problems understanding exactly what you mean, even if she's never heard of cookies before. Physical objects, body language, and interaction all serve as a sort of universal translator that helps kids make sense of their first words; it turns these words into comprehensible input. Later, once they've figured out what cookies are, you can ask them whether they want a cookie without actually holding one, and they'll know precisely what you're talking about.

In contrast, you can't teach a kid Japanese by merely showing him Japanese TV shows, even if you sit him in front of the TV for *hundreds* of hours. TV just doesn't make enough sense; it's missing that universal translator— real cookies and real interactions—and so it's *not* comprehensible input. At least until we make TVs that can bake and serve cookies, the only way to teach a kid a new language is by finding a real person to speak with them in that language. Later, with enough comprehensible input from people, kids can learn to understand television, at which point you and your cookie become much less interesting than Cookie Monster and *his* cookie.

If you ask linguists how kids do this, most of them will tell you about a language-learning machine hidden within the brain of every child. The nature of this machine has been the subject of raging linguistic debate—perhaps kids possess a language machine or perhaps it's a language + everything else machine—but both sides agree that kids have some sort of awesome, pattern-crunching machine in their heads. Every kid can take in sentences from their parents, chew them up, and automatically spit out perfect grammar by their sixth birthdays. And fortunately for us, the machine in their heads never stops working. If we want to learn a new language, we just need to learn how to use it.

The Grammatical Genius of Adults

How do we know that adults retain their language machines? This certainly doesn't *seem* true. Kids can boast a 100 percent success rate; no one fails to learn their native language by the age of six, and yet adults can spend years studying a language without any trace of success.

Since no one has actually *found* the language machine in our brains—after all, the idea came out of linguistics, rather than neuroscience—we can't poke it or zap it to see whether it's working. But we *can* look at the *output* of that machine: the sentences that kids produce when they're just starting to learn a language. And we can compare those sentences to what we observe in adults starting to learn a *second* language.

When kids learn languages, they follow a series of predictable stages. In English, for example, they begin with simple sentences that resemble our *SLEEP EAT WORK* stories from earlier: *birdie go* (The bird has gone), *doggie jump* (The dog is jumping). Shortly before they reach three years of age, they begin to use the *-ing* form of verbs (*doggie jumping*). Within six months, they've added the irregular past tense (*birdies went*) and *is* (*daddy is big*). Then, finally, come the regular past tense verbs (*doggie jumped*) and the present tense verbs in the third person (*Daddy eats*). Every English-speaking kid goes through these stages in the same order. According to researchers, you will *never* find a kid who learns to say "Mommy works" before "Mommy working."

If you look at the sentences produced by adults learning a second language, you wouldn't expect to see any patterns whatsoever. After all, where kids always learn language from their families and friends, adults learn languages in all *sorts* of ways. Some take structured classes, some move to foreign countries and immerse themselves, some read books, and some fall in love and learn from their boyfriends or girlfriends.[18] Add to this the thousands of possible native languages an

---

18. Word of the day: A boyfriend or girlfriend who teaches you a foreign language is euphemistically known as a *pillow dictionary*.

adult might speak originally, and you have a recipe for total irregularity. There's no reason to expect that a Japanese teenager learning English from his girlfriend will have *anything* in common with a German woman learning English from a textbook.

Yet if you monitor adults learning a second language, you find something completely mystifying. That German woman with her English textbook follows *the exact same* developmental stages as that Japanese guy with his American girlfriend. The German might progress through her stages *faster*—German, after all, is fairly similar to English—but she won't skip *any* of them. Not only that, but both of these English students will follow developmental stages that closely resemble the development of *child* speech. Like the kids, they start out with *-ing* (*He watching television*) and only later learn *is* (*He is watching*). They master the irregular past tense (*He fell*) before the regular past tense (*He jumped*). Toward the very end of their development, they master the third-person present tense (*He eats the cheeseburger*).

These results are baffling, in part because they don't have anything to do with the order of language textbooks and classes. English students usually encounter sentences from the last developmental stages—like "He *eats* the cheeseburger"—within their first week of classes. They can successfully learn to use a late-stage rule—*he* + *eat* = *he eats*—in the slow-paced world of homework and tests, but they invariably forget that same rule whenever they try to speak. Speech is too fast, and students just don't have enough time to apply their grammar rules consciously. In their speech, they have to walk through each of their developmental stages in order (*He eating carrot* → *He is eating a carrot* → *Yesterday he ate a carrot* → *He eats carrots daily*). Like kids, no English students will blurt out "He *eats* hamburgers" before "He *is eating*" unless they have enough time to plan out their sentences in advance, consciously apply the right grammar rules, and say them out loud.

As far as researchers can tell, this is simply the order with which the human brain picks up English, period. And while some learners can move through these stages more quickly than others, no amount of drilling a particular grammar rule—*I eat, he eats, we sit, she sits, they fall, it falls*—will enable a student to skip a developmental stage. Ever.

Naturally, it's not just English. While the developmental stages look different from language to language, *every* language has a particular developmental order, which children and second language learners alike will inevitably follow on their way to fluency. The most plausible explanation for these rigid, unavoidable developmental stages is this: our language machines never turn off. When we learn a second language, we develop like children because we learn like children. If we feed our language machines enough comprehensible input, then we will automatically learn our new language's grammar, just as we did as kids.

Kids seem to succeed at language learning where adults fail, but that's only because they get *much* more input than we do. In a kid's first six years of life, they're exposed to tens of thousands of hours of language. In *our* few years of language classes in school, we're lucky to hear more than a few *hundred* hours, and many of those hours are spent talking *about* a language rather than talking *in* a language. It's no wonder our language machines don't seem to work; they're starving for input. If we had Spanish-speaking adults talking to us for twelve to sixteen hours a day for six years, we would probably speak Spanish at least as well as your average Spanish-speaking six-year old.

To be fair, kids do possess some innate advantages over adults: they don't worry about making mistakes, and by the age of one, their ears are perfectly tuned to the sounds of their native language. But adults possess gifts of their own. We're very good at spotting patterns and we've developed better learning strategies than toddlers and pre-schoolers. Take that, kids. If we stop comparing kids with *thousands* of hours of language exposure to adults with *hundreds* of hours, we'll see a surprising trend: on average, adults learn languages *faster* than kids do.

Feeding Your Language Machine Efficiently

So far, we've discussed how learning a grammar rule won't affect when you'll use it instinctively. English students can repeat *he runs*, *she goes*, and *it falls* until they're blue in the face, but they'll *never* learn to produce those sentences spontaneously before they've mastered the *-ing* form (*he is running*), the article (*the dog is running*), and the irregular past tense (*the dog ran*). If that's the case, then it seems like drilling grammar exercises is a waste of time. And it is. But don't throw away your grammar book just yet.

As we've discussed, you can only feed your language machine with comprehensible input; you need to understand the gist of what you read and hear before you can learn from it. So you're not going to start with Chinese literature, just like you didn't start to learn English from *A Tale of Two Cities*.

But how can you understand something you don't yet understand? As a kid, you had adults chasing you around with cookies, milk, and bunches of simple sentences. As an adult, you probably can't afford this luxury (and you might not want to be eating that many cookies).

This is where you'll start using two abilities you've learned as an adult: the ability to find and use translations and the ability to learn grammar rules. We've discussed in depth the problems with translations—they're hard to memorize and they aren't great at giving you the whole picture—but they do a fine job of giving you the *gist* of an unfamiliar sentence. A simple translation like

Voulez-vous un cookie?
Want you a cookie?

can teach you the basic idea behind this sentence, even if it doesn't provide all of the magic, music, and mystery of each of its words. And you have a *ton* of well-made, well-translated sentences just waiting for you inside of your grammar textbook. It's a gold mine of comprehensible input.

That book isn't just useful for its translated sentences. Grammar rules, too, are worth learning; studies show that you'll learn a language faster when you learn the rules. You don't need to *drill* them—as we've discussed, grammar drills won't help you skip over any developmental stages—but a passing familiarity with grammar can help you logically break down complex sentences into chunks you can understand, and the more sentences you understand, the faster you'll learn.

Take a sentence like *He buys flowers for them*. There's one guy, many flowers, and many new flower owners. This isn't *They buy him a flower*, even though all of the main players in both sentences—*he, they, flower*—are the same. And we know they're different because the *grammar* tells us so.

Our sentence—*He buys flowers for them*—is complex; it's not the kind of sentence that will come spontaneously to a beginning English student's mouth: *buy* has turned into *buys, they* into *them, flower* into *flowers, for* comes out of nowhere, and the order of each component is essential. Our English student might be able to memorize each grammar rule that's operating here, but there's no way he's going to say this sentence automatically. And if you're learning French, you're not going to automatically spit out the French version—*Il leur achète des fleurs* (He–them–buy–indefinite plural article thingy–flowers)—even if you know the individual words and grammar rules. This is calculus, and as a beginning student, you're still learning algebra.

However, even a beginning student can still take his rudimentary knowledge of grammar rules and use it to *understand* our flower story, even if he can't produce it easily on his own. And by understanding that sentence, he feeds his language machine and progresses one step closer to fluency.

This is a subtle point. If every sentence you *understand* brings you closer to fluency, then what's the problem with grammar drills? Don't *they* count as comprehensible input?

Indeed they do. They're just not particularly interesting. If you're the sort of person who loves filling out conjugation tables (*I sit, you sit, he sits, she sits, it sits, we sit, they sit . . .*) then by all means, go ahead. These are understandable sentences, and they'll feed your language machine just fine.

But if you're *not* a grammar nut, you don't need to do workbooks full of grammar exercises. Instead, you can use your grammar book as a quick guided tour through your language. You'll read the explanations, learn an example or two, and skip over the (often monotonous) drills and exercises. The examples you learn will help you remember each grammar rule, and they'll serve as comprehensible input at the same time, feeding your language machine as it pieces together your new language's grammar in the background.

In Italian, for example, you'll run into the rules for plural nouns in the first couple of chapters of most Italian grammar books. You make plurals in Italian by playing around with the last letter of a word, so pizza is *pizza*, but pizzas are *pizze*. Your grammar book will tell you the rules, give you a few examples (one *calzone*, two *calzoni*, one *gnocco*, two *gnocchi*) and then launch into a page or two of exercises. You can skip those exercises completely. Just pick out an example or two that you find particularly interesting (I'm a fan of *pizze* and *gelati* myself), make a flash card for them (I'll give you suggestions later in the chapter), and poof, you'll have that grammar rule memorized forever. You can move on to the next section.

In short order, you'll get an overview of the entire grammatical system of your new language, which will enable you to understand and absorb almost *anything*. You'll also pick up a ton of vocabulary at the same time; you can't learn the plural for *fritelle* (ridiculously awesome doughnut balls from Venice) without also learning the word for "ridiculously awesome doughnut balls from Venice" (get the ones full of *crema*).

This process is exciting; you can feel your new language building itself in your mind. Instead of wasting your time on monotonous grammar drills, you're constantly encountering new words, new grammatical forms, and new ways to express yourself—a torrent of comprehensible input that feeds your language machine and helps you to understand more and more every day. This is what fuels language binges—entire weekends spent hunched over your textbook or laptop, learning new grammar and new vocabulary, making flash cards and absorbing your new language. It's my favorite part. And while your friends marvel at your work ethic, they're missing what's really going on. You're not working; you're just having fun.

KEY POINTS

- You'll learn fastest if you take advantage of your language machine— the pattern-crunching tool that taught you the grammar of your native language. This machine runs off of comprehensible input—sentences that you understand—so you'll need to find a good source of simple, clear sentences with translations and explanations.
- Take your first sentences out of your grammar book. That way, your sentences can do double duty, teaching you every grammar rule consciously while your language machine works in the background, piecing together an automatic, intuitive understanding of grammar that will rapidly bring you to fluency.

SIMPLIFY, SIMPLIFY: TURNING MOUNTAINS INTO MOLEHILLS

Like all magnificent things, it's very simple.

—Natalie Babbitt, *Tuck Everlasting*

When you look closely at what grammar can accomplish, you come to the inevitable conclusion that grammar is impossibly complex. After all, at any moment of any day, you can take a few common words and use them to create a sentence that has never been written or said in the history of the world, and impossibly enough, it will make perfectly good sense to anyone who speaks English. Hell, I can only find a *single* Google hit for the first few words of the last sentence: "after all, at any moment of any day." Grammar creates infinite possibilities out of a finite collection of words. It's an impossible kind of magic, and yet we use it on a daily basis without the slightest thought or effort.

When you open a grammar book, you'll find two hundred to six hundred pages of grammatical forms. These books aren't *infinitely* long, which is odd, given grammar's infinite potential, but they *are* long. Grammar, after all, has a lot of work to do. It needs to tell us who's doing what, when they're doing it, *how* they're doing it, and all sorts of other madness that comes into our heads and flows out of our mouths. In the end, grammar allows us to relate any idea to any other idea in any possible way, and to somehow send all of those relationships into the heads of the people listening to us. By all accounts, it should be completely impossible to describe, and yet the authors of grammar books accomplish the impossible on a regular basis.

Grammar is amazing in its complexity, but it is utterly *awe inspiring* in its simplicity. All of grammar's infinite possibilities are the product of three basic operations: we add words (*You like it → Do you like it?*), we change their forms (*I eat → I ate*), and we change their order (*This is nice → Is this nice?*). That's it. And it's not just English. *Every* language's grammar depends upon these three operations to turn their words into stories.

For instance, one of grammar's main storytelling jobs is to tell us who's doing what. In English, we indicate this by moving words around: *Dogs eat cats* versus *Cats eat dogs*. A language like Russian changes the *form* of its words to accomplish the same goal: if a dog is eating a cat, it's a *sobaka* (собака), but if that dog is getting eaten, it turns into a *sobaku* (собаку). Japanese adds little function words: a dog is an *inu* (犬), but if it's eating, it's *inu wa* (犬は), and if it's being eaten, it's *inu o* (犬を).

This simplicity makes grammar extraordinarily easy to learn, for even the most complex of grammatical forms is built out of these three basic pieces. Take English's passive voice, and consider the difference between *My dog ate my homework* (active) versus *My homework was eaten by my dog* (passive). This is a complex grammatical transformation; the two sentences barely resemble each other, and the change in meaning between them is subtle. Although the facts in both sentences are the same, we started with a story about a bad dog and ended with a story about a poor, unfortunate homework assignment.

But all of this complexity is the product of *simple* operations: There are a couple of new words (*was* and *by*), one new word form (*ate* turned into *eaten*) and the word order changed. This would be a lot to learn all at once, but it's *easy* to learn in bite-size pieces, and that's precisely what you'll do in your target language.

To learn a new grammatical form, all you have to do is find an example from your grammar book, understand the gist of the story in that example—you'll use your grammar book's explanations and translations—and ask yourself three questions:

· Do you see any new words here?
· Do you see any new word forms here?
· Is the word order surprising to you?

Then you'll make flash cards for any information you'd like to learn:

You'll notice in the above cards that I'm using an example sentence to teach myself the word *by*. This is how you'll learn abstract vocabulary. A word like *by* is difficult to visualize or define. You usually don't see a "by" on your way to work. And while you could wrestle with some obtuse definition—"*by* is the preposition that indicates the agent of a passive construction" —creating a definition from our example sentence is *much* easier: *By* is the word that fits into "My homework was eaten ____ my dog." That's what it really *means*, after all; it's the word we happen to use in that particular context. And since our example sentence for *by* is a real story, we can find a picture to help us remember that word—there are more than a million pictures of guilty dogs and chewed-up homework assignments on Google Images.

Can we use this strategy for *every* word? Almost. For functional words like *of* and *what*, this strategy works every time. These words don't mean much outside of their contexts, and so any examples can tell you precisely how to use them. *Of* is the word that fits into *I'd like a glass ____ water*, and *what* is the word that fits into ____*'s your name?* These might not be the *only* ways to use these words. *What*, for instance, shows up in all sorts of contexts: *What did you do today?* and *I'll eat what he's having!* But you can learn any surprising, new examples of a word by turning them into additional flash cards. In the process, you'll pick up a solid, intuitive feel for these words in a wide variety of contexts, which is a thousand times more useful than a clunky dictionary definition or a giant pile of translations (e.g., according to my dictionary, German's *bei* means "for, at, by, on, with, during, upon, near, in, care of, next to," and so on. Not. Very. Helpful.).

For some words that convey abstract concepts, like *change* or *honesty*, you may need additional help. You can learn how to *use* a word with any example sentence—*He's an honest man*—but you often need particularly good examples to help you remember what a word *means*: *Abraham Lincoln was an honest man*. In general, you're not going to run into this problem very often. You're using a grammar book, and it's designed to give you good, clear examples for the words and concepts you encounter. But when you *do* run into a problematic word, just skip it. As soon as you have a little more grammar under your belt, you'll be able to leave your textbook behind and seek out your own example sentences on the Internet, a strategy we'll discuss in the next chapter.

By taking example sentences from your grammar book and breaking them down into new words, word forms, and word orders, you get an enormous amount of mileage from every example you choose. As a result, you learn a lot faster than you're "supposed" to. While your grammar book is busy explaining the past tense of *eat* (*She ate her sister's birthday cake*), you're learning *everything* that sentence has to offer—where to put *her*, how *sister* turns into *sister's*, and so on. By the time your grammar book gets around to explaining the possessive form *her*, you'll already have it memorized. This turns into a fun game—it's like a race with your grammar book, to see whether you'll completely master a topic before your grammar book even talks about it. You win every time.

KEY POINTS

- Use your grammar book as a source of simple example sentences and dialogues.
- Pick and choose your favorite examples of each grammar rule. Then break those examples down into new words, word forms, and word orders. You'll end up with a pile of effective, easy-to-learn flash cards.

STORY TIME: MAKING PATTERNS MEMORABLE

[I] would rather decline two drinks than one German adjective.
—Mark Twain, "The Awful German Language"

You've chosen some example sentences from your grammar book and broken them down into new words, word forms, and word orders.

You're starting to get a feel for grammar, when suddenly you run face-first into the dreaded *declension chart*—an imposing mass of data that shows us the twelve forms of a Russian noun, the sixteen ways to decline a German adjective, or sixty-five ways to conjugate a French verb. Now what?

You could find sixty-five example sentences for your French verb, but what about the *next* verb? And the verb after that? Verb declension charts can literally fill books; I own three 550-page volumes of French, German, and Italian verb charts. If you tried to memorize every conjugation of every verb, one by one, you would be sitting in front of your textbook for a *very* long time. We need a route through this madness.

First things first: there's no need to memorize it all by rote. Any five-year-old French kid can recite most of the contents of my *501 French Verbs* book, and they've never sat down and memorized a French verb conjugation in their lives. They're using their language machines to do it. They've taken in and understood enough input to intuit the patterns of their language perfectly. And we're going to do the same.

As we've discussed, the only input that can feed our language machines is comprehensible input. We need *stories*, and sixty-five ways to say "to be" (*I am, you are, he is . . . I was, you were, he was . . .*) just won't cut it.

While your grammar book will usually supply you with *some* stories, it won't give you enough of them. In all likelihood, you'll see something like this: your book will start with a simple story like "I am a student." Then it will explain what that sentence means, which word does what, and so on. Finally, it will throw a verb declension table at your head (*I am, you are, she is, we are . . .*) and move on to the next topic. You'll need some way to remember all of the data in that declension table, but you only have one lousy story about a student. Now what?

You can create your *own* stories. Use that declension table to quickly generate a bunch of variations on whatever examples you find in your textbook. You can write *She is a doctor* and stick that story on a flash card within a few seconds. In contrast with the meaningless (or perhaps philosophical) *She is*, your "She is a doctor" story is easy to visualize, and it means something quite different than the original example from your textbook, "I am a student." You'll have an easy time remembering it, and it's the sort of clear comprehensible input that makes language machines thrive.

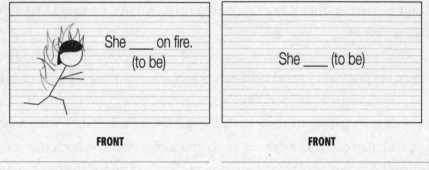

FRONT   FRONT

STORIES ARE MEMORABLE.   ABSTRACT GRAMMAR EXERCISES . . . AREN'T.

In the process of generating stories, you'll probably make some mistakes. Perhaps a "We are a teacher" will slip in somewhere. But not to worry—you'll catch your mistakes within a few days. By the end of this chapter, I'll show you where to get free native-speaker corrections for everything you write. If you make mistakes, then so much the better; you'll learn even *more* from your stories.

You can generate stories like these to learn all the forms of a single verb. You can even create little fragments of stories (*one potato chip, two potato chips*) for any adjective and noun forms you encounter. But how do you learn all the forms of *every* verb, adjective, and noun? Those sixty-five French verb forms are just the beginning of the story. If you're learning French, you have to learn a whole set of *new* verb forms for verbs ending in *-ir* (*finir, to finish*) or *-re* (*vendre, to sell*), not to mention one to two hundred *irregular* verbs. How on earth do those little illiterate French kids do this?

Kids rely on patterns, and even the most irregular languages are *full* of patterns. English, for example, is notorious for its irregular past tense forms: *go/went/have gone, do/did/have done, have/had/have had*. There are *hundreds* of these, and they drive English students crazy. But hidden within the chaos, there are always patterns—little islands of regularity, like *steal/stole/stolen, choose/chose/chosen,* and *speak/spoke/spoken*. When you're learning a grammatical form for the very first time—suppose you were learning English, and *steal/stole/stolen* was your first irregular verb—learn it with example sentences, as we did earlier: *Jon stole a delicious hamburger yesterday. George has stolen pizzas in fifty states.* But you don't need to make example sentences for your *next* irregular verb, *choose/chose/chosen.* You've already learned that pattern; you just need to somehow connect *choose* to the pattern you learned with *steal*.

This is where declension charts come in handy. While they're not very good for learning *new* patterns, they make it very easy to see patterns we've *already* learned. We're good at seeing patterns; it's why we speak our native languages so well. If you've already learned to use a verb like *steal*, you're going to have a much easier time learning all three forms of a similar verb—*choose/chose/chosen*—all at once. You can stick those three forms (or even a giant French declension chart) on the back of a flash card. Even if you're learning a French verb with sixty-five different declensions, you'll be able to remember it. After all, you're *not* really remembering sixty-five different verb forms at once; you're just remembering that *this* verb follows the pattern of some *other*, more familiar verb.

And we'll make this process easier and more enjoyable by playing a new version of our old, mnemonic imagery game.

KEY POINTS

- Languages are often full of complex, hard-to-remember patterns. You can learn these patterns easily by embedding them into simple, understandable stories.
- Whenever you encounter a confusing declension chart in your grammar book, take the nearest example sentence and use it to generate stories that cover every new form you need.
- You'll turn these stories into illustrated flash cards—the same new word/word form/word order flash cards discussed earlier—and you'll use those flash cards to learn your target language's patterns.

ON ARNOLD SCHWARZENEGGER AND EXPLODING DOGS: MNEMONICS FOR GRAMMAR

Kuato: What do you want, Mr. Quaid?

Douglas Quaid: The same as you; to remember.

—*Total Recall*, TriStar Pictures

Remember our exploding (male) German dog? In the last chapter, we attached mnemonic images to nouns, in order to turn an obnoxiously abstract concept—grammatical gender—into a vivid, memorable story. We assigned a vivid verb to each abstract idea—*burning* (feminine), *exploding* (masculine)—and in the process created a fun, powerful tool for memorization.

Now we're dealing with *new* obnoxious, abstract concepts. We've talked about how to memorize the basic patterns of your target language—those sixty-five French verb forms, for example—but how can you keep track of which words use which patterns? They can be unpredictable, after all; there's not always a simple way to know whether a word will follow one pattern (*teach / taught / had taught*) or another (*reach / reached / had reached*).

Suppose you could create mnemonic images that meant "*this* verb follows the same pattern as *teach / taught / had taught*" or "*this* Russian adjective follows the same pattern as this *other* Russian adjective." You could attach these images to every new word (i.e., *caught, thought,* and *bought*) that follows an old pattern (i.e., the *teach/taught/had taught* pattern) and make your life a lot easier.

Unfortunately, our old mnemonic images won't work here. They worked fine with nouns—exploding dogs and shattering horses make for memorable stories—but those same images break down if you try to use them with verbs or adjectives. How do you attach *exploding*—to a verb like *catch/caught/had caught*? Or *shattering* to *tall*? *Tall shattering* isn't a vivid, memorable story; it's a bad e. e. cummings poem.

You can even run into problems with nouns. German nouns have three possible genders and ten possible plural forms. If you're already using three mnemonic images for gender, how can you add *another* ten mnemonics for those plural forms? Our poor exploding dog can't do two things at once. He's already exploding; we can't expect him to *swim* or *sing* at the same time.

If you want to use mnemonics to help you learn grammar, you'll need a way to attach multiple mnemonic images to single words, and you'll need images that can work with verbs and adjectives.

Person-Action-Object: The Mnemonic Images of Memory Champions

Our solution comes from the wacky field of competitive memorization. There, in fierce, international competitions, participants memorize decks of cards, long poems, and thousands of numbers in exchange for cash prizes, fame, and glory. These competitions have created a sort of mental arms race, where competitors create new and improved mnemonic imagery techniques that allow them to memorize more and faster.

One of the core mnemonic weapons in any competitor's arsenal is known as the person-action-object (PAO) system, and we're going to use a simplified version of it to attach mnemonic images to our words.

PAO relies upon a simple premise: the three basic ingredients of a story are a person (*Arnold Schwarzenegger*), an action (*explodes*), and an object (*a dog*).

PAO can give you the flexibility you need to connect a mnemonic image to *any* kind of word. If you want to learn the ten ways to make German plural nouns, for example, you can choose ten people to represent them. Then you can use those people whenever you need them. *Arnold Schwarzenegger* (plural form 1) *explodes* (masculine gender) *a dog* is a weird, vivid, and compact story that could tell you the gender *and* plural form for our poor German dog. And if German *desks* follow the same patterns as German *dogs* (which they do—German desks are masculine, plural form 1), then I'm sure Arnold won't object to exploding a desk, too.

If you wanted to learn that *fight/fought*, *buy/bought*, and *think/thought* all follow the same pattern, you could put those verbs into the "action" slot of a PAO story. That lets you choose a mnemonic person or a mnemonic object to represent the "past tense ends in -*ought*" pattern.

For example, if you choose a mnemonic person—say, Patrick Stewart—you could imagine him *fighting* something, *buying* something, or *thinking* about something. If instead you choose an object—a toaster, perhaps—you could imagine *fighting* a toaster or *buying* some fancy toaster. Because these stories are visual, they're much easier to remember than some abstract verb form, especially when you're trying to learn a lot of verbs at once.

Adjectives can fit into PAO as well, but they're rarely complex enough to warrant some elaborate story like *Bruce Lee eats a large/cold/happy hot dog*. Instead, you can just use a simple mnemonic object. For example, French has five adjectives—*beautiful*, *new*, *crazy*, *soft*, and *old*—that follow a single, irregular pattern. We can connect them with a single object: *a beautiful football*, *a new football*, *a crazy football*—and easily remember the pattern in the future.

How do you keep track of all these stories? The same way you keep track of all your words: you can make a couple of flash cards for each of your mnemonic images and let your SRS sort it all out. Within a week or two, you won't be *able* to forget the strange and tawdry escapades of Sir Patrick Stewart and his stack of verbs.

What's this mnemonic signify? Mnemonic: Patrick Stewart	Verbs with past tenses ending in -aught/ought
	Examples: teach/taught/had taught buy/bought/had bought
FRONT	**BACK**

Mnemonics are a handy way to turn unwieldy declension charts into vivid, memorable stories. Instead of endlessly drilling verb forms or noun declensions, you can learn a pattern once, attach an image to it, and use that image to quickly memorize the pattern of every related word you encounter.

You don't always need mnemonics. In some languages, the spelling of a word may tell its particular pattern, and you don't need some crazy story involving Patrick Stewart and a baseball bat to remember it. But somewhere, you're inevitably going to encounter irregularities. After all, languages are human constructions, and we don't always make much sense. When you run into trouble, use mnemonics to make confusing irregularities easy and fun to memorize.

KEY POINTS

- Languages often have groups of "irregular" words that follow similar patterns. While you can learn each of these patterns easily with the help of illustrated stories, you may still need some way to remember which words follow which patterns.
- Any time you run into a tricky pattern, choose a person, action, or object to help you remember. For verb patterns, pick a mnemonic person or an object. For noun patterns, use a person or an action. Adjectives fit well with objects, and adverbs fit well with actions.

The Power of Output: Your Custom Language Class

Dude, suckin' at something is the first step towards being sorta good at something.

—Jake the Dog, *Adventure Time*

You've taken a few examples from each chapter of your grammar book, broken them down, and turned them into flash cards. You've learned how to learn patterns and how to attach them to new words using mnemonic images. You're well on your way toward learning the grammatical system of your new language. There's one last tool at your disposal, and it's where everything comes together: output.

You're going to write in your new language, but these aren't the tiresome essays you were required to write in school. Instead, you'll write about whatever you want to learn. If you want to pick up the ability to order food in France, then write about food. If you want to talk about Russian politics, then that's fair game, too.

Self-directed writing is the ultimate personalized language class. The moment you try to write about your upcoming vacation without the word for "vacation" or the future tense, you learn *precisely* what bits of language you're missing. Writing also trains you to take the patterns you've memorized and actually *use* them. This is where you learn to take raw information and turn it into *language*.

You can't learn much from writing without a source of corrections. You need native speakers to come in and tell you how to say whatever you want to say. Fortunately, those native speakers are out there on the Internet, and they're willing to correct your writing, as long as you're willing to correct theirs. You take a few minutes to correct someone's "He go to the store," and in exchange, you receive some of the best language training you could possibly hope for. Some of these exchange communities are *tremendously* helpful; I usually get a detailed correction from the Russians on *Lang-8.com* within an hour, and after a few hours, I often have *five* Russians commenting on my little paragraph. Insanity.

If you're uncomfortable correcting someone's writing, there are other communities—*italki.com* is one of the best—that can connect you to extremely affordable private tutors. Due to the magic of exchange rates and the allure of working from home, you can hire tutors in any language for extremely low prices.

Once you have a source for corrections, your goal in writing is to make mistakes. You don't need to craft a perfect essay, and in fact, you'll learn more if you write quickly and mess up a few times. Try to say what you want to say, and if you don't have the words or the grammar to say it, then use Google Translate (*translate.google.com*) to help. Once you get your corrections, you'll figure out *precisely* where your problems are, and you'll learn how a native speaker would express the same ideas. This is the best kind of input you could hope for; it's based upon your own writing and thoughts, so it's much more memorable than anything you could find in a grammar book.

Put every correction you receive into your flash cards. That way, you'll never forget a correction. This is one of the best features of SRSs; they give you the ability to remember *everything*. When you were learning a language in school, you could receive the same correction *hundreds* of times, and never actually remember it. With spaced repetition, you only need to receive a correction *once*, and within a few weeks, it will become a permanent part of your long-term memory.

 I went to Rome because I ~~want~~ eat gelato.
I went to Rome because I **wanted to** eat gelato

I went to Rome because
I ___ eat gelato.
(to want)

I went to Rome because
I **wanted to** eat gelato.

FRONT   **BACK**

KEY POINTS

- Use writing to test out your knowledge and find your weak points. Use the example sentences in your grammar book as models, and write about your interests.
- Submit your writing to an online exchange community. Turn every correction you receive into a flash card. In this way, you'll find and fill in whatever grammar and vocabulary you're missing.

Not sure what to write about? In the beginning, use your grammar book for inspiration. Take each new construction you learn and use it to write something about your life. What do *you* do for a living? What would *you* order in a restaurant? Turn the dialogues and examples in your grammar book into language that you'll actually use, and see what mistakes and missing words you can find.

Later on, we'll talk about using frequency lists—larger versions of our original 625 words—to make your writing exercises even more efficient. You'll learn key vocabulary at the same time as you learn grammar. But you have plenty to play with right now. Use writing to get a feel for the words and grammar rules in your textbook. In short order, you'll be ready to set aside your book and tackle the key vocabulary of your target language with the help of the Internet.

Do This Now: Learn Your First Sentences

In this section, we'll discuss where to find example sentences and then talk about what to do with the sentences you've found. To do this, you're going to rely upon a single skill: the ability to break a sentence down into tiny pieces. You'll use this skill over and over until you've mastered the grammar and vocabulary of your language.

This is the point at which your language begins to bloom. By taking words you've already learned and using them in sentences, you breathe grammatical life into your words. They aren't just spellings, pictures, and sounds anymore; they're *language*.

Find Your Sentences

Use your grammar book. It's there to make your life easier. You'll find a collection of easy-to-understand example sentences and dialogues, detailed explanations, and our favorite part of all, giant declension charts.

Take one chapter at a time and see what your book is trying to teach you. Usually, your book will begin by showing you how to greet people, say your name, talk about your occupation, and so on. Often, you'll find piles of examples—*one apple*, *two apples*, *one horse*, *two horses*. Go through and choose one or two of your favorites from each section. If you miss an important rule or exception (*one fish*, *two fish*), don't worry about it. At this point, you're just trying to get the basics into your head. You'll pick up more details as you learn more and more sentences.

Remember, you're going to be using an SRS, which basically gives you a perfect, photographic memory. You're going to remember *every tiny detail* about every sentence you choose. As such, you don't need fifty almost-identical examples for "how to form a plural noun." Just take one or two, turn them into flash cards, and then move on to the next topic.

Break Each Sentence into New Words, Word Forms, and Word Order

Take each sentence and break it down. Here are a couple of sentences from the first chapters of a made-up English textbook. For a moment, let's assume that you're starting to learn English. We'll go through the whole process step-by-step.

My name is George. I have a pet monkey.

NEW WORDS

Your first step: go through the words and see which ones are new. If you didn't know *any* of them, you have eight words to learn (*George* doesn't count).

Next, figure out which of these words lend themselves to simple pictures. *Name, I, pet,* and *monkey* all fall under this category (and two of these words—*name* and *I*—show up in the 625-word list). You'll take these words and make flash cards in the same way you did in the last chapter, by playing Spot the Differences with Google Images, adding in personal connections, and using mnemonics for gender (if needed). That leaves you with four more words: *my, is, have,* and *a.*

Let's deal with *a* first. *A* is a strange beast known as the indefinite article. It means that it's not particularly important *which* monkey George has; he doesn't have *the* monkey—he has *a* monkey. If your language has something like this, your grammar book will explain it in detail. Read that explanation, and then use your example sentence to remember it: *A* is the word that fits into *I have ____ pet monkey.*

FRONT   **BACK**

You can use this strategy to define all of the other words. *Have,* for example, is the word that fits into *I ____ a pet monkey*. Granted, it's not the *only* word that fits into the blank. George could *walk* his pet monkey or *disintegrate* said monkey. Nonetheless, *I ____ a pet monkey* can teach you *have* for three reasons.

First, you're going to be finding pictures of George and his monkey, and if George isn't actively *walking* or *disintegrating* that monkey, you're not going to think about those words.

Second, you're going to turn this monkey story into ten or more flash cards. With that much stimulation, there's *no way* you're going to have trouble remembering the word *have*.

Third, and the most important of all, *you're making these cards yourself*. Back when we discussed learning simple vocabulary, I stressed the importance of making your own cards. I pointed out that the *real* learning occurs when you're playing Spot the Differences on Google Images, choosing a personal connection, and so on. The flash cards you create are just a tiny reminder of a much bigger experience. And while you could probably share your flash cards with friends and teach them a few simple words (This is a *ball*, this is a *horse*), *you're* the only person who can get the full benefits from your cards.

Grammar is even more personal than vocabulary. You can't share any of your grammar cards with friends. These flash cards only mean *anything* because of the experience you had while creating them. You're starting with an example sentence from your grammar book and comparing that sentence to its translation. You're spending a few seconds looking at *I* have *a pet monkey* and searching for an accompanying image. In every step of this process, you're building connections between those words (I–have–a–pet–monkey) in your mind. Your flash card is just a way to reactivate and deepen those connections.

You're picking an image or two, but the image you eventually choose barely matters; by the time that you decide upon one, you've already created the connections you need to remember your sentence forever. Remember that abstract image of "Apples are delicious" from Chapter 2? The main purpose of pictures here is to help make your sentence more memorable. You may end up with some terrible clip art of a monkey paw-print. No one else who sees that image on a flash card would ever think, "Oh! Monkey paw-print! That must mean 'have,' as in 'I have a pet monkey.' " But as long as *you* chose that image and designed your flash card yourself, your sentence (and the missing word in it) will be memorable and clear.

Every now and then, you may run into problems. Occasionally your grammar book may include *terribly* vague example sentences, and a sentence like "____ *is a good thing*" just isn't going to do a good job of teaching you the meaning of a word like *integrity*, no matter how many flash cards you make. In cases like these, just skip those words. You'll learn them using the tools in the next chapter, when you start to find your own example sentences with Google Images and supplement them with a monolingual dictionary.

NEW WORD FORMS

It's not always clear when you're looking at a new word, and when you're looking at a new word form. Take the word *my*, for instance. *My* isn't really a new word; it's just a different form of the word *I*. Intuitively, you might not think this, but if I said to you, "I favorite monkey's name is George," you would probably correct me with "*My* favorite monkey's name is George."

When you start learning your target language, you won't necessarily notice these sorts of connections, and if you don't, it's not a problem. You'll learn *my* as if it was a new vocabulary word, in the same way we learned *a* and *have*, above.

But suppose you *did* notice. Suppose you also noticed that *is* is a special form of the verb *to be*. This is where you can learn your word forms. *My* is the word that fits into ____ *name is George* (*I*), and *is* is the word that fits into *My name* ____ *George* (*to be*). The only difference between new *words* and new word *forms* is that here you'll give yourself an extra clue (*I* or *to be*). This makes your flash cards somewhat easier to remember and links closely related concepts.

FRONT   BACK

WORD ORDER

You've learned all of your words. Now you just need to remember where to put them. This part's easy. Remove a word from your sentence: *I a pet monkey*. Now put it back into the sentence on the back side of a flash card. Where does *have* go? Do this once or twice in a sentence—*I have a monkey* (insert *pet*)—and you'll have the order of the words memorized for every similarly worded sentence.

FRONT   BACK

This process will look different in every language—you'll get a different mix of new words, word forms, and word orders—but the steps are identical. Here's the Italian version of our story:

Mi chiamo George. Ho una scimmietta.
Me—I call—George. I have—a (feminine)—little monkey pet.

The Italians convey just as much information in their six words as we convey in our nine. They do this by jamming a bunch of information into their word forms: *chiamo* (I call) is a special form of *chiamare* (to call). *Ho* (I have) is a special form of *avere* (to have). To learn a pair of Italian sentences like these, you'd make a couple of flash cards for the new words (and perhaps for *una*), a giant pile of word form cards, and a couple of word order cards.

You might do this whole rigmarole for your first few sentences, but from then on, you'll have much less work to do. If you made flash cards for the word order of *I have a pet monkey*, you'd now know precisely where to put *have* and *pet* in a sentence. From now on, you could skip the word order cards in *She has a kid* or *That pet monkey has a gun!* This applies to new words and word forms as well. Any time the position of a word, the form of a word, or the word itself surprises you, then learn it. But if you're not surprised by it, then skip it and move on to the next sentence.

Find Pictures

Pictures are there to make your life easier. They trick your brain into thinking about the *story* within each sentence rather than some abstract grammatical relationships. This makes every aspect of grammar more memorable and more *useful*. You don't need to know that the third person present indicative tense of "to have" is *has;* you *do* need to know how to talk about George and his monkey, and you can trick yourself into training *that* skill by adding a picture of a monkey to your *George _____ a monkey (to have)* flash card.

Unless you're using a Leitner box and drawing your pictures, you'll use Google Images. If you're not learning new, concrete words, then you don't need to search for images in your target language. We're not playing Spot the Differences here, so if you need a picture of a man with a monkey, feel free to search for "man with a monkey." This will save you some time and allow you to find practically any picture you can imagine. After all, the Internet is mostly in English; there are 625 million men with monkeys out there, and only a million *hommes avec singes*.

When you're picking apart a sentence into a bunch of little pieces, you can carefully search for the perfect picture of a man/monkey and reuse it in every flash card, or you can haphazardly pick up a handful of *different* pictures of men and monkeys. The former—using the same, single image on every card—will probably take you less time, and the latter—different images on every card—will be easier to remember.

Try both variants out and see how your brain reacts. I like to use multiple images to highlight different aspects of the sentence. For my *George ____ a pet monkey (to have)* flash card, I might have a picture of a monkey and a grabbing hand, to emphasize the possessive nature of *have*. Experiment. You'll find that after a few weeks, you'll develop a sense for the sorts of images that work best for you.

Note that not every sentence comes with an obvious picture. *Honesty is the best policy* doesn't contain any references to monkeys. In cases like these, find a picture of whatever comes to mind. You might grab an image of George Washington or a hand swearing on a Bible or Pinocchio. When all else fails, find a picture of *anyone* who would say your sentence—there are *billions* of images of people on the Internet (just search for "man talking"). Pick your favorite. *Any* picture will help turn an abstract grammatical idea into a concrete story. As a result, you'll have a much easier time remembering your sentence.

Dealing with Declension Charts

Deal with declension charts (I *am*, he/she *is*, we *are*, etc.) in the same way you dealt with example sentences; turn them into the same kinds of picture flash cards described above. The only real difference is that your grammar book won't supply you with every example sentence you need. So make those sentences yourself. Take an example sentence from your grammar book (I *am* a student) and turn it into a bunch of *new* sentences (She *is* an architect, he *is* a duck inspector).

Whenever possible, make each sentence unique; it's relatively easy to keep track of *I ____ a student* and *She ____ an architect*, whereas four nearly identical flash cards for *I/he/she/you* ____ *a student* can become confusing.

Once you've typed out your examples, submit them for corrections. You have two wonderful options here: *Lang-8.com* and *italki.com*.

Lang-8 is free. Register on the site, write out your entry, and click the submit button. Within a day, you should get your corrections. Turn the corrected sentences into flash cards to learn the new words, new word forms, and word orders you encounter. If you correct someone's English entry every time you submit an entry of your own, your writing samples will consistently jump to the top of the correction pile, and you'll get your corrections sooner.

If you want to get corrections even faster, search for native speakers of your target language who are learning English and request to add them to your profile as friends (Click on Add Friend). If they agree, they'll see and correct your submissions before anyone else's (and you'll see their submissions first, too).

italki.com has free services, but for writing, those services are similar to Lang-8, and Lang-8 does a better job. Use italki for its wonderful paid services. Register on the site and start searching for a language teacher. You'll find both professional teachers (more expensive, better trained) and untrained tutors (less expensive, untrained, but often *really* helpful). The site is designed for speaking lessons—you're basically paying for private tutoring sessions via video chat—but you can use it to find a teacher who will correct your writing and email it back to you. Contact a few teachers and see what kind of arrangement they'll make for writing corrections. By means of example, one of my website readers got seriously addicted to writing (he was writing out a full page of German *every day*). His tutor on italki corrects his writing for around a dollar a page.

Creating Your Own Sentences

Writing is your proving ground. It's where you can play around with the words and grammar rules you've learned and see what you can create with them. We've discussed the importance of turning declension charts into memorable stories, but there's no reason to stop there. Write about your life, your interests, or anything else.

Any time you have a question—"How do I say x?" "Can I do y?"— just write out a few sentences, submit them for corrections, and get your answers. If you have *absolutely no idea* how to write something, use Google Translate (*translate.google.com*) to get yourself in the ball-park.[19] Then submit your sentences for corrections and see what the native speakers say.

After you get your corrections, turn them into new-word / word form / word order flash cards. These are just variations of the same sentence game. At this point, you know how to play with a sentence, so there's nothing to prevent you from playing with *lots* of sentences. Go have fun.

Once you've played your way through a few chapters of your grammar book, move on to the next chapter in *this* book, where you'll find a few more tools to add to your repertoire.

For the Intermediates

Learning grammar is an improvisatory dance at *every* level. As you encounter texts in your grammar book or elsewhere, you're constantly asking yourself the same question: "Does this sentence contain something *new*?" Do you know all the words? Have you seen those word forms before? Is the word order surprising? Use your flash cards to take whatever you find interesting. Your SRS will make sure that you never forget it.

In the beginning of the next chapter, we'll discuss using Google Images to provide you with example sentences for any word and any grammatical construction. Since you have a bit of vocabulary and

---

19. Be careful not to get *too* reliant upon Google Translate for your writing. Eventually, you'll need to make new grammatical constructions on your own if you want them to stick, so if you roughly know how to say something, then try to do it without Google's help. Remember, you have access to native speakers to help turn your mistakes into new, useful flash cards.

grammar already under your belt, you can start using that tool immediately. Read the Words About Words section and start using it to supplement your grammar book; it's an incredible tool.

A note about writing: if you're trying to refresh a language you've forgotten, writing is one of the *best* ways to reactivate those old memories. Write as much as you possibly can, and turn all of the corrections you receive into flash cards. There's no better review for grammar and vocabulary.

CHAPTER 6

The Language Game

It is a happy talent to know how to play.

—Ralph Waldo Emerson

By learning the sounds of your language, you gain access to words. By learning words, you gain access to grammar. And with just a little bit of grammar, you gain access to the rest of your language.

This is the language game. It's the moment when a new language unfolds before your eyes and you can choose your own games to play and your own paths to follow.

On some level, these paths are simple, even obvious: to improve your vocabulary, you need to learn vocabulary; to learn how to read, you need to read; to learn how to speak, you need to speak. But there are better and worse ways to walk these paths, and so we're going to take a tour of the landscape. We'll walk through the process of customizing and learning vocabulary. We'll discuss how to approach your first books and your first TV shows. Finally, we'll talk about strategies for speaking and where to find native speakers.

Wander this landscape in any way you choose. You may enjoy reading French magazines or watching Russian TV shows. You may fall in love with Chinese vocabulary, or you may fall in love with a new Italian friend. This is *your* language. Take it wherever you want to go.

SETTING GOALS: YOUR CUSTOM VOCABULARY

If you don't know where you are going, you'll probably end up somewhere else.

—Yogi Berra

How many words should you learn? *Which* words should you learn? The answer depends upon you: what do *you* want to do with your language?

Back in Chapter 4, we discussed using frequency lists to help streamline your vocabulary acquisition. I gave you a list of 625 basic words to learn and showed you how to learn them quickly. When you combine those words with a healthy dose of grammar from your textbook, you'll have everything you need to master the rest of your vocabulary.

Begin with the top thousand words in your new language. There won't be many new words—you'll have learned most of them already from the 625-word list—and they'll let you understand nearly 85 percent of the words you hear and 75 percent of the words you read.

Your next steps depend upon your individual needs. If you just want to chat in restaurants, those top thousand words may be enough. If you want to get a doctoral degree at the Sorbonne, then keep going. The second thousand words will give you a 5 percent boost to your reading and listening comprehension—you'll understand 90 percent of what you hear and 80 percent of what you read.[20] On the surface, those 5 percent may seem like a relatively small payoff for a thousand new words, but in practice, they make a significant difference. Instead of running into issues with every fourth word you read, you'll have pushed it back to every *fifth* word. At this point, you're doing pretty

---

20. The 80 percent figure only applies to nonfiction texts. If you're reading fiction, the top two thousand words will bring you to nearly 90 percent comprehension.

well, but you're not quite prepared for your doctorate yet. Your academic texts will feel something like this:

> If current planting rates are ___ with planting ___ satisfied in each ___ and the forests milled at the earliest opportunity, the ___ wood supplies could further increase to about thirty-six million ___ meters ___ in the ___ 2001–2015. The ___ ___ wood supply should greatly ___ ___ ___ , even if much is used for ___ production.

With two thousand words, you're at 80 percent comprehension. You can pick up the gist of a text—this paragraph is about wood supplies—but you're missing many of the important bits. To understand more, you can either learn a *lot* more words (90 percent comprehension takes approximately 5,500 words, and 95 percent comprehension takes 12,500 words) or you can start to specialize.

Every field speaks its own language. Academics use different words than politicians, and musicians use different words than farmers. In our native languages, we've learned enough vocabulary—fifteen thousand to thirty-five thousand words—to function in a wide variety of contexts. We can listen to political speeches, attend university lectures, and get our hair cut without much trouble. Occasionally, we'll run into problems with an abstruse art critique or a baffling article on particle physics, but for the most part, our native vocabularies serve us in any environment.

You don't necessarily need this capability in a new language. You may never attend a university lecture in French, or on the other hand, you may use your French *primarily* in a university setting. Not everyone needs to learn the same words, and you can save a great deal of time by customizing your vocabulary to suit your needs. If you need to read academic texts, you could, for instance, learn a small collection of frequently used academic words like *affect, confirm,* and *facilitate.* Here's a new version of our wood supplies essay. In addition to the top 2,000 words, I've added just 570 *academic* words:

> If current planting rates are *maintained* with planting targets satisfied in each *region* and the forests milled at the earliest opportunity, the *available* wood supplies could further increase to about thirty-six million ____ meters ____ in the period 2001–2015. The ____ *available* wood supply should greatly *exceed domestic requirements*, even if much is used for *energy* production.

Now you've reached 90 percent comprehension, and you can understand most of this text (you're missing *cubic*, *annually*, and *additional*). You'd need a fifty-five-hundred-word vocabulary to reach this level of comprehension in *every* context, but here, in an *academic* context, you've accomplished the same result with half the work.

Whether or not you're going into academia, you can take advantage of vocabulary customization to save you time. Start by learning the top one thousand to two thousand words to form a solid foundation and then add key words based upon your interests. Where can you find these words? Get a thematic vocabulary book—the publisher Barron makes the best ones—and check off any words you want. These books give you lists of words based upon specific themes: home, business, automotive, and so on. If you're a musician, you can skip directly to the music section and pick out your favorite music vocabulary. Later, if you want to learn thirty words for pasta dishes, skip to the food section and pick out what you need from there. Choosing your vocabulary is one of the most enjoyable parts of learning a new language: it's like a personalized shopping trip for your brain.

KEY POINTS

- To learn vocabulary efficiently, begin by learning the top thousand words in your target language.
- If you're aiming for a high degree of fluency, then keep going until you know the top fifteen hundred to two thousand words.
- Once you're done building a foundation, choose additional words based upon your individual needs. You can find these words by skimming through a thematic vocabulary book and finding key words for every context you need—travel, music, business, and so on.

Words About Words

Un dictionnaire, c'est tout l'univers par ordre alphabétique.
A dictionary: the entire universe in alphabetical order.

—Anatole France

In the last chapter, we talked about learning new grammatical constructions and complex words with the help of example sentences from your grammar book. You can take these sentences, turn them into fill-in-the-blank exercises, add a few pictures, and learn a bunch of new words and word forms. The word *Where*, for instance, might go with ____ *are you going? I'm going to France!*

This strategy can teach you the words in your grammar book, but what about the *rest* of your vocabulary—that list of words we discussed in the last section? You need a way to find quality examples and explanations for every new word, and it wouldn't hurt if you learned some grammar at the same time.

We're going to use three tools: Google Images, self-directed writing, and monolingual dictionaries. We've already encountered the first two, and with some grammar and vocabulary under your belt, you can use them to their full potential. The last tool, a dictionary in your target language, will soon become one of your best friends. It will let you learn *any* word in your target language, no matter how complex. First, let's reintroduce ourselves to Google Images.

Google Images, the Sequel

You saw in Chapter 4 how to use Google Images to find helpful images for your words and to play the Spot the Differences game. But with the help of some grammar, you can use Google Images in a different way. Suppose you needed to learn the French word *dernier* (last). A quick search for *dernier* on Google Images provides you with this little illustrated story:

nouvellesargentines.fr
The **last** Argentine dictator
sentenced to life imprisonment

And if you move your mouse over the text, you get the original French headline:

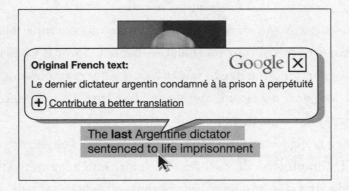

Suddenly you're not just learning one word. You're picking up the words for "Argentine" (*argentin*), "dictator" (*dictateur*), and "sentenced" (*condamné*). You're learning the phrase for "life imprisonment" (*prison à perpétuité*), and you're getting bits and pieces of grammar all over the place. This is a language gold mine, and it will take you *seconds* to learn. What's *dernier* mean? It's the word that fits into this story: *Le ____ dictateur argentin condamné à la prison à perpétuité.*

Le ___ dictateur argentin condamné à la prison à perpétuité.	dernier
FRONT	**BACK**

Granted, *dernier* isn't the *only* word that could fit into our story. Perhaps Argentina's *first* or *seventeenth* dictator also went to prison. Nonetheless, you'll still remember *dernier* every time you see this story and its accompanying picture. After all, that story is just a reminder of a much richer experience: searching for *dernier*, skimming through nineteen *other* illustrated stories—Justin Bieber at his *dernier* concert, Arnold Schwarzenegger's *The* Dernier *Stand*—and finally choosing that Argentinian dictator. All of these experiences link together in your memory, and your flash card becomes merely a reminder that brings those memories back.

Google Images can also produce illustrated examples for any grammatical construction. Need a good story for French's *avait fait* (he / she / it *had done*)? Search for *"avait fait"* and you'll find 1.6 million different examples of that construction, complete with images and translations.

Self-Directed Writing

Google Images is a wonderful (and fast) way to find good example sentences for your words. But if you want to learn a heap of grammar at the same time, write out your own examples and definitions. After you get your corrections, you can use the example sentences to teach you your words and use the corrections to teach you your grammar.

This is a tremendously efficient use of your time. Not only are you learning vocabulary and grammar simultaneously, but you're also creating particularly memorable examples for your words. These aren't just stories you've read somewhere; they're *your* stories, and accordingly, they'll stay in your head.

You can also write *anywhere*, provided you have a translated list of words to learn and a small notepad or smartphone. You'll probably make mistakes—Hungarian has two words for "red"; did you use the right one?—but every time you do, a native speaker will catch it, and you'll learn even more from the experience.

I like to write whenever I'm stuck on a long commute. I'll finish my daily flash card reviews and then begin writing example sentences and definitions for new words. It's an endless source of portable entertainment.

Monolingual Dictionaries

A good monolingual dictionary is an extraordinary source of input. Inside, you'll find every word you could possibly desire, paired with a complete *explanation* of that word in your target language. And if you don't understand some words in that explanation, you can just look them up and find new explanations of *those* words. Every time you read a new definition, you automatically learn a few new words and a bunch of grammar. It's like having a French guy in your pocket who is willing to discuss any word in his language at any hour of the day.

If you get a *really* good dictionary, then you'll even find premade example sentences for your words. If you're lucky enough to find a dictionary like this, you're holding a one-stop shop for all of your vocabulary needs. Take those examples and definitions, grab a few accompanying images from Google Images, and move on to your next word.

At intermediate and advanced levels, you'll start relying more and more upon monolingual dictionaries, in part because they're awesome and in part because they'll show you the subtle distinctions between your words. A couple chapters back, we were avoiding synonyms. Now we can embrace them, because we can use dictionaries to tell us the differences between our *policemen* (formal) and our *cops* (informal).

Up until this point, I've recommended using example sentences to learn abstract words, but that has limits. Sometimes it's hard to find a good example sentence to help you remember an abstract word like *determination.* In the last chapter, I suggested that you skip any tricky words and learn them later. Now, with the help of a monolingual dictionary, there's nothing you can't learn.

Even with access to definitions, don't stop using example sentences. They make your words easier to remember and they show you how to *use* your words fluently. A dictionary adds an *additional* layer of depth and helps you figure out the differences between words like *eat* and *devour*.

Using a dictionary may take a little bit longer than you're accustomed to. Before, you could grab a picture of a cat and make a flash card in a few seconds; now you'll search for pictures, good example sentences, *and* definitions. But for every word you learn in this way, you get a bunch of *new* words added to your passive vocabulary and a great deal of comprehensible input. This reinforces every part of your language and dramatically accelerates your learning. And if you use an *online* dictionary, you won't need much more time at all. You can search for a new word, copy the information and add it to your flash cards in less than a minute.

KEY POINTS

- Use Google Images to find quality example sentences and pictures for your words. It's fast, it provides clear examples, and the combination of images and sentences is easy to memorize.
- If you run into problems or you're away from your computer, write out your own example sentences and definitions for new words. Get them corrected and use those corrections to learn both grammar and vocabulary.
- Once you have enough vocabulary under your belt, add a monolingual dictionary to your toolbox. When you do, you'll gain the ability to learn every word in your target language, and as a bonus, your passive vocabulary will grow every time you research and memorize a new term.

READING FOR PLEASURE AND PROFIT

The more that you read, the more things you will know.
The more that you learn, the more places you'll go.

—Dr. Seuss, *I Can Read with My Eyes Shut!*

We have huge vocabularies in our native languages. Words can be hard to count (is *jump* different from *jumping*?), but if we're counting *word families* (e.g., the *jump* family includes *jumped* and *jumping*), then we know fifteen thousand to thirty-five thousand of these families by our twentieth birthdays.

How on earth did we learn so many words? Most of us didn't spend our teenage years leafing through dictionaries, and most of the words we know are rarely, if ever, spoken aloud. When's the last time you said "excavate"? There's only one feasible source left: as it turns out, we learn the vast majority of our words through reading, and we can do the same in a foreign language.

Reading in a foreign language often evokes some ugly associations: hours spent trudging through some excruciatingly long *masterpiece* of literature, painstakingly looking up every other word in a dictionary. But we don't need to torture ourselves. We possess an extraordinary ability to learn words from context alone, without the aid of a dictionary—this is how we learned most of our English words, after all. That part of our brain doesn't simply shut down as soon as it encounters a word *en français*.

Measure It Yourself!

You can accurately measure your English vocabulary at *TestYourVocab.com*. The tests are fun and only take five to ten minutes. Try it, and then get all your friends (and especially their children) to do it. The website is run by linguists who are trying to understand how vocabulary levels change with age and education. The more people who take it, the better data they'll get, and the more we'll all know about vocabulary growth.

Practically speaking, we'll automatically learn an unknown word 10 percent of the time we encounter it. Sometimes we'll catch it the first time we see it—*The dog's farok wagged excitedly*—and sometimes we'll pick up a word more gradually. If a character in our book chugs a single *doboz* of beer, then we can be pretty sure *doboz* is some sort of can or bottle. If he later crushes that *doboz* in his hands and throws it in the recycling bin, it's probably not made of glass.

You can take advantage of this ability by reading as much as you can, as quickly as possible. Every novel-length book you read—whether it's Tolstoy or Twilight—will automatically increase your vocabulary by three hundred to five hundred new words and dump buckets of grammar into that language machine in your head. As such, you don't need to start with hard-core literature. You can just read whatever's most fun. The Harry Potter series has been translated into a bajillion languages (or at least sixty-seven), and you can find trashy romance novels or detective stories in every language. Choose whatever you find most appealing.

For your very first book, try to find a familiar story—a translation of something you've already read or a book that's been turned into a movie you've seen—and read it *along with an audiobook.* The audiobook will carry you along and help you read faster than you otherwise would. You won't have the time to get bogged down with unknown words, and you'll pick up the rhythm of the spoken language.

In the previous chapters of this book, I've directed your attention toward the pronunciation of individual words, but I haven't talked much about the sound of sentences. Even familiar words can sound different in the context of rapid speech, and audiobooks are the easiest way to familiarize yourself with real, spoken language. You're listening to a native speaker talk for twelve to eighteen hours in a row, you have the words right in front of you, and you have a good story to concentrate on. It's perfect. Along the way, you'll get a ton of comprehensible input, pick up a bunch of vocabulary, and have fun in the process.

You also get an opportunity to focus on a story rather than painstakingly decoding the precise meaning of every word in every sentence. It's not always important to know whether a wizard's wand is made of *yew* or *alder;* sometimes you just need to know what that wizard *did.* This is yet another skill that will serve you in the future; you need the ability to skip over holes in your vocabulary. You're not *going* to know the precise meaning of every word you encounter, but that doesn't necessarily prevent you from understanding a story or a conversation. By reading books, you can learn to let go of the words you don't understand and get yourself swept up in the magic of a good story.

KEY POINTS

- Reading without a dictionary is the simplest, easiest way to grow your passive vocabulary. On average, a single book will teach you three hundred to five hundred words from context alone. By reading just one book in your target language, you'll make all future books and texts of any kind *much* easier to read.
- By reading in conjunction with an audiobook, you'll have a much easier time moving through a long text, and you'll pick up invaluable exposure to the rhythms of your language in action. This will improve your pronunciation, your listening comprehension, your vocabulary, your grammar; in short, it will provide a huge boost to *every* aspect of your language.

LISTENING COMPREHENSION FOR COUCH POTATOES

If you want to use television to teach somebody, you must first teach them how to use television.

—Umberto Eco

Learning to listen can be tricky. Out in the real world, speech can come *fast*, and even familiar vocabulary can sound foreign in someone else's mouth. You may learn to comfortably read and write, and even begin thinking in a language, when suddenly you run into a real-life French teenager and realize that you don't understand a word she's saying. Whole fragments of sentences—*Je ne suis pas* (I'm not)—turn into single mumbled words—*shwipa*—and you're left scratching your head, wondering if she's actually speaking French.

And this is before you even begin to worry about regional accents and dialects. When I moved to Austria, I arrived with an *official German fluency certificate*. I strutted my way to the farmers' market, bought a basil plant, and asked the farmer how to care for it. He replied in Austrian German. After five minutes of smiling and nodding, I picked up *one* word. Water. Apparently, I needed to do something with *water* to keep my basil plant alive.

If you want to understand real-world speech, you need to listen to real-world speech. But you can't just start by listening to foreign news radio all day. It's just too hard. You'll get frustrated and you'll tune out, at which point you might as well be listening to random noise.

You could listen to music, which might be a bit more engaging, but music isn't great either. How often do you pay serious attention to the lyrics of a song? How often do you even *understand* the lyrics of a song? Music carries us away, and when the drums are beating and the guitars are playing, we will happily sing "Slow motion Walter, fire engine guy" regardless of the *real* lyrics, "Smoke on the water, fire in the sky." We don't always listen to music for the *stories*; we listen for the *music*. So if you want to listen to French music, go ahead. It might get a few new words banging around in your head, but it's not going to prepare you for that mumbling French teenager.

Instead, watch movies and television. In these genres, you *are* listening for the stories, and so you'll pay very careful attention to everything you hear. Unlike news radio, you can see the facial expressions and body language of every speaker, and you can see precisely what they're doing while they speak. These visual clues can help you understand what you're hearing. TV and film are just like real life, only a bit more story driven. They're perfect for learning how to listen.

DVDs of movies and TV shows often come with subtitles in English or your target language. Don't use them. The problem with subtitles is that reading is easier than listening. We learn with our eyes more than our ears, and so when subtitles are present, we don't improve at listening.

A film with English subtitles is basically an English storybook with some foreign language background noise. It's useless for our needs.

Sure, you might hear a couple hours of French or Spanish, but you aren't actually *listening* to the dialogues; you're just reading the story.

If the subtitles are in your target language, then you're *still* just reading a story, although this story is significantly more useful. This can be a wonderful source of input; it's not much different than reading a book with an audiobook. But it won't help you with that damned mumbly teenager. You need to put yourself in a situation where you're relying entirely on your ears, and subtitles take that away from you.

Still, you'll probably need some help. With subtitles, you won't train your ears, but without them, movies and TV shows can feel overwhelming. You can dial back the difficulty in two ways: by choosing your first shows very carefully and by reading about those shows ahead of time on Wikipedia.

First things first: TV series are easier than films. When you watch *anything*, your first, hardest task is to figure out who's who and what's going on. This task is equally difficult in TV and film, but in a TV series, you only have to do it *once*. By the second or third episode, you basically understand what's happening and you can sit back and enjoy yourself. In a film, you may *never* understand what's going on, which is extraordinarily frustrating. It feels like you just threw away two hours of your life, and you didn't even have fun doing it. So start with a TV series. At least after the first couple of episodes, you'll have a much easier time.

Which TV series should you watch? Choose whatever you like, as long as it's not comedy. There is nothing quite as terrible as listening to a long German joke, reaching the end, and realizing that you don't understand the punch line, because it's a crappy pun on some rare word that only exists in some ridiculous German dialect. Don't do this to yourself. Watch *House* or *24* or *Some Guy Runs Around and Shoots People*. In all likelihood, these shows have been professionally dubbed into your target language. You can follow along without too much trouble ("What's he doing? Oh, he's shooting someone again"), you'll pay attention, and you won't throw your TV set out the window after a terrible German "joke." If you choose your show carefully, you can get yourself seriously *addicted* to foreign language TV. This is the best case scenario. I got through forty-eight episodes of *24 Heures Chrono* (the French dub of *24*) in a two-week TV binge, and it did *wonders* for my French.

Don't worry about the dubbing; today's high-budget TV shows have come a long way from the lip-flapping kung-fu dubs of the past. They *had* to; American TV is played around the world, and no one wants to watch a terrible dub of their favorite series. As such, they hire translators who pay close attention to both the words *and* timing of the English originals, so you barely even notice that everyone's lips are slightly off. Still, if it bothers you, feel free to find a TV series originally made in your target language. But don't be surprised if all the fun, mindless violence of American TV is replaced by *drama* or, worse, *comedy*. Blech.

You'll have a much easier time understanding a TV show or movie if you read a summary of it first, particularly if that summary is in your target language. This trick got me through the first couple of seasons of *Lost* in Russian. Go to Wikipedia (in English), look up your TV show, and then switch to your target language (you'll find a link on the bottom left side of the page). There you'll usually find information about your show and summaries of the episodes. When you read one of these summaries, you pick up a bunch of the vocabulary used in each episode. This strategy can also help you handle films, since you can introduce yourself to the characters and plot ahead of time. It feels like reading a short book and then watching the movie adaptation of that book, which *definitely* beats staring at a movie screen and only figuring out the plot after the movie is over.

Later, once you're comfortable watching TV, you can begin to drop your crutches. You won't need to read summaries on Wikipedia, and you'll be able to handle films without much trouble. If you're really adventurous, you might even be able to handle comedy (but don't bother if you're learning German). Then, if you want, you can make the step to audiobooks (without a book in hand), podcasts, and radio.

KEY POINTS

- Listening is a fast-paced skill that can sometimes feel overwhelming. Take baby steps, and gradually ramp up the challenge until you can handle the fastest and hardest of listening challenges (radio, podcasts, ridiculous garbled train station announcements).
- Start with an interesting foreign TV or dubbed American TV series without subtitles. You can dial down the difficulty by reading episode summaries ahead of time, in order to prepare yourself for the vocabulary and plot twists of each episode.
- As your comfort level grows, wean yourself off of summaries and begin watching and listening to more challenging media.

Speech and the Game of Taboo

"I can't do this," I said. "I don't know what to say."

"Say anything," he said. "You can't make a mistake when you improvise."

"What if I mess it up? What if I screw up the rhythm?"

"You can't," he said. "It's like drumming. If you miss a beat, you create another."

—Patti Smith, *Just Kids*

There is a party game called Taboo. Perhaps you've played it. In Taboo, you try to make your teammates say a certain word—"baseball," for instance—out loud. However, you're not allowed to *say* "baseball," nor can you say "sport," "game," "hitter," "pitcher," or "ball." Those words are forbidden—they're taboo—and in order to win, you have to find a path *around* the forbidden words. You improvise. You talk about an event where players get together, hit spheres with bats, and run around on a diamond. If all goes well, your team shouts out, "Baseball!" and you win a point. If not, then you find other routes—it's America's favorite pasttime, it's what the Dodgers do, and so on.

Fluent speech and the game of Taboo are practically the same thing. When you speak in a foreign language, you try to communicate the thoughts in your head, but you don't always have the right words to express them. You want to tell your German friend about a baseball game, but you don't know the word for "baseball." Perhaps you don't even know the German words for "sport" or "game." How do you communicate your thoughts to your friend?

Your first tendency will be to switch to English. Your friend probably understands English, and you'll get your point across. Unfortunately, your German won't get any better. If, on the other hand, you *stay* in German, a remarkable thing occurs: you begin to improvise. At that moment, you take a giant leap toward fluency.

Fluency, after all, isn't the ability to know every word and grammatical pattern in a language; it's the ability to communicate your thoughts without stopping every time you run into a problem. If you can successfully tell your friend about that baseball game—*We were . . . watching the Dodgers*—then you've just practiced fluency. You've gotten better at using the words you *know* to express yourself. If you can do this for every thought in your head, then you're done. You've won the language game; you're fluent.

This is a learned skill, and it's a skill you can practice using a simplified version of Taboo. There's only one rule: no English allowed. Every time you speak with a native speaker or another language learner, you'll stick to your target language *exclusively*. At some point, a thought will arrive in your head, and you won't have the words to express it. That's the moment that matters most. Seize it! It's the opportunity to turn your memorized vocabulary and grammar into fluent spoken language, and you only get it when you stubbornly refuse to speak in English.

This is the most important game in this book. Everything we've done until now has been designed to help you reach this final game. So don't let anyone take it from you. You're going to run into people who have no interest in playing Taboo. They might be fellow language learners who switch to English whenever they run into problems, or native speakers who want to use you to practice their English. They will (sometimes unconsciously) encourage you to speak in English. Don't do it. Find other people to hang out with. Your language will thank you.

Finding Fellow Taboo Players

The world is full of people who speak the language you're learning. You can find them at home, abroad, or somewhere in between:

AT HOME: VIDEO CHATS IN YOUR LIVING ROOM

Five to ten years ago, your only local options for speech practice involved classes or local tutors. Then high-speed Internet came and changed everything. You can load up a website, click a few buttons, and video-chat with a native speaker in the comfort of your own home. It's a brave new world.

The Internet's offerings change all the time, but there are a few communities that stand out and deserve mention: Verbling, Live Mocha, and italki.

Verbling.com is an instant gratification machine. You tell it what language you're learning, and it pairs you up with someone who speaks your target language and wants to learn your native language. You chat for five minutes in one language, a bell sounds, and then you chat in the other language. It's language learning in the style of speed dating, and it's a nice way to meet and chat with real, live native speakers. You can make some friends, play a bit of language Taboo, and generally have a good time.

Verbling is great because it's fast; you don't need to spend time finding language exchange partners and arranging times to chat. You get a lot of exposure to wildly varying accents, which can help you understand those accents in the future. As you might expect, the conversations don't get very deep; you generally just introduce yourselves and talk about where you live and what you do. If you really hit it off, you can exchange contact information and chat later using a video-chat service like Skype (*Skype.com*).

LiveMocha.com is one of many language exchange websites. Other notables are *Busuu.com*, *MyLanguageExchange.com*, and *Language-*

Exchanges.org. They resemble dating websites for language learners. You put up a profile—*I'm an English-speaking tax attorney, seeking a like-minded Russian speaker for video chatting*—search through other users' profiles, and try to make friends. Once you find a few interesting people, you set up video-chat dates (usually via Skype), where you chat and alternate languages until you decide to stop. If you find a few dedicated language learners on LiveMocha and set up regular chat dates, you can get a lot of speaking practice. The real challenge is figuring out what to talk about once you've made your introductions. At that point, you'll either need to find mutual interests to talk about or shift into party games (e.g., *YouRather.com*: *Would you rather always be naked or always be itchy?*).

italki.com brings money to the table, which changes the game dramatically. It can connect you with native speakers and professional teachers, who are willing to chat with you exclusively in your target language. This cuts the English out of your practice sessions and makes them much more efficient. Since these teachers get to work in the comfort of their own homes, they usually charge very little.

This arrangement gives you a lot more control over your learning. Once you've tried out a few people and found a good match (most teachers offer cheap, thirty-minute intro sessions), you can schedule regular meetings and plan out conversation topics in advance.

If you're aiming for efficiency, then pull out a word frequency list and discuss every word you don't know in order. This is what I do with my private English students, and it always provokes interesting, fun conversations. When we try to suss out the difference between a *bar* and a *pub*, for instance, we invariably get caught up in long discussions about German and American drinking cultures. In the end, we've managed to chatter for five to ten minutes, play *countless* games of Taboo, and definitively learn the difference among a *bar*, a *pub*, and a *Biergarten*. Then we move on to the next word and have a totally new conversation.

Take notes on everything you learn. This is your chance to pick up all the slang that's missing from your textbook. If you want, you can even work with your tutor to generate example sentences for new flash cards. In the process, you'll run into new grammar and new vocabulary, all while speaking in your target language. It's a great use of time and money, and it's one of the best ways to practice speaking at home.

ABROAD: LANGUAGE HOLIDAYS

You *can* learn a language at home, but there is no substitute for travel. When you travel to a country, you learn something about the *soul* of a language—its people, its food, its culture—that can't be captured in books. I learned Italian in Perugia, Italy. I lived with a man from Naples, who once sat me down and explained the difference between ordinary pizza and real, Neapolitan pizza. His monologue was a ten-minute rhapsody on pizza, after which he began to run out of words and simply gestured wildly while saying, *"È come . . . come . . . è come un orgasmo"* (It's like . . . like . . . it's like an orgasm). I learned some Italian that day, but that wasn't really the point; I learned about the Italian soul.

If you want to add some structure to your language holiday, consider enrolling in classes. There are language institutes in almost every country, many of which are surprisingly affordable. The experience you get in return is invaluable. You learn a thousand things you would never have otherwise learned—etiquette at the Viennese opera house, the strange workings of the national healthcare system, the taste of *real, Neapolitan* pizza—and in the process, you fall in love with a people and a culture.

Be aware that most people speak English, so try to find the people that prefer to speak in your target language. Even if you're taking classes with an international group of students, you'll find that most students speak English in the breaks. And if you speak English natively, people will actively seek you out to practice their English skills. This makes our game of Taboo much more difficult.

So if you're on a language holiday in a foreign country, arrange activities that put you in contact with locals. Go on museum tours *in Italian*; take cooking classes *in French*; go to bars, local religious services, or community events. Create an environment in which you can speak your target language as much as possible. There's nothing *wrong* with speaking English with Italians, but this is your money and your time abroad. Seek out people who hate speaking English and hang out with them instead. Or just tell everyone you're Albanian and you don't speak English. No one speaks Albanian.

IN BETWEEN: IMMERSION PROGRAMS

I'm a big fan of immersion programs, particularly those offered at Middlebury College in Vermont. You show up at a secluded university with a group of forty to two hundred people, you all sign a contract forbidding the use of English, and you speak exclusively in your target language for seven to eight weeks. It's language-learning boot camp, and the game of Taboo is the law of the land. You study in your target language, eat in your target language, and after a few weeks, you even dream in your target language.

These programs are wonderful because everyone is working toward the same goal. As a result, you feel much less inhibited when you speak. It can be embarrassing or scary when you're the only non-native speaker in a room. This happens a lot when you're studying abroad. In an immersion program, *everyone* is making mistakes, so it's not that big a deal if you make some as well. You spend most of your days taking classes, chatting with friends, helping less experienced students, and learning from more experienced students.

There's a slight downside to spending so much time with students—you can pick up bad habits, particularly when it comes to pronunciation. Even if you arrive with an excellent accent, you may start sounding a little American if you spend most of your time listening to American-accented German. Still, there's no way to beat the amount of speaking practice you get in one of these programs— you're playing Taboo *constantly*—and you can minimize any damage to your accent by spending time with the native-speaker teachers (and by watching foreign language TV when you need a break from socializing).

These programs can be expensive, but they offer plentiful, grant-based financial aid and their results are beyond compare. If you have the opportunity to go, jump on it. You'll never forget it.

KEY POINTS

- With the advent of ubiquitous, high-speed Internet connections, you can get quality speech practice anywhere.
- Whenever and wherever you practice, follow the golden rule of Language Taboo: no English allowed. By practicing in this way, you'll develop comfortable fluency with the words and grammar you know.

DO THIS NOW: EXPLORE YOUR LANGUAGE

Go explore. Read one book or twenty. Write a novel. Jump on a plane to an intensive program abroad. You have the tools you need to turn your language into whatever you desire, and you can use them in any way (and in any order) you choose.

That being said, it can be nice to have some suggestions about what to do first and what to do next. I'm happy to oblige.

Over the previous three chapters, I've suggested the following:

1. Sound Play: Learn how to hear and produce the sounds of your target language and how spelling and sound interrelate.

2. Word Play: Learn 625 frequent, concrete words by playing Spot the Differences in Google Images, finding personal connections, and if needed, adding mnemonic imagery for grammatical gender.

3. Sentence Play: Begin turning the sentences in your grammar book into flash cards for new words, word forms, and word order. Use written output to fill in the gaps missing from your textbook.

Here's what I suggest you do next:

1. If you haven't already done so, learn the first half of your grammar book. Make flash cards for everything you find interesting.

2. Learn the top thousand words in your target language. Write out definitions and examples whenever you're not entirely sure what a word means. About halfway through, you'll find that you can understand a monolingual dictionary. Use it to help you learn the rest of your words.

3. Go back to your grammar book, skim through it, and grab any remaining bits of information you'd like.

4. Read your first book while listening to an audiobook.

5. Watch a full season of a dubbed TV show, reading episode summaries in your target language ahead of time.

6. Get a *ton* of speech practice. Get as much as you possibly can, either through an immersion program, a language holiday abroad, or through teachers on *italki.com*. If you get a private teacher, talk about the next thousand words from your frequency list and add specialized words for your particular interests. Together with your teacher, create example sentences and enter them into your SRS.

Then rinse and repeat as desired.

Note: even when you're focusing on a book or TV show, never stop doing flash card reviews. Your flash cards get more and more useful the longer you use them. I like to review my flash cards for a full year before I stop completely. That way, I'll have an easier time retaining all my words and grammar, even without doing any maintenance later.

Also, never *entirely* stop creating and learning new cards. In the past, I've run into situations where I wanted to maintain one of my languages without learning anything new. I did my daily reviews, but I stopped learning new flash cards. It got boring fast. At least in my experience, flash card reviews are only fun when you're learning new things at the same time. So make sure you always have something new to learn—even just a couple of new words a day makes a huge difference.

Resources

FREQUENCY LISTS AND DICTIONARIES

You'll find frequency list recommendations in Appendix 1 for the top eleven foreign languages. If you're learning a different language, check my website (*Fluent-Forever.com/language-resources*) for reviews and suggestions. When all else fails, you can find acceptable quality frequency lists for most languages on Wikipedia (*en.wiktionary.org/wiki/Wiktionary:Frequency_lists*).

You'll also find dictionary recommendations in Appendix 1 and on my website. If you can find an online monolingual dictionary, stick it into Google Translate (*translate.google.com*). This will give you the ability to use a dictionary *very* early in your learning process.

BOOKS

The world of books is gigantic. By the time you're ready to read a book, you'll also be ready to search the Internet in your target language and find booksellers who will happily ship you copies of your desired book and its audiobook. From personal experience, I can highly recommend the Harry Potter series. The translations are great, and there are *lots* of audiobook versions. Whenever possible, I've linked to booksellers on my website.

FILM AND TV

Film and TV can be a bit tricky to find, in part because the big media companies have reacted poorly to the Internet and tried to lock down their intellectual property in inconvenient ways. As such, you may need a special DVD player to play DVDs from a different country. And if you want to rent foreign films or TV episodes from an iTunes store in another country, you need to either get access to a foreign credit card or buy a foreign iTunes gift card off of eBay. This can be aggravating when all you want to do is buy and watch a TV show.

However, producers and TV stations are starting to wise up. You can frequently find foreign language DVDs on Netflix, and you can even occasionally find legal streams of your favorite dubbed TV shows on the websites of some foreign television stations.

The easiest way to find streaming or purchasable media is through Wikipedia. To search for your TV show, you need to figure out your TV show's foreign title (*The West Wing*, for example, is called *À la Maison Blanche* in French). Wikipedia is the simplest way to find it. Look up your show in English, switch to your target language (on the bottom left of the page), and you'll find the title you're looking for. Then search for that same title on Google, and you'll usually find some decent purchasing options.

SPEAKING OPPORTUNITIES

We've already gone through the main options in the Speech and the Game of Taboo section of this chapter, but we'll summarize them here for convenience.

AT HOME: Depending upon where you live and what language you're learning, you may have access to local classes and tutors in your target language (*Craigslist.com* is a good way to find a tutor). But as long as you have a high-speed Internet connection, you also have these options:

- *Verbling.com* (fast, in the style of speed dating)
- *Livemocha.com* (longer conversations, in the style of general dating websites)
  - Also consider *Busuu.com*, *MyLanguageExchange.com*, and *Language-Exchanges.org*
- *italki.com* (paid professional teachers and tutors)

If you're looking for conversation topics, try:
- *Fluent-Forever.com/conversation-questions* (a handy list of conversation topics)

- *ConversationStarters.com* (*What is one thing you miss about being a kid?*)
- *YouRather.com* (*Would you rather always be naked or always be itchy?*)
- Gregory Stock's *Book of Questions* (*Do you tend to listen or talk more in conversations?*)
- Smith and Doe's *Book of Horrible Questions* (*For one million dollars, would you eat a human foot [with the bone removed]?*)

ABROAD: If you're looking for intensive programs abroad, then you'll have to rely upon Google ("Learn French in France") and word of mouth. At the moment there's no centralized service that collects information about these programs and reviews them. You'll find the cheapest (and often the best) programs in centralized universities and community colleges: the *Università per Stranieri* (University for Foreigners) in Perugia, Italy; the *Escuelas Oficiales de Idiomas* (Official Schools of Language) throughout Spain; and so on.

IN BETWEEN: The most intensive, immersive language courses are offered at Middlebury College (*Middlebury.edu*) in Vermont. I'm not aware of any other schools that take an official, mandatory no-English policy. If your language isn't offered there, then there are several intensive programs in the United States that you might want to consider. You'll find them listed at *Fluent-Forever.com/immersion*.

For the Advanced Students

If you're in a position to use the tools in this chapter, you've already reached at least an intermediate level. But suppose you really knew a *lot* about your language. Perhaps you've studied it for years, and you've just forgotten much of what you've learned. Or perhaps you're just looking for a way to feel a little more comfortable with the four main skills—speaking, writing, listening, and reading.

My advice for you is roughly the same as my advice for anyone else; if you want to get more comfortable listening, then listen, and if you want to get more comfortable speaking, then speak. But I can recommend some strategies that might help you do this more efficiently.

If you're looking for a way to refresh and maintain a language with the least amount of effort, then watch a lot of TV. I did this recently with my French—I had forgotten a lot over the course of learning Russian and Hungarian, and I wanted to bring it back—and so I started watching ridiculous amounts of television and film. Within a month, I got through three seasons of 24 and five films. By the end of that month, I was once again dreaming in French. It's a tremendously fun way to maintain a language.

With a bit more effort, you can steadily *improve* an advanced-level language. The most efficient way to do this is by writing on *Lang-8.com* and speaking with tutors (on *italki.com*). Turn every mistake you make and every new word you want to learn into flash cards. Use a frequency list as conversation/essay fodder. Find the words you don't know, discuss them with a tutor (or write about them), and make as many mistakes as you can (and tell your tutor to catch them). If you're constantly speaking and writing, and you're using your SRS to learn from all of your mistakes, then you're going to improve at breakneck speed.

CHAPTER 7

Epilogue: The Benefits and Pleasures of Learning a Language

The brain is like a muscle. When it is in use we feel very good. Understanding is joyous.

—Carl Sagan

You bought this book along with a small pile of other books and/or software—a textbook, a phrase book, a dictionary or two, a pronunciation guide, and so on. You may have enrolled in a class or found a private tutor or even signed up for an immersion program. You've spent hundreds of hours making and reviewing thousands of flash cards. So what do you get for your time, effort, and money? What reward is at the end of your journey?

If you break it all down, you get a *lot*.

From an economic standpoint, you've opened up a world of new employment opportunities, both at home and abroad. Despite the prevalence of English, the demand for foreign language ability has only increased in recent years, as we grow more and more interconnected. The United States, in particular, has found itself lagging behind the rest of the world in this regard. Due to an increasingly global economy, the U.S. Bureau of Labor Statistics has projected a 42 percent growth in demand for interpreters and translators between 2010 and 2020—placing these jobs among the top ten occupations with the highest projected growth.

If translation's not your thing, you might want to consider secret agent. Seriously. If you've learned a so-called *mission critical language*—Arabic, Chinese, Dari, Korean, Pashto, Persian, Russian, or Urdu—then the CIA will eagerly snap you up and hand you $35,000 per language as a hiring bonus on your first day, not to mention additional monthly "language maintenance" bonuses. Every time I've been to an immersion program at Middlebury College, the CIA recruiters are always there in their crisp suits and snappy haircuts, putting on recruitment seminars. They're *desperate* for multilingual people.

Even if you don't change careers, you've potentially increased your salary by 5–20 percent. Employers are willing to pay more for bilingual employees, even when those employees never need their extra languages to do their work. Employers see language skills as a sign of intelligence and competence, and that puts you—their newly bilingual employee—in higher demand.

These employers aren't basing their decisions on appearances. You don't just *seem* smarter when you know another language; you *become* smarter. By learning a language, you permanently change structures in your brain. Bilingual brains are *measurably different* than monolingual brains—certain brain regions are more developed—and recent studies show that you don't need to be bilingual from birth to show these telltale signs of bilingualism. You just need to learn a language and maintain it; the better you learn it and the longer you maintain it, the more your brain will change.

How does this affect you in your daily life? When you learn a language, you permanently improve your memory—you'll be able to memorize faster and easier. You'll multitask better. Bilingual people are better at focusing on tasks and ignoring distractions. They're more creative. They're better problem solvers. Bilingual students beat monolinguals in standardized tests of English, math, and science.

All of these advantages—collectively known as the *bilingual effect*—

aren't the result of natural, inborn intelligence. Most bilinguals never choose to be bilingual; they just happen to grow up in bilingual families. The bilingual effect is a kind of *learned* intelligence, and by picking up a new language, you get it too.

Why does the bilingual effect exist? There's a lot of research left to do, but current results point to a particularly peculiar cause: learning a language makes it *harder to think*.

When you learn French, you effectively implant a little Frenchman in your head who *never shuts up*. Even when you're trying to think in English, he sits in the background, mumbling away in French. There's no off switch. Remember those tip-of-the-tongue moments from Chapter 2? Bilinguals get them more frequently than monolinguals, because they have twice as many words to search through. Bilinguals even have a harder time naming simple objects—*that's a* table, *that's a* cat. While they usually find the words they're looking for, they take longer to find them, because they're always wrestling with that damn mumbling Frenchman.

On the surface, this sounds terrible, like a kind of learned schizophrenia. But your brain adapts. In the process of learning to speak a new language, you necessarily learn to muffle and ignore your native language. You learn to focus in the face of constant linguistic distraction, and as a result, your brain gets better at focusing *in general*. It's like walking around with weights attached to your ankles; after a while, your body adapts—you get stronger—and you forget all about them. Language learning is a form of strength training for your brain.

Not only does your brain get stronger, it gets healthier, too. Bilingual brains are more resistant to the wear and tear of age. Studies show a marked delay in the onset of dementia and Alzheimer's disease for bilinguals. On average, elderly bilinguals will show symptoms of dementia five years later than monolinguals, and if they've learned *more* than two languages, then the effects are even stronger.

Beyond all the economic and mental benefits of language learning lies the greatest treasure of all: language learning is good for your soul. It connects you to new people and a new culture in ways you could never imagine. Italians are *different* when they're speaking Italian, and German poetry is exquisitely beautiful—but only in German. You get to see different sides of people and cultures—sides which are hidden from the English-speaking world. You even get to see different sides of yourself.

I gesture in Italian. I *have* to gesture in Italian. When I speak Italian, I yearn to travel and see beautiful things, relax in the sun, and eat delicious food. All on its own, the Italian language fills my mind with happy memories, because all of my words are connected to the moments in which I learned and used them. *Gelato* isn't the Italian word for "ice cream"—it's a six-week, almost religious quest for the best gelato in Italy; it's strawberry gelato in Rome and pistachio gelato in Perugia—it's eating the best coconut gelato you could ever imagine while watching the waves roll into a sunny harbor in the Cinque Terre. My Italian words *aren't* just the everyday words that I've used all my life; they're a distinct set of memories that I formed with my own hands and brain. In learning that language, I created a new mind and a new personality for myself. *That* is the dearest gift of language learning—you get to meet a new you.

And this isn't just my own insanity speaking; I've seen this in all the multilingual people I've met. One of my French teachers was an American woman who had married a Frenchman and moved to Paris. When she spoke French, she was one of the most elegant, intelligent women I have ever met. On the last day of our French program, we finally switched to English. In an instant, that same elegant woman suddenly transformed into a quick-witted, sailor-mouthed party girl from Texas. That's not to say that her French persona was somehow *fake*; it was just a different side of her personality, and it came to the surface in her French.

At times, a foreign language can feel like a mask. It's a game of make-believe. You're playing the role of Some French Guy, and you're acting out a conversation with some friends. In these moments, you occasionally catch yourself saying things you *never* would have said in English. You're more open. You speak more freely. After all, it's not *really* you; it's just a game.

But that's not quite true.

It *is* you.

And you can only meet that side of yourself in a foreign language.

THE TOOLBOX

THE GALLERY: A GUIDE TO THE
FLASH CARDS THAT WILL TEACH YOU
YOUR LANGUAGE

This book is about many things: language, the human brain, the learning process, the essence of words. But when you get down to brass tacks, it's about learning languages with flash cards.

We have all encountered flash cards in school. They usually had a prompt on one side (Prompt: *the dodo bird*) and an answer on the back side (Answer: *This is an extinct flightless bird that once lived on the island of Mauritius . . .*), and you may have made stacks of them for your school tests. If you did, you shuffled through them, saw which ones you knew already, and then quizzed yourself again on the ones you didn't. If you were *really* anxious about an upcoming test, you might have turned the stack of cards over and seen whether you knew them in the *other* direction (New prompt: *This is an extinct flightless bird . . .* New answer: *the dodo bird*). Then you'd take your test and shelve your cards (or throw them out).

Flash cards like these can be a bit boring, but they do a good job of preparing you for tests. If you study them in one direction (Prompt: *the dodo bird*), you're prepared for certain test questions (*What is a dodo?*). If you study them in the *other* direction (Prompt: *This is an extinct flightless bird . . .*), you're prepared for *other* test questions (*What flightless bird once lived on Mauritius?*), and if you study them in *both* directions, you could handle *either* dodo-related scenario.

If you wanted to become a dodo *expert*, you could make a giant stack of flash cards, covering every aspect of the dodo in as many directions as possible. *Where did the dodo live? (The Island of Mauritius.) How big was the dodo? (Three feet tall, between twenty-two and forty pounds.) Could the dodo fly? (Nope.)* And so on. The more ways you study the same information, the better you know your material.

I want you to become an expert in your language, but you should have some fun in the process. So I'm going to make some changes to this tired, index-card-shaped theme.

First and foremost, we're sticking all of your flash cards into an SRS, which will tell you when to study each and every card. As we discussed in Chapter 2, this makes them a lot more effective and a lot more fun. You're playing a constant game with yourself, trying to see how long you can go before you forget one of your cards. Because of this game, your flash cards stay challenging, and you get a constant sense of accomplishment when you review them.

Second, you're going to use these flash cards to remember multi-sensory experiences, rather than just facts. You'll take a word like *déjeuner* (lunch) and connect it to a tasty memory. Then, every time you see *déjeuner*, your mind will instantly wander to that crispy baguette full of butter and brie (and honey and walnuts) that you once bought from a street vendor in Paris. You can accomplish this in three ways: by using pictures instead of translations (*a delicious brie baguette*), by finding fitting memories for each word (*lunch in Paris*), and by leaving little reminders of those memories on your flash cards (*Paris, 2002*). This will make your review process much more enjoyable, and *much* more effective.

Last, you're not studying for a boring test; you're teaching yourself about intensely *interesting* topics. You're looking for the mysteries hidden beneath the surface of every word and grammar rule. What makes a word like *gato* different from *cat*? How can you use German grammar to think in a completely new way? Rather than learning forgettable translations, you're learning to become a treasure hunter, and you're going to use your flash cards to remind you of your adventures.

Let's begin. We'll start with the basic principles that underlie these cards, and then walk through each category of cards in order: sound (Chapter 3), basic vocabulary (Chapter 4), grammar (Chapter 5), and advanced vocabulary (Chapter 6). You'll stick the cards you've created into your SRS, play the game on a daily basis, and end up with a fully formed language in your head, ready for reading Japanese comics, watching German films, or chatting with Brazilian waiters.

The Basic Design Principles

We're building upon ideas introduced in Chapters 2 and 3. If you haven't read them yet, do that now. Chapter 2 explained why we're using flash cards, how to use an SRS to schedule your review sessions for maximum efficiency, and how to make each flash card as memorable as possible, by linking sounds, spellings, concepts, and personal connections to every fact you learn. At the end of Chapter 3, we investigated the "more is less" paradox—that learning *more* information about a topic can help you learn in *less* time.

We'll add two basic design principles to these ideas:

· Many simple cards are better than a few complex cards.
· Always ask for one correct answer at a time.

The first of these principles is mostly a matter of attention. You can only focus on one thing at a time. SRSs can help you learn and retain large numbers of facts quickly, but they can't enable you to think of many different facts at once. The English word *set* has 464 definitions. If, for some crazy reason, you wanted to learn *all* of them, you're not going to do it with a single flash card. You'll need around 464 of them to help direct your attention to each definition in its turn.

We're not going to write 464 flash cards for every word; you don't *need* to memorize your words in such depth. But you will need multiple flash cards. After all, you're creating complex structures in your mind. You'll want each word to bring out an explosion of associations: sounds, spellings, multiple definitions, grammatical features, memories, and emotions. You'll build these associations fastest if you tackle them one flash card at a time.

The second principle—always ask for *one* correct answer—is just an extension of the first. We want these flash cards to be easy. You won't have a good time if you're stuck trying to remember the spelling and pronunciation of all twelve months of the year at once; as we've said, you can only focus on one thing at a time. So when a flash card asks you a question with more than one right answer—*How do I make a "k" sound in English?* (Answer: *With a C, a K, or a CK*)—accept *any* right answer (*with a C!*) as correct. You can make sure you know *all* the answers by creating additional flash cards (e.g., *What sound does the* CK *in* rock *make?*). This way, your flash card review sessions will stay fun, quick, and effective.

How Many Flash Cards Do You Need?
Different Tracks for Different Needs

The more flash cards you make for the same information, the easier time you'll have. Suppose you're learning the word *chèvre* (goat). You could make one flash card that asks "What's a *chèvre*?" and another flash card that asks "What's *this*?"

Both flash cards will teach you about the same word, but they train different *chèvre*-related skills. If you use *both* types, you'll have a much easier time remembering *chèvre* when you're studying.

We could keep going:

- How do you pronounce "*chèvre*"?
- How do you spell the word pronounced "sheh-vre" (ʃɛvʀ)?

- What's a food that *chèvres* eat?
- What colors do *chèvres* come in?
- What's your least favorite memory of a *chèvre*?

But eventually, you're going to get sick of *chèvres*, and your flash cards will be too easy. You'll get bored and you'll spend *forever* creating your flash cards. There's a balance here, naturally, and you'll need to find your own comfort level as you progress.

I'll give you three different tracks for three different scenarios:

- INTENSIVE TRACK: You're learning Chinese, Arabic, Japanese, or Korean, and you've never learned another language before. You need some extra cards to help you remember your words and grammar rules, because they're so distant from the words and grammar rules you already know.
- NORMAL TRACK: You're studying some other language (say, French) for the first time. You need some help remembering your words and grammar rules, but not as much as a learner of Chinese. This is the balanced approach you'd want for a language that isn't one of the hardest four.
- REFRESHER TRACK: You've taken four years of French in school, but you've forgotten a lot of it. You just need a few reminders about your words and grammar rules.

The only real difference among the three tracks is how many cards you make per sound, word, or grammatical concept. If you've taken French already, you may only need a single flash card to keep a word like *portefeuille* (wallet) in your head. Of the three cards listed in the Words section of the Gallery, you'll just make the card labeled "Refresher Track."

On the other hand, if this is your *first* encounter with French, you might need two flash cards to remember that same *portefeuille*. You'll make the two cards labeled "Normal Track." In the same vein, if this is your first time with Arabic, you'll probably need all three cards labeled "Intensive Track" to remember محفظة (wallet).

Strategies for Chinese and Japanese

Chinese and Japanese (and, to a much lesser extent, Korean) use a set of characters known as logograms. In contrast with alphabets, logograms correspond to words or chunks of words rather than sounds. These can be tricky to learn. If you're learning either of these languages (or if you really want to learn something wacky like ancient Egyptian hieroglyphs), then go to *Fluent-Forever.com/logograms* for a handful of supplementary flash card designs and strategies to make them easier.

These guidelines are just that: guidelines. If you're having a hard time with a specific concept (e.g., *chèvres*), then by all means add additional cards that put a slightly different spin on closely related information: *What's a baby* chèvre *called?* (*a* chevreau); *What's a* chevreau *turn into when it grows up?* (*a* chèvre). Any time you have a lot of trouble with a word or grammatical rule, just make a few new cards on a closely related theme, and it'll become much easier to remember.

If you're using a Leitner box instead of a computer, you'll need more time to make cards than your Anki-using friends. They can press a single button and create three cards at once; you have to make each one yourself. If card creation on the Intensive/Normal Tracks seems overwhelming or tedious, jump down to the Refresher Track, even if you're just starting with a language. While you'll have fewer cards to review, you may find that you don't need as many reviews, because you've spent extra time and effort physically making your cards. You can always add new cards later if you need them.

THE ART OF FLASH CARDS

How to Make Them, How to Review Them

In each chapter of this book, we talked about ways to explore your target language. We began with sound, and discovered a world of new sounds to hear and create. We looked at words, and found that beneath every translation, a symphony of images and associations waits for us. And we looked at sentences, and discovered how grammar can take a handful of words and string them into thoughts of limitless complexity.

The process of *exploring* a language is the core of *learning* a language. Every time you discover a new sound, a new word, or a new grammatical construction, you've planted a seed in your mind. These seeds will grow into fluency, provided you can retain them. To do this, you'll be using flash cards. Each flash card will contain a small memento or two of your exploration process—just enough to remind you of your journeys and discoveries.

The flash card creation process is relatively simple, and we'll walk through every step in this section. We'll look at model flash cards that you can use and we'll talk about which ones you need. Then, when you're ready to learn, you'll utilize those flash cards as models for your own.

If you're making your flash cards by hand, you'll simply copy the models over, substituting in *your* words, images, and memories for the ones in this book. If you're using Anki, then you'll type, copy, and/or drag your information into the appropriate boxes:

Then you'll click the Add Card button and get something like this:

The cards you make are your own. On this card, "Lily" helps me remember *my* favorite *macska*, but it won't do much for *you*. Similarly, the picture helps remind me of *my* experience on Google Images, looking at bunches of Hungarian cats. I even remember downloading a recording from *Forvo.com* and trying to mimic the tricky Hungarian ɒ vowel (a cross between our "ah" and "oh"). Each of these experiences was fun for me, and so my flash card brings back all sorts of enjoyable, *macska*-related memories. When you review *your* flash cards, they'll do the same for you.

The Review Process

The first thing you'll see whenever you review a flash card is the front side. It poses the following question: "What's on the back side of this card?" You might be looking at a picture of a cat and need to remember the Hungarian word *macska*, or you might see the word *macska* and need to remember a picture of a cat.

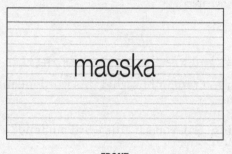

FRONT

You're building a connection in your mind between a stimulus (the word *macska*) and a response (a picture of a cat). But let's get a little more specific: Do you need to remember *a picture* of a *macska*? How to *say* the word?

These connections are more complex than a single thread connecting two ideas; you're creating *networks* of connections among sounds, spellings, and images. This is a good thing; after all, memories *are* networks, and the more connections they contain, the easier they are to recall—*neurons that fire together wire together*. You want as many neurons as possible to fire every time you encounter your *macska*.

Ideally, you want your word to provoke an explosion of associations in your brain: the spelling *m-a-c-s-k-a*, the pronunciation (mɒtʃkɒ - "moch-ko"), how you'd use it in a sentence, a thousand images of each *macska* you've ever met. You'd even want to hear *other* words—related words like *farok* (tail) or words with similar sounds and spellings, like *matrac* (mattress). You're trying to create as loud and varied a response as possible, and you'll do it one flash card at a time.

To accomplish this, you need balance. If you spend ten minutes ruminating about every *macska* you've ever seen whenever you pick up a flash card, you're not going to learn Hungarian very quickly. You need a way to add connections to your words without wasting time.

So when I introduce a flash card design, I'll identify the most essential facts. In this case, you won't get very far with *macska* if you don't know what *macska* means or if you can't actually say the word out loud. These are the essential facts we *need*:

ESSENTIAL FACTS (YOU NEED TO REMEMBER THESE!):
- **Picture**: Can you remember what this word means? What's it look like?
- **Pronunciation**: Can you say this word out loud?

But there are also a lot of facts that would be *nice* to remember. We'll call these bonus points. You get a bonus point whenever you add a nonessential connection to a word. While it's *essential* that you remember how to say "*macska*," it'd be nice if you remembered that *matrac* (mattress) starts with the same letters. If you remember both, you get a bonus point. Yay! You'll remember *macska* (and *matrac*, for that matter) better the next time you see it. If you don't, that's fine. They're just fake points anyway, and you might get one next time around. Here are bonus points for our *macska* card:

BONUS POINTS (IF YOU CAN THINK OF SOME OF THESE WHEN YOU REVIEW, YOU'LL HAVE AN EASIER TIME REMEMBERING NEXT TIME):
- **Personal Connections**: Can you think of any personal connections with this word? (Do you *like* cats? Can you think of a cat you know?) (*My cat's name is Lily.*)
- **Similar-Sounding Words:** Can you think of any other (Hungarian) words that start with the same sound or spelling? (*Matrac [mattress] also starts with "ma."*)

- **Related Words**: Can you think of any other (Hungarian) words that relate to this word in meaning? *(farok [tail], kutya [dog], állat [animal])*

When you review your cards, give yourself five to ten seconds. Recall whatever you can, then turn the card over (or press the Turn Card Over button if you're on a computer), and check your answers on the back side:

ESSENTIAL FACT!
Pronunciation (with a recording and/or phonetic spelling)

ESSENTIAL FACT!
Image

BONUS POINT
Personal Connection (My cat's name is Lily)

macska
mɒtʃkɒ

Press to play recording
[Digital cards only!]

"Lily"

BACK

If you remembered all of the essential facts, you win. If you're using a Leitner box, you'll move this card into the next section in your box and you'll review it again in a few days or weeks. If you're using Anki, you'll click the "I remember this" button, and it'll make sure you see the card less often.

A Time-Saving Tip

If you're using Anki, get my (free) demo deck. It's all set up to generate every card in this book automatically. You assemble the information (spelling, recordings, personal connection, etc.), and it spits out all the cards you could want. You'll find it at *Fluent-Forever.com/gallery*.

If you forgot an essential fact, then you'll want to see this card more often. With a Leitner box, you'll move that card back into the first section of your box. With Anki, you'll click on "I Forgot." You'll see that card more frequently until it sticks for good.

If you remembered some bonus points, then you can pat yourself on the back. You just made your reviews easier for the rest of your learning process. If not, you still won the game. Congratulate yourself anyway. You remembered that *macska* is a cat, and it's pronounced mɒtʃkɒ—"moch-ko"—your two main goals. Take a few seconds to think of a connection or two you could make next time: think of your favorite *macska* or some other word you've learned that has anything to do with a *macska*. Then move to the next card.

The Three Tracks

The more cards you make per word, sound, or grammatical concept, the easier time you'll have. Every time I introduce a new card design, I'll also discuss whether you'd use it on the Intensive Track, the Normal Track, the Refresher Track, or all three.

Later on, for example, I'll show you a flash card that asks you specifically about the *spelling* of a new word. When I do, you'll see something like this:

FRONT

Notice the checklist on the right. This card is *only* for the Intensive Track; it's designed to help you remember complex characters like 猫 (*cat* in Chinese). If you're on the Normal Track—perhaps you're learning Spanish—you probably won't need an extra card to learn the spelling of every word in your language. You'll skip it, and only make the cards labeled "Use this card on: ✓ The Normal Track."

We're just about ready to start making flash cards. We'll do a quick recap of what you've done already and then delve into each chapter's cards.

What You've Done Already

FROM CHAPTER 2 (SETTING UP YOUR SRS)

If you've chosen Anki, you've watched tutorials on how to use it. They've taught you how to make a basic flash card, how to insert audio files and images into your cards, and how to review those cards once you're ready to learn. You've also downloaded and installed my demo deck, so your main job involves finding information and recordings, putting them in the right boxes, and clicking the Add Flash Cards button.

If you've chosen a Leitner box, you've read Appendix 3, gone out to your local office supply store, and purchased your materials. You have an index card file-box full of dividers, a stack of blank index cards, some pencils, and a calendar in front of you (today is day 1!).

You also remember my earlier caveat: Since paper flash cards can't talk, you're going to take extra care to learn a phonetic alphabet and to listen to recordings of example words when you write your flash cards.

THE FIRST GALLERY:
DO-IT-YOURSELF
PRONUNCIATION TRAINERS

Cards for Chapter 3

In this section, I'm going to show you how to build a pronunciation trainer for your new language. These trainers are a lot of fun to use; you listen to a bunch of crazy new sounds and learn weird spellings and example words (and alphabets, depending upon your language). Then you press buttons on your computer/smartphone or shuffle around flash cards in your Leitner box until those sounds and spellings are deeply implanted in your brain. Aside from being fun, they save you an *enormous* amount of time, because they make the rest of your language much easier to remember (perhaps you still remember our discussion about *mjöður* in Chapter 2).

Before we begin, a caveat: these trainers can take time to create. They combine a great deal of information at once—recordings, spellings, phonetic alphabets, and bunches of example words. I'll show you how to make them step by step, but there's another option that skips all of this hullabaloo: In all likelihood, I've made a trainer for your language already. If you look at the upcoming instructions and feel the least bit squeamish, then go get a trainer off of my website (*Fluent-Forever.com/chapter3*). They're effective, they're a lot of fun, and I'm not aware of any faster or easier way to learn the pronunciation of a new language. I made them because I want this process to be as easy as possible. I'd rather you not run off screaming before you even start to learn vocabulary.

If I *haven't* yet made a pronunciation trainer for your language, or if you're more of a do-it-yourselfer, then we'll get started now.

Step 1: Get Your Bearings

Open your grammar or pronunciation book and read the introduction to your new language's alphabet and sound system. Usually, any problem sounds will be singled out and discussed in depth. Read about them and listen to them, either using the recordings that came with your book or *Forvo.com*. Sounds that are difficult to *hear* are your first priority, and your book will likely discuss them and give you minimal pairs as examples. (Korean textbooks often start with the dreaded and nearly indistinguishable *pul* [grass], *ppul* [horn], and *bul* [fire], for example). Listen to them repeatedly or turn them into minimal pair tests using one of my online tutorials until you begin to get a sense of which sound is which.

> ### Resources at Your Disposal
>
> You'll find a full list of pronunciation resources in the Do This Now section of Chapter 3. For minimal pair tests, go to *Fluent-Forever .com/chapter3*.

Once you can hear the differences between each of the sounds, focus on every new sound that doesn't seem to agree with your tongue. If your book doesn't discuss *how* to produce those sounds, go to Appendix 4 and see how they fit into your mouth. Keep imitating your recordings while you're paying attention to your tongue, lips, and throat until you roughly understand how to form each sound. If you're having a seriously difficult time with a certain sound, consult YouTube or work with a tutor on *italki .com* until you're comfortable.

Now you can start making some flash cards. You'll create 80 (Spanish) to 240 (Japanese) cards, which will take you one to three hours to design and three to eight days to learn at thirty minutes a day. In the process, you'll learn a bunch of new words, listen to a bunch of recordings, and begin to acquaint yourself with your new language.

If you're using Anki, you'll be downloading recordings of example words and putting them into your flash cards. If you wish, feel free to ignore all of the phonetic transcriptions (fə'nɛtɪk træn'skrɪpʃənz) on the example flash cards in this book. On the other hand, if you're using a Leitner box, you'll be relying *heavily* on those phonetic transcriptions. While you're at it, make sure that you also regularly listen to recordings as a supplement. There's no use in memorizing that German's *ä* sounds like ɛ if you don't know what ɛ sounds like. (It sounds like "eh.")

Step 2: Get Your Information

We're going to connect three chunks of information for each sound in your new language:

- **Sound**: What's this sound? What is it like? (If it's a new sound for you, how does it fit in your mouth?)
  - *Resources:* Your grammar/pronunciation book, Appendix 4, Wikipedia's "IPA for Spanish/French/Whatever" articles, Forvo.com

- **Spelling**: How do I spell this sound?
  - *Resources:* Your grammar book, your dictionary of choice, or a Lonely Planet pocket phrasebook.

- **Example Word**: What's an example word for this sound?
  - *Resources:* The glossary section of your grammar book or the dictionary section of a pocket phrasebook.

Step 3: Make Your Cards

Intensive / Normal / Refresher Tracks: *Two card types per sound (I've already stripped these cards down to the bare essentials, so all three tracks are the same.)*

Card Type 1: *What does this spelling sound like?*
(e.g., *ä* as in German's *Lächeln* [smile] sounds like [recording]/lɛçln)

German Fact of the Day

German capitalizes all of its nouns, which is why I'm doing it here!

Card Type 2: *How do you spell this example word?*
(e.g., [recording of *Lächeln* (smile)]/**lɛçln** is spelled *L-ä-c-h-e-l-n*)

CARD TYPE 1: WHAT DOES THIS SPELLING SOUND LIKE?

Here's where you'll begin to tie spellings to sounds. You'll need example words for every spelling/sound combination in your language. You'll probably find a good list of these in the beginning of your grammar book, but if not, you can refer to Wikipedia (search for "IPA for Spanish," "IPA for French," and so on). If you're using Anki, feel free to ignore the phonetic alphabet part; you're just going to take the example words and find recordings of each.

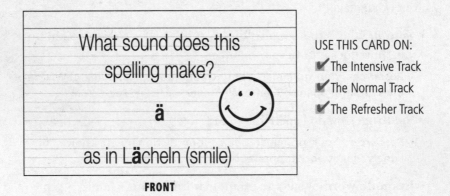

FRONT

USE THIS CARD ON:
- ✔ The Intensive Track
- ✔ The Normal Track
- ✔ The Refresher Track

ESSENTIAL FACT (YOU NEED TO REMEMBER THIS!):
- **Sound**: What sound does this spelling make? Can you say it out loud? If this spelling can make a few different sounds (as in English's infamous *tough/though/through/thought*), then you'll make a flash card for each of these different sounds, with an appropriate example word for each one. (Here the *ä* in *Lächeln* sounds like "eh.")

BONUS POINTS (IF YOU CAN THINK OF SOME OF THESE WHEN YOU REVIEW, YOU'LL HAVE AN EASIER TIME REMEMBERING NEXT TIME):
- **The Whole Word**: Can you pronounce the *whole* word rather than just the sound in the middle of it?
- **Example Word**: Can you think of any other word that uses this sound? Can you remember how it's spelled, how it's pronounced, or what it means?

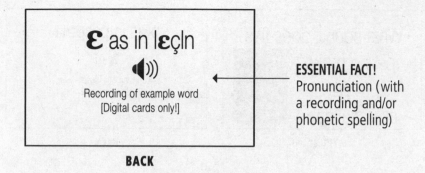

ɛ as in |ɛçln

Recording of example word
[Digital cards only!]

ESSENTIAL FACT!
Pronunciation (with
a recording and/or
phonetic spelling)

BACK

Use a recording of the entire example word (*Lächeln*) rather than the individual sound ("eh"). In part, this is because it's difficult to *find* recordings of every individual sound in a language. It's even hard to *make* them. Remember that these are sounds, rather than just letters, and sometimes sounds don't show up on their own. While we know how to pronounce the letter *u*, it's pretty difficult to pronounce a good, accurate "u" as in *put* without a *p* and a *t* nearby. So instead, just grab complete recordings of example words. You'll be able to find them quickly on *Forvo.com*.

Whenever possible, choose example words that are easy to visualize. Generally, your textbook will give you a list of example words and spellings in the first chapter or two. If these are concrete and easy to visualize (*p* is for *pizza*, *gn* is for *gnocchi*), use them. If not (*a* is for *abstraction*), find some similarly spelled words in the glossary at the end of your book. If your textbook doesn't discuss pronunciation at all, throw it away and get a better one. (And send an angry letter to the author, while you're at it.)

Once you have good examples for every sound/spelling, grab a picture of each example word from Google Images and stick it on the front of each card. This will help you remember your spelling, sound, and example word in the future.

You can use these cards to learn a new alphabet. Here we're learning the Russian *p*, which looks like the mathematical symbol for pi (п). To learn it, we'll use the Russian word for "passport," which sounds like "pahspert."

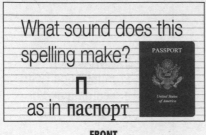

FRONT   BACK

IF YOU'RE STUDYING CHINESE OR JAPANESE

Both of these languages use characters that mainly correspond to words rather than phonetic information. Since we're currently focusing on sound, we'll use alternate writing systems. For Chinese, you should learn your sounds in Pinyin (Nǐ Hǎo, as opposed to 你好), and in Japanese, you should do this in Hiragana and Katakana, the two writing systems used in Japanese that contain sound information.

CARD TYPE 2: HOW DO YOU SPELL THIS WORD?

You can reuse each of your example words to help ingrain the spelling rules of your new language. Here we'll reuse the German word *Lächeln* (smile). The cards look like this:

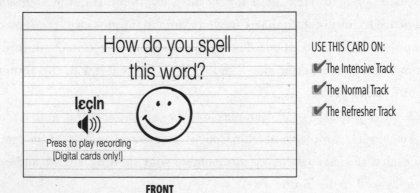

FRONT

ESSENTIAL FACT (YOU NEED TO REMEMBER THIS!):
· **Spelling**: Can you remember how to spell this word?

NO BONUS POINTS! SPELLING'S COMPLEX ENOUGH AS IT IS!

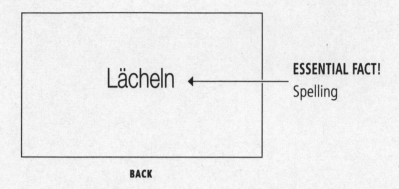

These cards may be tricky in the beginning. Each card combines a bunch of spelling rules at once. Since you haven't even learned all of them yet, you may have a hard time remembering each word's spelling. Don't worry. Within a few days, you'll cover all possible spellings and sounds, and you'll start to have a much easier time. Your SRS will make sure that you review your flash cards efficiently, and you'll be spitting out German words in no time.

Step 4: Follow Your Spaced Repetition System and Learn Your Cards

Learn thirty flash cards a day. As you learn them, you'll tell your SRS what you remember. If you're using Anki, you'll be clicking one of the buttons that correspond to "Yup, I remember" or "Oops, I forgot," and it will automatically schedule your cards accordingly, so that you review each of your cards near the ideal moment, right before you forget them. If you're using a Leitner box, you'll follow the rules of the Leitner box game, moving cards you remember forward and cards you forget back. Once you've done this for a week or two, you'll be ready to move on to vocabulary (Chapter 4).

Cards for Chapter 4

Remember those 625 words from Chapter 4? Here's how you'll learn them. These flash cards are a lot of fun to create (you get to play with all sorts of cool tools: Google Images, mnemonics, recordings, and personal experiences), and they're extremely effective. Because you're not using English, you're learning to *think* in your target language, which makes each of these words easier to remember and a lot more useful in the long run than a simple (and boring) translation.

In the First Gallery, we had two cards per sound/spelling. In this gallery, we have up to three, depending upon which track (Refresher, Normal, Intensive) you choose. We'll discuss these basic three types of flash cards and then talk about a few special scenarios: what you'll do when your word has multiple definitions (a bar for drinks vs. a bar of chocolate) or synonyms (a dish, a plate), how to learn category words (*fruit, animal, noun, verb*), and how to learn words with easily confounded pictures (*to kiss* vs. *a kiss, girl* vs. *daughter, sea* vs. *ocean*).

Then we'll cover a couple of card types for mnemonics, if you wish to use them in your studies.

When you're done, you'll have 625–1,875 cards, which will take you one to three months to learn with your SRS (or less time, if you review for more than thirty minutes a day). You'll leave with a solid foundation in the words and sounds of your language. Once you get to grammar, you'll already know most of the vocabulary you need, so you can focus on stringing your words together into thoughts and stories.

The Discovery Process: Get Your Information

We're trying to connect four or five chunks of information for every word in your new language:

- **Spelling:** How do I spell this word?
  - *Resources:* The glossary at the end of your grammar book, the dictionary at the end of a pocket phrase book, a standard dictionary

- **Pronunciation:** How does this word fit into my mouth?
  - *Resources: Forvo.com* for recordings, *Wiktionary.org* for IPA pronunciation, your own dictionary's phonetic transcriptions

- **Picture—the Spot the Differences Game:** What does this word really mean? Is it different than I expected? How can I capture that in a picture?
  - *Resources:* Google Images (ideally, Google Images inside of Google Translate; see *Fluent-Forever.com/chapter4*)

- **Personal Connection—the Memory Game:** What's this word mean *to me*? When's the last time I encountered this thing/ action/adjective?

Save Time with Multisearch

There's a neat way to automate your web searches, so you can type in your word *once* and it automatically searches as many websites as you want at the same time. I usually search a bilingual dictionary, a monolingual dictionary, Google Images inside of Google Translate, and *Forvo.com* for each word, and it only takes a single mouse click. You can find a guide to setting this up (it only takes a few minutes) at *Fluent-Forever.com/multi-search*.

- **Gender—the Mnemonic Imagery Game [if your language uses grammatical gender]**: If this word is a noun, what's the gender of the word? If you're using mnemonic imagery, can you imagine your mnemonic interacting with your new word?

In the process of investigating these four or five facts, you'll form deep, multisensory experiences with each word you learn. The whole process is relatively quick (one to three minutes per word) and a lot of fun. You're *discovering* your words rather than simply memorizing them, and as a result, you'll remember them for much longer. Then, you'll take little reminders of your discoveries and turn them into flash cards.

Make Your Cards

Intensive Track: Three card types per word
Normal Track: Two card types per word
Refresher Track: One card type per word

WE'LL LOOK AT THREE CARDS FOR THE FRENCH WORD *CHAT* (CAT):

Card Type 1: *What's this word mean? Can you say it out loud?*
(e.g., *Chat* is a [picture of a] cat, pronounced "shah" [ʃa in IPA].)

Card Type 2: *What's the word for this image? Can you say it out loud?*
(e.g., a [picture of a] cat = *chat*, pronounced ʃa)

Card Type 3: *How do you spell this word?*
(e.g., a [picture of a] cat, pronounced ʃa = c-h-a-t)

The Three Tracks

Our three types of flash cards focus on three different aspects of each word: comprehension, production, and spelling. These cards work together to help you remember what a word means, when to say it, and how to spell it.

Like the rest of the cards in this book, I've included suggestions about how many cards to make; if you're studying Chinese, Japanese, Korean, or Arabic, you should make all three cards for every word you learn (Intensive Track). If you're studying another language (Normal Track), you can skip the third card on spelling. If you're already an intermediate speaker (Refresher Track), then you can also skip the second card, which matches an image to a word. You'll only make the first card for each word.

Stick to these guidelines once you've learned a few hundred words and you feel comfortable with your progress. But if you're an absolute beginner, start by making all *three* cards, regardless of your language. In this early stage, your cards are doing double duty, teaching you about your language's phonetic system at the same time as they're teaching you vocabulary. You'll need a little bit more help before you get comfortable with spelling and pronunciation, so don't skip the spelling cards, even if you're learning a relatively straightforward language like Spanish (phonetically straightforward, that is). You'll know when you don't need them anymore. In Hungarian (which has a *very* friendly spelling system), I got sick of my spelling cards after 240 words. At that point, I dropped back down to two cards per word. If I were learning a language with a new alphabet and/or a more complex spelling system, like Greek, Thai, or French, I'd stick to three cards per word for longer.

CARD TYPE 1: WHAT DOES THIS WORD MEAN? (COMPREHENSION)

FRONT

USE THIS CARD ON:
- ✓ The Intensive Track
- ✓ The Normal Track
- ✓ The Refresher Track

ESSENTIAL FACTS (YOU NEED TO REMEMBER THESE!):
- **Picture**: Can you remember what this word means? What's it look like?
- **Pronunciation**: Can you say this word out loud?
- **Gender [if your language uses it]**: If this word is a noun, what's the gender of the word?

BONUS POINTS (IF YOU CAN THINK OF SOME OF THESE WHEN YOU REVIEW, YOU'LL HAVE AN EASIER TIME REMEMBERING NEXT TIME):
- **Personal Connection**: Can you think of the first/last time you encountered this thing/action/adjective or an example of this word that is relevant to your life?
- **Other Words**: Can you think of any other words with similar spellings or related meanings?

CARD TYPE 2: WHAT'S THE WORD FOR THIS PICTURE? (PRODUCTION)

FRONT

USE THIS CARD ON:
- ✔ The Intensive Track
- ✔ The Normal Track
- ☐ The Refresher Track

ESSENTIAL FACTS (YOU NEED TO REMEMBER THESE!):

- **Pronunciation**: What word does this picture correspond to? Can you say it out loud?

- **Gender [if your language uses it]**: If this word is a noun, what's the gender of the word?

BONUS POINTS (IF YOU CAN THINK OF SOME OF THESE WHEN YOU REVIEW, YOU'LL HAVE AN EASIER TIME REMEMBERING NEXT TIME):

- **Spelling**: Do you remember how to spell this word?

- **Personal Connection:** Can you think of the first/last time you encountered this thing/action/adjective or an example of this word that is relevant to your life?

- **Other Words:** Can you think of any other words with similar spellings or related meanings?

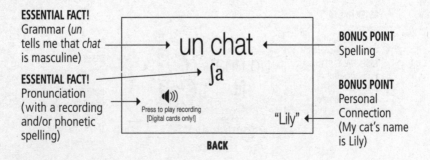

ESSENTIAL FACT!
Grammar (*un* tells me that *chat* is masculine)

ESSENTIAL FACT!
Pronunciation (with a recording and/or phonetic spelling)

un chat
ʃa

◀))
Press to play recording
[Digital cards only!]

"Lily"

BONUS POINT
Spelling

BONUS POINT
Personal Connection (My cat's name is Lily)

BACK

Ess-Pee-Ee-Ell-Ell

Do you spell by visualizing letters in your mind's eye? Do you say spellings out loud (see-aitch-ay-tee = *chat*)? If you do the latter, you might want to take this opportunity to learn the letter names of your target language. You can learn them by making a flash card for each letter (*How do you pronounce the letter D? Dee*). You'll pick up the ability to easily spell your name / address / whatever when speaking and understand spellings whenever a native speaker says them out loud. You can find example flash cards for letter names at *Fluent-Forever.com/gallery*.

CARD TYPE 3: HOW DO YOU SPELL THIS WORD? (SPELLING)

FRONT

USE THIS CARD ON:

☑ The Intensive Track

▪ The Normal Track

▪ The Refresher Track

ESSENTIAL FACT (YOU NEED TO REMEMBER THIS!):
- **Spelling:** Do you remember how to spell this word?

BONUS POINTS (IF YOU CAN THINK OF SOME OF THESE WHEN YOU REVIEW, YOU'LL HAVE AN EASIER TIME REMEMBERING NEXT TIME):
- **Gender [if your language uses it]:** If this word is a noun, what's the gender of the word?
- **Personal Connection:** Can you think of the first/last time you encountered this thing/action/adjective or an example of this word that is relevant to your life?
- **Other Words:** Can you think of any other words with similar spellings or related meanings?

BACK

With these three card types, you can memorize almost any of the basic 625 words. You'll discover that they're a lot of fun to create and a lot of fun to review. When you're creating your cards, you'll find all manner of silly French cat pictures or German grandmothers. When you review, you'll remember how you felt when you first found each of these images, and you'll even add a burst of excitement to that memory ("I can't *believe* I still remember that!"), which makes each word that much more memorable.

Next, we'll go through a few special cases, where we'll slightly modify the basic three card types to handle a greater variety of words.

Four Special Scenarios: Multiple Definitions, Synonyms, Category Words, and Easily Confounded Images

MULTIPLE DEFINITIONS

Suppose you were learning the English word *bar*. A bar is usually for drinks, but bars of gold and chocolate bars certainly exist. Cards like these aren't a problem:

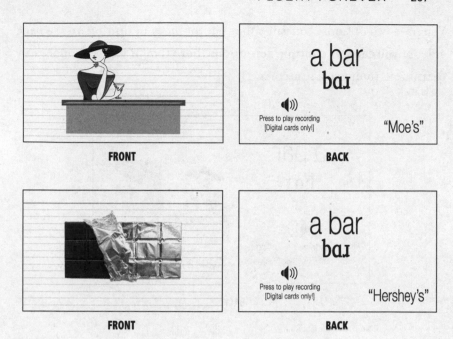

But the other direction is trickier. What goes on the back side of this card?

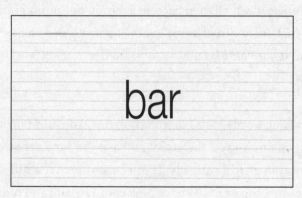

You have two options. You can either put the *main* definition on the back side, or you can put multiple definitions there (and if you remember *any* definition, then mark it as correct):

BACK

There's no large advantage of one approach over the other, and you can use them interchangeably. In both cases, you'll tend to remember one definition best, which then becomes the anchor point for new definitions. With that anchor in place, it's very easy to connect a new concept to the first one. (*Chocolate bars use the same word as normal bars!*)

SYNONYMS

For your first 625 words, don't learn synonyms. You don't need them. No one is going to stop you on the street and ask you for a synonym of *plate*, and you have enough to do already. If you encounter a few different translations for a word you want to know, pick your favorite and move on.

When you come back to synonyms in the future, bear in mind that no two words are *exactly* alike. *Policeman* and *cop* might refer to the same person, but these words differ in their formality. While you can eat off of a *plate* or a *dish*, you probably don't know anyone with a metal *dish* in their heads. Once you have some grammar and a sizable vocabulary under your belt, you can begin to learn the subtle differences between similar words, but until then, learn one basic word and move on.

Every once in a while, you'll *have* to learn a synonym early in your studies. You may learn one word—*dish*—and find that your grammar book uses a synonym—*plate*—instead. You can learn them like this:

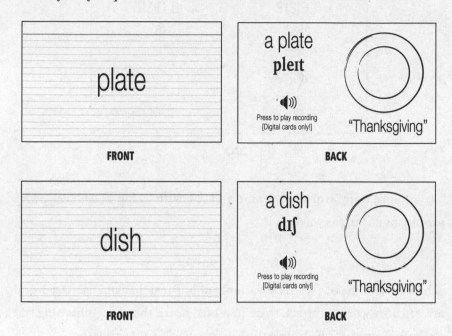

You may want a third card with a picture on the front side, like this:

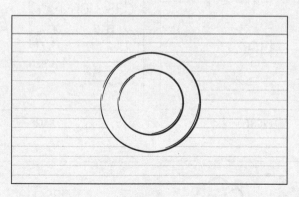

FRONT

Like our multiple-definition scenario, you have two options for this card (this time, on the back side). You can either make it with both words or with your favorite word. Remember that *any* correct answer (plate *or* dish) is correct; you don't need to sit there and list synonyms for your pictures.

BACK

Choose your favorite back side and run with it. But in general, avoid synonyms as long as you can.

CATEGORY CARDS

While most of the 625 words are simple nouns (cat, banana, man), several are category words (animal, fruit, person). Learn these by combining two or three simple words. Here's the German word *Tier* (animal):

FRONT · BACK

FRONT

BACK

How do you know that *Tier* means "animal" rather than "mammal" or "organic material that is sometimes gray on the outside"? Remember that *you're* the one making these cards. *You're* choosing the collection of words that says "animal" to you. If you decide that *animal* is best represented by a pig, fish, and goat, there's no way you're going to forget what those pictures stand for. You're not suddenly going to think, "Pig, fish, goat? This must mean 'objects smaller than a cow that are made of meat!'" You're going to think *animal*.

You can use this strategy even for abstract words like *noun* (= cat, banana, man . . .) and *verb* (= to kiss, to eat, to run . . .). This will enable you to do some fancy footwork when dealing with very similar-looking words (e.g., *to kiss* vs. *a kiss*), as we'll soon see.

WORDS WITH EASILY CONFOUNDED IMAGES

Suppose you wanted to learn the German words for "daughter" (*Tochter*) and "niece" (*Nichte*). Both of these girls may *look* the same, but each word means something quite different. You need more information than a picture alone can provide, but you don't know enough German to write a full definition (like "the daughter of my brother or sister"). You have two good options: you can add a personal note to these cards—your niece's name, for example—or you can add a short German clue using words from your 625 list—since daughters have mothers (and fathers), and nieces have aunts (and uncles), you could use *Mutter* (mother) or *Tante* (aunt).

First I'll learn *Nichte* (niece) using my niece's name, Eliana. Note that *die Nichte* isn't as violent as it sounds. It's just German's friendly way of indicating that *nieces* are feminine:

Then I'll learn *Tochter* (daughter) with another German word, *Mutter* (mother), which I've taken from my list of 625 common words:

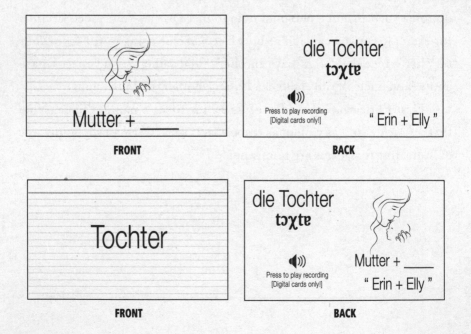

We're making simple definitions using a picture and a familiar name or new word. We could do the same thing for "to kiss" (*küssen*) and "a kiss" (*Kuss*), by sticking the German words for "verb" (*Verb*) and "noun" (*Substantiv*) under a picture of two people kissing. We could stick the German word for "border" under a picture of a beach to get "coastline," or write the word *Atlantic* under a picture of an ocean to distinguish it from a sea.

As you learn more vocabulary, you'll be able to define more and more words using this technique. With a touch of grammar, you'll be able to write out full definitions of your words, and learn to understand abstract words in terms of the words you know already. This ability grows and grows, and eventually you'll find a fully formed language hiding out in your brain.

For now, begin at the beginning, with simple words, straightforward flash cards, and an SRS to get those words into your head. In one to three months, you'll be ready to tackle grammar head-on, without needing to learn vocabulary, pronunciation, and spelling at the same time.

There's one last flash card type you may need, which can help you keep track of any mnemonic images you might want to use.

Mnemonic Imagery

These cards are *not* vocabulary, so don't worry about the three tracks, bonus points, and all that jazz. You'll just use these cards to help you keep track of mnemonic imagery; you wouldn't want to accidentally explode some poor feminine noun when it should be burning instead.

If you're just using mnemonic imagery for noun genders, you'll only need to memorize two or three images. This might be fairly easy to remember, even without flash cards. Still, we have this lovely SRS, and it would be a shame not to use it whenever it can make your job easier.

Later, if you decide to make mnemonic images for every spelling, preposition, and verb conjugation in your language (see Chapter 5), you'll *definitely* want to make these flash cards. Mnemonic imagery can prove addictive, and if you get hooked, flash cards can help you sort out which image is which.

There are two basic card types, and they're relatively simple:

FRONT   BACK

MNEMONIC CARD 1: WHAT'S THE MNEMONIC FOR ___?

FRONT   BACK

MNEMONIC CARD 2: WHAT'S THIS MNEMONIC MEAN?

THE THIRD GALLERY:
USING AND LEARNING YOUR
FIRST SENTENCES

Cards for Chapter 5

In this section, we're going to play with sentences. You'll learn how to use them to learn abstract words, to learn how words change in different contexts, and to learn the ways that word order affects meaning. And you'll do it all without a trace of English on any of your flash cards. Think of it like a portable language immersion program that you've built yourself.

There are three main categories of cards here: new words, word forms, and word orders. You can use these cards to memorize every last bit of information from any sentence. We'll go through them in detail, and then cover a few special scenarios: how to deal with declension charts, how to handle corrected writing, and how to make easy cards a bit more challenging.

Once you start using these cards, you'll find that they're very efficient. As soon as you learn where to stick a verb in *one* sentence, you'll get a feel for where it belongs in almost *every* vaguely similar sentence. You don't need to learn anything twice. This puts you on a constant quest for new, surprising constructions to learn, which is a thousand times more satisfying than a workbook full of boring grammar drills.

Sentence Play: Get Your Information

By its very nature, a sentence connects words, grammar, and stories. All you're going to do is memorize those connections in bite-size pieces.

Ideally, you'll find all of the following information in your grammar book or dictionary, but if you're missing something, then don't worry about it. Skip over it and learn it later. Your only goal is to stick a bunch of information into your head. You don't need to know everything. You'll need:

- **A Good Sentence, Phrase, or Dialogue**: You want to find a sentence, a short phrase (*two apples*), or a snippet of dialogue (*"Where are you going?" "I'm going to Disneyland!"*) with some new content. It should have some new words, some new word forms, and/or a surprising word order.

  - *Resources*: Your grammar book. It's *full* of quality sentences and dialogues, and in the beginning, almost all of those sentences will contain a lot of new, interesting content. Use those first. Later, once you've learned some grammar, you'll start getting most of your sentences from Google Images or your own corrected writing samples.

- **The Story**: What's going on in this sentence or dialogue? When might you encounter this situation?

  - *Resources*: Your grammar book. It will give you translations and/or supply you with enough contextual information that you can figure out what's going on (e.g., a conversation in which Susie asks, *"Comment t'appelles-tu?"* and John Smith responds, *"Je m'appelle John Smith"* is probably one in which Susie asks John his name, and he tells it to her.)

- **The Chunks**: What does each word mean individually? What role does each word play in this sentence? If needed, how do you pronounce each word?

  - *Resources*: Your grammar book, a dictionary, *Forvo.com* (if needed). Here's where you might not find all the information you'd ideally want. That's fine. If you're baffled by the role of a word, skip it and learn it later.

  - *A Note Regarding Pronunciation*: By now, you're going to have the pronunciation of 625 words under your belt. In most languages, this will give you a pretty accurate intuition about the pronunciation of every word, so pronunciation probably isn't going to be a problem. Feel free to skip it if you're confident that you're pronouncing everything correctly. Whenever you're a little unsure, look it up in your dictionary or at *Forvo.com*, and if it's not what you expect to hear, add it to your cards.

- **The Base Forms**: If you encountered these words in a dictionary, would they look the same? If not, what's the dictionary entry for each word look like?

  - *Resources*: Your grammar book, a dictionary. You might not always know whether or not you're looking at the base form of a certain word. That's fine. Just assume it is. Learn it like you would learn any other new word.

- **Pictures**: What are some good pictures for this sentence? Can you use a few *different* pictures to help you remember the meanings of each individual word?

  - *Resources*: Google Images (or, if you're using a Leitner box, your own imagination). In general, just search in English; it's faster and easier than searching in your target language. Use *images.google.com* (you can see more images at once) or *TinyURL.com/basicimage* (the images are smaller and easier to copy/paste).

- **Personal Connections [optional]**: In my experience, personal connections are harder to find for complex vocabulary and grammatical constructions. I don't have any particularly memorable encounters with the word *when*. Still, when appropriate (you *may* know a particularly "caring" person), then feel free to play around with personal connections in your words. In practice, you'll find that you don't need personal connections nearly as much as you did in the beginning. Grammar ties words together, which makes your words *much* easier to memorize.

Collecting this information can take time—usually a few minutes per sentence—but it supplies you with a *ton* of flash cards. When I'm working on grammar, I usually average around one minute per flash card when all is said and done.

The research and construction process feels a lot like a puzzle game. You're trying to figure out how many different things you can teach yourself with one sentence. You get a feel for it pretty quickly, and then it starts getting exciting, because all those words you've already learned start turning into a real language before your eyes.

Make Your Cards

Intensive Track:

New words / Word forms: Two to four cards per word

Word Order: 1 card per word

Normal Track:

New words / Word forms: Two to three cards per word

Word Order: 1 card per word

Refresher Track:

New words / Word forms / Word order: One card per word

WE'LL PLAY AROUND WITH THIS SENTENCE: "He lives in New York City."

New Words: *We'll learn the word* in.

Card Type 1: *Which word fits in the blank?*
   (e.g., "He lives __ New York City" → *in*, pronounced ɪn)

Card Type 2: *What's a sentence/phrase that includes this word?*
   (e.g., *in* → "He lives *in* New York City.")

Card Type 3: *Which word fits into this* other *blank?*
   (e.g., *The Cat __ the Hat* → *in*, pronounced ɪn)

Card Type 4: *How do you spell this word?*
   (e.g., Pronounced ɪn, fits into "He lives __ New York City" → *i-n*)

Word Forms: *We'll learn the word form* lives.

Card Type 1: *Which word fits in the blank?*

   "He __ in New York City" [to live]
   (e.g., *lives*, pronounced lɪvz)

Card Type 2: *What's a sentence with the word* lives? *What's the base*
   word form?
   (e.g., "He *lives* in New York City." [*to live*])

Card Type 3: *Which word fits into this* other *blank?*

   "No one __ forever" [to live]?
   (e.g., "No one *lives* forever.")

Card Type 4: *How do you spell this word?*
(e.g., Pronounced lɪvz, fits into "He __ in New York City" → *l-i-v-e-s*)

Word Order: *We'll learn where to put the word* He.

Card Type 1: *Where do you put* He *in "Lives in New York City"?*
(e.g., "*He* lives in New York City.")

New-Word Cards—Type 1: Which Word Fits in the Blank?

There might be a few different words that fit in the blank of your example sentence. Ideally, you're looking for sentences that are relatively unambiguous (e.g., *He lives _____ New York* is better than *_____ is good*), although with the help of pictures, you can make even the most ambiguous of sentences clear ("[Picture of delicious turkey] is good").

Still, you'll occasionally run into situations where you come up with a perfectly fine answer that doesn't match the back of your card. This is fine. Remember, *any* correct answer counts as a correct answer.

FRONT

USE THIS CARD ON:
✔ The Intensive Track
✔ The Normal Track
✔ The Refresher Track

ESSENTIAL FACTS (YOU NEED TO REMEMBER THESE!):
- **Pronunciation:** What word fits in the blank? Can you say it out loud?
- **Gender [if your language uses it]:** If this word is a noun, what's the gender of the word?

BONUS POINTS (IF YOU CAN THINK OF SOME OF THESE WHEN YOU REVIEW, YOU'LL HAVE AN EASIER TIME REMEMBERING NEXT TIME):
- **Spelling:** Do you remember how to spell this word?

- **Personal Connection:** If this word isn't a totally abstract function word, can you think of the first/last time you encountered this thing/action/adjective or an example of this word that is relevant to your life?

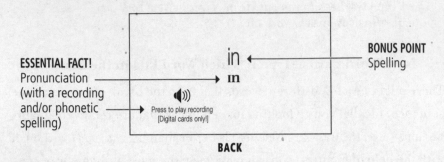

BACK

New-Word Cards—Type 2: What's a Sentence or Phrase That Includes This Word?

There are an infinite number of sentences that include your word. If you can come up with *any* of them, you win. (In all likelihood, though, you'll just come up with the one on the back side of your card.) Note that you don't need to reproduce an entire sentence perfectly, word for word. A relevant fragment of that sentence—*in New York*—will work just fine.

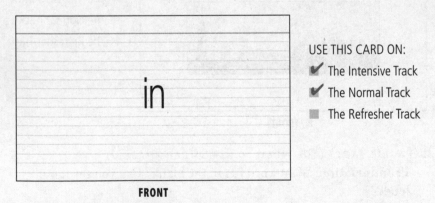

FRONT

ESSENTIAL FACTS (YOU NEED TO REMEMBER THESE!):

- **A Sentence or Phrase:** What does this word mean? Can you think of a sentence or phrase that would use it?

- **Pronunciation:** Can you say this word out loud?

- **Gender [if your language uses it]:** If this word is a noun, what's the gender of the word?

BONUS POINTS (IF YOU CAN THINK OF SOME OF THESE WHEN YOU REVIEW, YOU'LL HAVE AN EASIER TIME REMEMBERING NEXT TIME):

- **Other Meanings:** Can you think of any *other* sentences or phrases that would use this word in a different way?

- **Personal Connection:** If this word isn't a totally abstract function word, can you think of the first/last time you encountered this thing/action/adjective or an example of this word that is relevant to your life?

BACK

New-Word Cards—Type 3: Which Word Fits into This *Other* Blank?

This is identical to card type 1. You're just adding another sentence, ideally with a slightly different use of the same word. This is how you'll learn multiple definitions for a single word. If you wanted to learn all 464 definitions of *set*, you'd do it with these types of cards (or with the slightly expanded versions in the next gallery): *I ____ the table, I bought a ____ of silverware, My TV ____ broke*, and so on. Every time you do this, your *set* gets a little more nuanced and multidimensional, and you'll have an easier time remembering it in *all* contexts. You'll find new sentences for old words in your grammar book, in your dictionary, or on Google Images (discussed in detail in Chapter 6).

FRONT

USE THIS CARD ON:
- ✔ The Intensive Track
- ✔ The Normal Track
- ◼ The Refresher Track

ESSENTIAL FACTS (YOU NEED TO REMEMBER THESE!):
- **Pronunciation**: What word fits in the blank? Can you say it out loud?
- **Gender [if your language uses it]**: If this word is a noun, what's the gender of the word?

BONUS POINTS (IF YOU CAN THINK OF SOME OF THESE WHEN YOU REVIEW, YOU'LL HAVE AN EASIER TIME REMEMBERING NEXT TIME):
- **Spelling:** Do you remember how to spell this word?
- **Personal Connection:** If this word isn't a totally abstract function word, can you think of the first/last time you encountered this thing/action/adjective or an example of this word that is relevant to your life?

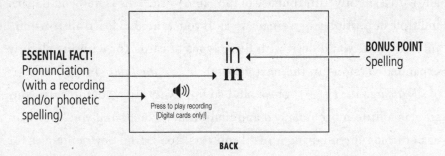

ESSENTIAL FACT!
Pronunciation (with a recording and/or phonetic spelling)

in
in

Press to play recording
[Digital cards only!]

BONUS POINT
Spelling

BACK

New-Word Cards—Type 4: How Do You Spell This Word?

It is extraordinarily unlikely that you'll need these cards, unless you're learning Japanese or Chinese, in which case you'll use them to learn your Kanji/Hanzi characters.

In most other languages, once you've learned your first 625 words, you'll tend to pick up proper spelling automatically from the other three card types. Still, every once in a while, you *might* find an occasion to use one of these cards. Hungarian, for instance, has some lovely, ridiculously long words that can be difficult to remember, like *fényképezőgép* (camera). If some of these words cause you trouble, then add spelling cards as needed.

FRONT

ESSENTIAL FACT (YOU NEED TO REMEMBER THIS!):
- **Spelling:** Do you remember how to spell this word?

BONUS POINTS (IF YOU CAN THINK OF SOME OF THESE WHEN YOU REVIEW, YOU'LL HAVE AN EASIER TIME REMEMBERING NEXT TIME):
- **Gender [if your language uses it]:** If this word is a noun, what's the gender of the word?
- **Personal Connection:** If this word isn't a totally abstract function word, can you think of the first/last time you encountered this thing/action/adjective or an example of this word that is relevant to your life?

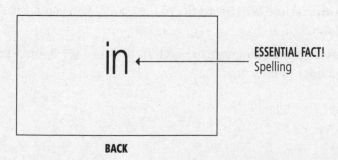

BACK

Using these four card types, you'll be able to memorize practically any word you see, regardless of how abstract it is. Usually, if you run into problems, it's only because the example sentences from your grammar book are too ambiguous to teach you a word (e.g., ___ *is good* won't work very well for the word *caring*). For now, skip over those words. You'll be able to learn them with the tools discussed in Chapter 6—Google Images, monolingual dictionaries, and self-directed writing.

Word Form Cards—Type 1: Which Word Fits in the Blank?

Word form cards are basically identical to new-word cards. The main difference is that instead of *He ___ in New York City*, you're giving yourself a hint, in the form of the basic form of the word (the one you'd see in your dictionary): *He ___ in New York City (to live)*. This makes these cards significantly easier to remember and helps to teach you how your language plays around with the forms of its words in order to change the meaning of a sentence (the difference between *a cat* and *cats*, for instance).

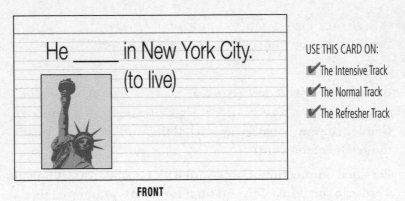

FRONT

ESSENTIAL FACTS (YOU NEED TO REMEMBER THESE!):
- **Pronunciation**: What word fits in the blank? Can you say it out loud?
- **Gender [if your language uses it]**: If this word is a noun, what's the gender of the word?

BONUS POINTS (IF YOU CAN THINK OF SOME OF THESE WHEN YOU REVIEW, YOU'LL HAVE AN EASIER TIME REMEMBERING NEXT TIME):

- **Spelling:** Do you remember how to spell this word?

- **Other Forms:** Are there other forms of this word that you're aware of? When would you see them? (While it's not necessary, I find it very helpful to list a few of these forms on the back of my word form cards.)

- **Personal Connection:** If this word isn't a totally abstract function word, can you think of the first/last time you encountered this thing/action/adjective or an example of this word that is relevant to your life?

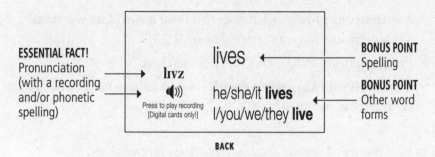

Word Form Cards—Type 2: What's a Sentence or Phrase That Includes This Word?

Like we discussed in the new-word cards, any sentence fragment will work here. In addition, you're trying to remember the base word form of the word you see (i.e., if you see *lives*, you're trying to remember *to live*).

In this example, we run into another layer of complexity: if we see the word *lives*, how do we know whether this is a verb (as in *to live*) or a noun (as in *a life*)? We don't. Fortunately, our old, trusty rule—*any correct answer is always correct*—is still in effect. If you see *lives* and think *Cats have nine lives* instead of *He lives in New York City*, then so much the better. You'll now remember *both* of those sentences the next time you see this card.

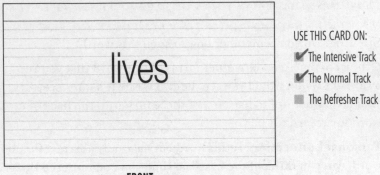

FRONT

ESSENTIAL FACTS (YOU NEED TO REMEMBER THESE!):

- **A sentence or phrase**: What does this word mean? Can you think of a sentence or phrase that would use it?

- **Pronunciation**: Can you say this word out loud?

- **Gender [if your language uses it]**: If this word is a noun, what's the gender of the word?

BONUS POINTS (IF YOU CAN THINK OF SOME OF THESE WHEN YOU REVIEW, YOU'LL HAVE AN EASIER TIME REMEMBERING NEXT TIME):

- **Other Meanings**: Can you think of any *other* sentences or phrases that would use this word in a different way?

- **Other Forms**: Are there other forms of this word that you're aware of? When would you see them?

- **Personal Connection**: If this word isn't a totally abstract function word, can you think of the first/last time you encountered this thing/action/adjective or an example of this word that is relevant to your life?

BACK

Word Form Cards—Type 3: Which Word Fits into This *Other* Blank?

Same old story. You'll find that you won't need very many of these. Card types 1 and 2 will do a fine job of teaching you new word forms on their own. Still, if you ever feel uncertain about a particularly complex word form ("I *have been living* in Paris since 2004"; "You *have been drinking* lactose-free milk for ten years"), then add cards like these until you feel comfortable.

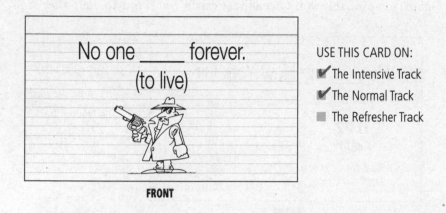

FRONT

USE THIS CARD ON:
✔ The Intensive Track
✔ The Normal Track
▪ The Refresher Track

ESSENTIAL FACTS (YOU NEED TO REMEMBER THESE!):
- **Pronunciation**: What word fits in the blank? Can you say it out loud?
- **Gender [if your language uses it]**: If this word is a noun, what's the gender of the word?

BONUS POINTS (IF YOU CAN THINK OF SOME OF THESE WHEN YOU REVIEW, YOU'LL HAVE AN EASIER TIME REMEMBERING NEXT TIME):
- **Spelling**: Do you remember how to spell this word?
- **Other Forms**: Are there other forms of this word that you're aware of? When would you see them?
- **Personal Connection**: If this word isn't a totally abstract function word, can you think of the first/last time you encountered this thing/action/adjective or an example of this word that is relevant to your life?

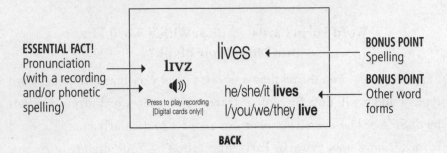

BACK

Word Form Cards—Type 4: How Do You Spell This Word?

Again, you probably won't need these cards, but if you do, here they are:

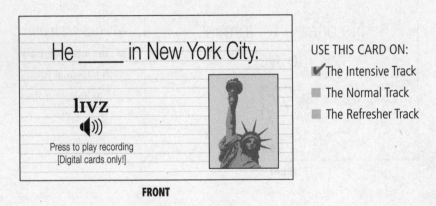

FRONT

ESSENTIAL FACT (YOU NEED TO REMEMBER THIS!):
- **Spelling:** Do you remember how to spell this word?

BONUS POINTS (IF YOU CAN THINK OF SOME OF THESE WHEN YOU REVIEW, YOU'LL HAVE AN EASIER TIME REMEMBERING NEXT TIME):
- **Gender [if your language uses it]:** If this word is a noun, what's the gender of the word?
- **Personal Connection:** If this word isn't a totally abstract function word, can you think of the first/last time you encountered this thing/action/adjective or an example of this word that is relevant to your life?

BACK

Word Order Cards: Where Does This Word Go?

Word order cards teach you the order of a sentence. Use as many as you need. In the beginning, try using two per sentence (just pick a couple of words at random). That should be enough to teach you the precise order of the words. Within a few weeks, you'll get a feel for how these cards work, and you'll be able to use them more sparingly.

FRONT

USE THIS CARD ON:
- ✔ The Intensive Track
- ✔ The Normal Track
- ✔ The Refresher Track

ESSENTIAL FACT (YOU NEED TO REMEMBER THIS!):
- **The Full Sentence**: Where does this word belong in the sentence?

NO BONUS POINTS! (SORRY.)

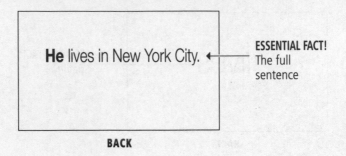

BACK

Four Special Scenarios: Dealing with Declension Charts, Dealing with Short Phrases, Eliminating Clues, and What to Do When You're Stumped

All of these cards are just variations on the same themes we've been using: a fill-in-the-blank sentence, a picture, and a missing word. Mostly, this is just an excuse to show you a few more examples. Enjoy!

DEALING WITH DECLENSION CHARTS

Let's return to our tired old friend *He lives in New York City*. We just learned *lives* in this way: *He _____ in New York City (to live)*. This assumes that we already know *to live*, and we're just learning how to conjugate it. But how do we learn *to live* in the first place?

We'll make a special sort of new-word card. It looks like this:

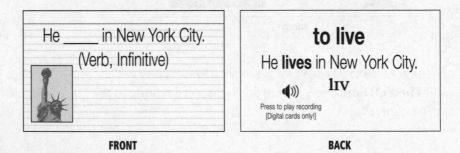

FRONT   **BACK**

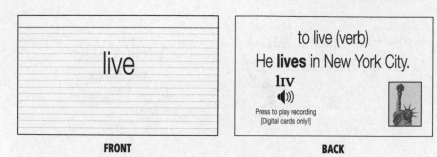

FRONT   BACK

Alternatively, you could make a different kind of fill-in-the-blank and copy the format of your word form cards from earlier:

FRONT   BACK

Both sorts of cards will teach you the same thing. I prefer the first version because it's a little more challenging, and it forces me to master all of my base forms.

SHORT PHRASES

What do you do with a dialogue like this?

Waiter: Here's your coffee!
Customer: Thank you.
Waiter: **You're welcome.**

In this case, "You're welcome" is just the thing you say after "Thank you." It doesn't have much to do with *welcoming* someone. So when you learn a phrase like this, you have a choice. You can either learn each word individually, like this:

Waiter: Here's your coffee! Customer: Thank you! Waiter: You're _____	**welcome** **wɛlkəm** 🔊 Press to play recording [Digital cards only!]
FRONT	**BACK**

Or learn them all at once, like this:

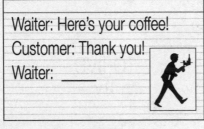

Waiter: Here's your coffee! Customer: Thank you! Waiter: _____	**You're welcome** **jʊəɹ wɛlkəm** 🔊 Press to play recording [Digital cards only!]
FRONT	**BACK**

Either option works fine. Personally, I prefer to learn words individually whenever I can. It's easier to remember one word at a time, and if I can turn a short phrase into *several* flash cards instead of two, then I'll tend to learn more from it.

ELIMINATING CLUES

Sometimes your example sentences provide clues about your word that make your resultant flash cards too easy. In Russian, for instance, a single adjective (a *red* traffic light) can tell you *much* more than the color of your traffic light; it can tell you the precise role, number, and gender of a missing word in your sentence.

You can get a small taste of this in English. Suppose you were learning the word *automatic* with the sentence *She was holding an _____ rifle.* The *an* in this sentence gives you a big clue about the word: it starts with a vowel. In practice, you might find that this flash card feels too easy. So take the clue away, like this:

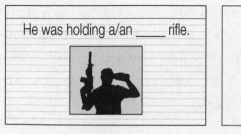

FRONT   BACK

WHEN YOU'RE STUMPED

Sometimes you'll run into a grammatical construction and you won't have any idea how to teach it to yourself. You might not be able to figure out whether to make a new word card, a word form card, a word order card, or all three.

Alternatively, you may have already *made* flash cards for a given grammatical rule, but you'd like more reinforcement. Perhaps someone found and corrected a mistake on something you wrote. You just want a little more practice, and you don't want to go through the whole new-word/word form/word order rigmarole.

In either of these cases, turn your sentence into a basic, nondescript, fill-in-the-blank test with a picture or two, like this:

FRONT   BACK

Use these cards whenever you're not quite sure *what* to do. In practice, they're slightly more difficult to remember than new-word/word form/word order cards, but you'll be able to memorize them without *too* much trouble.

Teaching yourself grammar without using English is something of an improvisatory art. You'll be able to use these cards to learn almost anything, but from time to time, you may run into something totally unexpected. Don't be afraid to try out new flash card designs and see what works. They're just flash cards. Write whatever you want on them (and whenever possible, throw in a picture).

THE FOURTH GALLERY:
ONE LAST SET OF VOCABULARY CARDS

Chapter 6

In this section, we're only going to talk about one thing: learning the last bits of your vocabulary with the help of a monolingual dictionary. Since you're invariably going to run into a few words that are difficult to define by context alone—words like *honest* or *fascinating*—you need to learn how to add definitions to your flash cards.

The Language Game: Get Your Information

To make these cards, you'll want a good example sentence or two; a good, concise definition; and a picture to help you remember.

- **A Good Example Sentence**: Look for an example sentence that includes a few words you know already and a few words you don't. That way, you'll pick up a few new words passively.

  - *Resources*: Google Images in Google Translate (as discussed at the beginning of Chapter 6), your own writing (corrected at *Lang-8.com* or *italki.com*), or your grammar book.

- **A Good, Concise Definition**: Try to find a definition that's less than ten words long (or just use a short excerpt of the definition). You don't want to have to read an essay about your word every time you review your flash cards.

- *Resources*: Your trusty monolingual dictionary. If you use a dictionary online, stick it into Google Translate. That way, you'll be able to start using your dictionary much earlier and learn faster.

- **Pictures:** If you're using Google Images to find example sentences, they already come with pictures. Awesome. If you're using other sources, then search for images in English to save time.

   - *Resources:* Google Images (or, if you're using a Leitner box, your own imagination).

Expect to spend around two to three minutes per word. You're exposing yourself to a *lot* of material—a bunch of example sentences, subtle definitions, pictures, and so on. Have fun exploring; each word you learn here will boost your passive vocabulary by around three to five additional words and teach you a bunch of grammar in the process.

Make Your Cards

Intensive Track: Two to four card types per word
Normal Track: Two to three card types per word
Refresher Track: One card type per word

WE'LL PLAY AROUND WITH THE WORD *HONEST*.

Card Type 1: *Which word fits in the blank?*
   (e.g., "He was an __ man" → *honest*, pronounced ɑnɪst)

Card Type 2: *What's a sentence/phrase that includes this word?*
   (e.g., *honest* → "He was an *honest* man.")

Card Type 3: *Which word fits into this* other *blank?*
   (e.g., "It was an __ mistake." → *honest*, pronounced ɑnɪst)

Card Type 4: *How do you spell this word?*
   (e.g., Pronounced ɑnɪst, fits into "He was an __ man" → *h-o-n-e-s-t*)

Card Type 1: Which Word Fits in the Blank?

Now that you're adding definitions to your words, there's not much room for ambiguity. Every fill-in-the-blank will only have *one* correct answer. If you think you're looking at a synonym for a word you've learned already, then look deeper into your monolingual dictionary; you'll almost always discover some tiny difference between so-called synonyms, and now's your chance to find that difference and indicate it on your flash cards.

He was a/an _____ man.
Adjective: You don't lie, cheat, or steal

FRONT

USE THIS CARD ON:
- ✔ The Intensive Track
- ✔ The Normal Track
- ✔ The Refresher Track

ESSENTIAL FACTS (YOU NEED TO REMEMBER THESE!):
- **Pronunciation**: What word fits in the blank? Can you say it out loud?
- **Gender [if your language uses it]**: If this word is a noun, what's the gender of the word?

BONUS POINTS (IF YOU CAN THINK OF SOME OF THESE WHEN YOU REVIEW, YOU'LL HAVE AN EASIER TIME REMEMBERING NEXT TIME):
- **Spelling**: Do you remember how to spell this word?
- **Personal Connection**: If this word isn't a totally abstract function word, can you think of the first/last time you encountered this thing/action/adjective or an example of this word that is relevant to your life?

ESSENTIAL FACT!
Pronunciation
(with a recording
and/or phonetic
spelling)

Honest ←

→ ɑnɪst

🔊

Press to play recording
[Digital cards only!]

BONUS POINT
Spelling

BACK

Card Type 2: What's a Sentence or Phrase That Includes This Word?

You don't need to remember the *precise* definition here. As long as you can think of any typical use for this word, you win.

honest

USE THIS CARD ON:
✔ The Intensive Track
✔ The Normal Track
▪ The Refresher Track

FRONT

ESSENTIAL FACTS (YOU NEED TO REMEMBER THESE!):

- **A Sentence or Phrase**: What does this word mean? Can you think of a sentence or phrase that would use it?

- **Pronunciation**: Can you say this word out loud?

- **Gender [if your language uses it]**: If this word is a noun, what's the gender of the word?

BONUS POINTS (IF YOU CAN THINK OF SOME OF THESE WHEN YOU REVIEW, YOU'LL HAVE AN EASIER TIME REMEMBERING NEXT TIME):

- **Other Meanings**: Can you think of any *other* sentences or phrases that would use this word in a different way?

- **Personal Connection:** If this word isn't a totally abstract function word, can you think of the first/last time you encountered this thing/action/adjective or an example of this word that is relevant to your life?

ESSENTIAL FACT!
Pronunciation (with a recording and/or phonetic spelling)

ESSENTIAL FACT!
Example sentence

He was a/an _____ man.
Adjective: You don't lie, cheat, or steal

ɑnɪst

🔊
Press to play recording
[Digital cards only!]

BACK

Card Type 3: Which Word Fits into This *Other* Blank?

These cards work best for capturing a different definition or use of a word, like this:

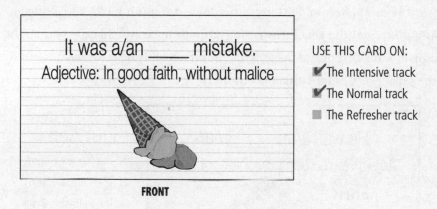

It was a/an _____ mistake.
Adjective: In good faith, without malice

USE THIS CARD ON:
✔ The Intensive track
✔ The Normal track
■ The Refresher track

FRONT

ESSENTIAL FACTS (YOU NEED TO REMEMBER THESE!):

- **Pronunciation:** What word fits in the blank? Can you say it out loud?

- **Gender [if your language uses it]:** If this word is a noun, what's the gender of the word?

BONUS POINTS (IF YOU CAN THINK OF SOME OF THESE WHEN YOU REVIEW, YOU'LL HAVE AN EASIER TIME REMEMBERING NEXT TIME):

- **Spelling:** Do you remember how to spell this word?

Personal Connection: If this word isn't a totally abstract function word, can you think of the first/last time you encountered this thing/action/adjective or an example of this word that is relevant to your life?

ESSENTIAL FACT!
Pronunciation
(with a recording
and/or phonetic
spelling)

honest ←

→ ɑnɪst

🔊
Press to play recording
[Digital cards only!]

BONUS POINT
Spelling

BACK

Card Type 4: How Do You Spell This Word?

At this point, you'll only need this card if you're learning Japanese or Chinese. In extraordinarily rare circumstances, when the spelling of the word is completely and utterly ridiculous—something like *floccinaucini-hilipilification* (the act of describing something as worthless)—you might consider making one of these cards, but it's mostly here for the benefit of the Japanese/Chinese learners out there.

He was a/an _____ man.

Adjective: You don't lie, cheat, or steal

ɑnɪst
🔊
Press to play recording
[Digital cards only!]

USE THIS CARD ON:
✔ The Intensive Track
■ The Normal Track
■ The Refresher Track

FRONT

ESSENTIAL FACT (YOU NEED TO REMEMBER THIS!):
   · **Spelling**: Do you remember how to spell this word?

BONUS POINTS (IF YOU CAN THINK OF SOME OF THESE WHEN YOU REVIEW, YOU'LL HAVE AN EASIER TIME REMEMBERING NEXT TIME):

- **Gender [if your language uses it]**: If this word is a noun, what's the gender of the word?

- **Personal Connection**: If this word isn't a totally abstract function word, can you think of the first/last time you encountered this thing/action/adjective or an example of this word that is relevant to your life?

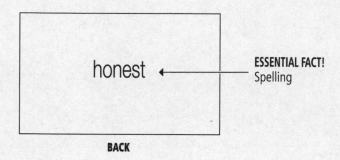

BACK

You now have all the tools you need to learn whatever you want to learn. Go forth and have fun!

A GLOSSARY OF TERMS AND TOOLS

From italki to Verbling, levels of processing to verb declensions, we've discussed a *lot* of potentially new terms and tools in this book. For your convenience, I'm collecting all of them here, along with a brief explanation, and when appropriate, a website address.

625 WORDS

A list of extremely common, concrete English words that are easy to visualize and simple to translate. If you learn them, they'll reinforce the pronunciation work you did in Chapter 3, and they'll provide a solid vocabulary foundation for when you're ready to approach grammar in Chapter 5.

AMYGDALA

A companion organ to the hippocampus that tells it what to keep and what to throw out. It is stimulated by recall tests more than simple reading.

ANKI

My favorite computerized SRS. It's free, it runs on every platform, and it handles both pictures and audio without a problem.

ankisrs.net—Download link

Fluent-Forever.com/chapter2—Video Tutorials

AUDIOBOOKS

Foreign language audiobooks are one of the best ways to begin reading in your foreign language. You buy the audiobook and the actual book, and then listen to the recording as you read along. The recording will help you move through a large text quickly, and you'll pick up a great deal of pronunciation information at the same time. You can find many audiobooks in French, German, Italian, Portuguese, Russian, and Spanish at *Amazon.com*. For other languages, you'll have to use your newfound language abilities to search for them on the net. As I find good audiobook sources myself, I'll add them to my website.

Fluent-Forever.com/language-resources

BACK CHAINING

A tongue exercise whereby you take a long word and say the last phoneme alone, then say the last two phonemes, then the last three, gradually building up to saying the whole word from the beginning to the end. This makes short work of hard-to-pronounce words.

BILINGUAL DICTIONARY

A translating dictionary that lets you look up words in one language and find a translation in another. It's useful for finding words that you're missing in your target language (What's the word for "dog" in French?), for figuring out the meaning of new words (What on earth is an *aiguillage*?), and for finding out grammatical and pronunciation information about a new word (What's the phonetic transcription for *aiguillage*? What's the gender of *aiguillage*? What type of verb conjugation does *finir* [to finish] use?).

BILINGUAL EFFECT

A phenomenon in which bilingual individuals outperform monolingual individuals as a direct result of their language knowledge. Learning another language is a kind of strength training for the brain, which results in increased intelligence and more resilient mental health.

BROKEN WORD

A word that you've learned through reading but don't pronounce correctly. When you encounter it in spoken language, you're going to think it's a totally new word and get confused. This is one of the reasons why pronunciation training in the beginning can save you time in the long run.

CASE

I don't specifically discuss case in this book, I just hint at it in Chapter 5. But since you're looking, *case* is just another word for "role," as in "What's the role of *dog* in this sentence?" In *Dog eats cat, Cat eats dog, Man gives dog a bone,* and *Cat eats dog's food,* the word *dog* keeps switching cases.

COMPREHENSIBLE INPUT

Any foreign language sentences that you can basically understand, either through the help of context clues, body language, translations, or some combination of the above. If I say *"Voulez-vous un cookie?"* and offer you a cookie, you've just taken in comprehensible input, even if you don't speak French. Your brain uses comprehensible input to piece together the grammatical system of a language.

CONJUGATION

Changes in the verb form based upon its context. The proper conjugation of *to be* is *am* when it's in the context *Help! I ____ on fire!*

CONSONANT

A phoneme made by blocking the air coming out of your lungs in some manner. *P, t,* and *sh* are all consonants.

CONSONANT LOCATION

Also known as consonant place, this is one of the three components of any consonant. Location is the difference between "p" (lips) and "t" (tongue against alveolar ridge).

CONSONANT TYPE

Also known as consonant manner, this is one of the three components of any consonant. Type is the difference between "t" (tongue blocks air completely and then pops open) and "s" (tongue blocks air slightly, allowing air to hiss out).

CONSONANT VOICING

This is one of the three components of any consonant. Voicing is the difference between "z" (vocal cords buzzing) and "s" (vocal cords not buzzing).

DECLENSION

Basically synonymous with *conjugation*. Linguists use *conjugation* to refer to the changing forms of verbs and *declension* to refer to the changing forms of everything else (e.g., *one dog/two dogs, he/him/his, they/them/their*, etc.).

DECLENSION/CONJUGATION CHART

A list of verb conjugations or noun/adjective declensions (e.g., *I am, you are, he is, we are, they are* . . .).

DVDS (FOREIGN LANGUAGE TV AND FILM)

You can find foreign language DVDs on Netflix and Amazon, but for many languages, you'll need to search for your shows elsewhere on the Internet. Find the titles for the shows you're looking for on Wikipedia, and try to find stores that accept international credit cards. Hopefully, this will all get easier in time, as the world continues to globalize and the Internet knocks down barriers.

FEEDBACK

The process of taking a test and finding out whether or not you got the right answer. If you get immediate feedback when you review your flash cards (by checking the back of every card to see if you answered correctly), you'll improve the effectiveness of your study sessions.

FLUENT-FOREVER

My language-learning website. It basically contains everything that didn't fit in this book, along with links and tutorials for everything that *did* fit in this book. You'll find in-depth explanations of everything you read here and quite a bit that you haven't yet read.

Fluent-Forever.com

FOREIGN SERVICE INSTITUTE COURSES

The US Foreign Service Institute has put forty-one languages' worth of free textbooks (and their accompanying recordings) online. They're mostly from the 1960s and 1970s and can be a bit dry, but their content is usually excellent.

fsi-language-courses.org

FORVO

A giant database of over 2 million recordings in over 300 languages. You can find a native speaker recording of almost any word in almost any language, and if it's not there, you can request a recording, and you'll get it within a few days. It's free, and it's wonderful. Use it to learn the pronunciation of your target language.

Forvo.com

FREQUENCY DICTIONARY

A dictionary that contains words in your target language, arranged in order of frequency, along with English translations of these words. Often, it will contain example sentences of the words in context. These dictionaries are wonderful tools for expanding your vocabulary efficiently. They're not yet available in every language, but if you're studying a relatively common language, you may be in luck.

Fluent-Forever.com/language-resources

FREQUENCY LIST

Ranging from the 625 words introduced in Appendix 5 to the free lists available at *en.wiktionary.org/wiki/Wiktionary:Frequency_lists*, these lists of words are arranged in order of frequency and usually don't come with translations (so you need to do that step yourself).

GENDER

Grammatical gender has little (if anything) to do with *actual* gender. The original meaning of the word was "kind," and that meaning still persists in related words like *genre*, *genus*, and *generic*. Languages use gender to put nouns into groups. Some languages use male and female, some languages use male/female/neuter, and some use people, body parts, animals, small cute things, thin objects, objects that usually come in pairs, and so on. If you replace the word *gender* with *random, arbitrary group of nouns*, it will make a great deal more sense.

GOOGLE IMAGES

An image search engine run by Google. As of this book's publication, it contains more than forty-six billion images from websites in more than 130 languages. There are three different ways to use Google Images, which you can access at the following URLs:

Regular Google Images: In its regular form, you can type in any word (*cat*), hit enter, and you'll see a giant wall of images of that word.
   images.google.com

Google Images Basic Version: Every image in Google Images has an associated caption, which is hidden by default. If you turn these captions on, you'll be able to use Google Images to find illustrated examples of every word in your target language.
   TinyURL.com/basicimage

Google Images Basic Version, Translated: The captions under each image in Google Images Basic Version will be in your target language, which you may not understand yet. Fortunately, if you configure your browser just right, you can see side-by-side translations for all of those captions. This makes those captions much easier to use when you're just starting out.
   Fluent-Forever.com/chapter4

GOOGLE TRANSLATE

The best machine translator on the Internet. You can type in a sentence in any of its seventy-one languages, and it will translate it into any of its other languages. You can also type in a website address (say, a French monolingual dictionary), and it will translate that website. You can Google Translate in a few ways:

   1. If you encounter a strange written passage in your target language, you can type it into Google Translate and get a decent translation back into English.

2. If you're not sure how to write something in your target language, you can write it in English and have it translated (badly) into your target language. Then you can submit that translation to a language exchange website like Lang-8 and get it corrected by native speakers.

3. You can type in the address of a monolingual (French-French) dictionary. This will give you much better explanations of your words than a bilingual (French-English) dictionary, and if you put your mouse cursor over any of the translations, you'll see the original text, which you can use in your flash cards.

translate.google.com

GRAMMAR BOOK

Just one author's take on the easiest way to introduce you to a language. Grammar books start simple and gradually grow more complex, showing you how to use verbs, nouns, and adjectives and how to indicate time, hypothetical situations, and so on. They save you a lot of work, since each example has been chosen so that it builds upon previous examples and doesn't overwhelm you.

HEBB'S LAW

Neurons that fire together wire together. This is how we build memories. If you see a cookie, smell a cookie, and eat a cookie, you will associate those three experiences in the future.

HIPPOCAMPUS

A mental switchboard that helps interconnect neurons and tells you where to find them in the future.

IMMERSION PROGRAMS

A place where *all* of your time is spent in the target language, even outside of class. These programs can be expensive, but they're a *phenomenal* way to learn to speak fluently.

INTERNATIONAL PHONETIC ALPHABET (IPA)

An alphabet in which every letter corresponds to a single sound. If you know it, you can use it to tell you precisely what any foreign word sounds like and even how to form a new foreign sound in your mouth.

ITALKI

A language exchange community with a well-thought-out payment system. You can use italki to find a professional teacher or untrained tutor in your target language and work with him through email or video chat for extremely low prices. There are free options on the site, which can help you find language exchange partners, but I mostly recommend italki for its paid services.

italki.com

LANG-8

A free language exchange community devoted to providing writing corrections. You sign up, submit some writing, correct someone else's writing, and get a correction of your own, usually in less than a day.

Lang-8.com

LANGUAGE EXCHANGE

A language-learning arrangement between you and a speaker of your target language. You'll meet up, typically via Skype video chat, and talk for a predetermined time in your language and for the same amount of time in your partner's language.

LANGUAGE EXCHANGE WEBSITES

Websites that are designed to help you find language exchange partners. *Livemocha.com*, *Busuu.com*, *MyLanguageExchange.com*, *italki.com*, and *Language-Exchanges.org* are some of the better-known language exchange websites.

LANGUAGE HOLIDAYS

A trip abroad for the purposes of learning your target language and exposing yourself to the culture of your target language's home.

LEITNER BOX

Paper-based spaced repetition systems. They use a flash card file, a carefully designed schedule, and a few simple game rules to create the same sort of spaced repetition magic you'll find in a computer program like Anki.

LEVELS OF PROCESSING

One of the mental filters that determine what you remember and what you forget. You'll best remember things that you know how to spell (structure), you know how to pronounce (sound), you understand/see (concept), and you relate to personally (personal connection).

LIVEMOCHA

One of the more popular language exchange websites. Feel free to ignore its language courses; its main use is to connect you with a language exchange partner.

LiveMocha.com

MEMORY GAME

A game you can play with any new word to help memorize it. Can you find a personal connection with this word? If so, you'll remember it 50 percent better.

MINIMAL PAIRS

Pairs of words that differ by only a single sound, like *niece/knees* or *bit/beat*.

MINIMAL PAIR TESTING

A test using pairs of words that differ by only a single sound. If you test yourself with minimal pairs (*Do you hear "rock" or "lock"?*) and get immediate feedback (*It was "lock"*), you can permanently rewire your brain to hear new sounds.

Fluent-Forever.com/chapter3

MNEMONIC IMAGERY GAME

The process of attaching a mnemonic image (say, masculine = *exploding*) to a word (say, *dogs*, which are masculine in German) to form a mnemonic story (*kaboom goes the dog*). The more vivid and weird you can make your story, the better you'll remember it later.

MNEMONICS

Memory aids that turn something that's abstract (e.g., the masculine gender in German) into something that's concrete (an explosion). They take advantage of our extraordinary visual memory, and you can use them to memorize many irregular, nonsensical patterns in your target language.

MONOLINGUAL DICTIONARY

A dictionary that is 100 percent in your target language. It provides full definitions for your words rather than simple translations. Once you reach an intermediate level, you can use a monolingual dictionary to learn even the most abstract of words in your target language. You'll find good ones in print, but at least toward the beginning, you'll want to find one online, because you can use it in conjunction with Google Translate to get translations for those definitions. This gives you the best features of a bilingual dictionary (it's usable right from the beginning) and a monolingual dictionary (it teaches you tons about your words) at the same time. You'll find dictionary recommendations on my website.

Fluent-Forever.com/language-resources

MORE IS LESS

The idea that the more things you learn about a topic, the easier it is to remember all of it. This is why you'll have an easier time learning a language like Chinese if you make many more flash cards than you otherwise might for a language like Spanish.

NEURON

Nerve cells that transmit signals within your brain and connect your brain to the rest of your nervous system. A memory is what happens when a group of neurons fires together and interconnects.

OUTPUT

Writing, for the most part. When you write, you test out grammar and find your weak spots. Output is the way you turn the hundreds or thousands of little facts you've learned into a usable language.

PERSON-ACTION-OBJECT (PAO)

A memory technique used in competitive memorization. The basic premise is that you can pick a relatively small number of people, actions, and objects and connect them to form a great number of weird, memorable stories. We can use it to add flexibility to our mnemonic imagery (e.g., connecting a mnemonic person and/or object to a verb we're learning, or a mnemonic person/action to a noun we're learning).

PHONEME

A single sound in a language (rather than a single letter); *sh* is just one phoneme in English.

PHONETIC TRANSCRIPTION

Converting a word—like *enough*—into phonetic letters: ɪnʌf (usually into IPA).

PHRASE BOOK

A small, cheap travel companion that tells you how to say various canned phrases (e.g., "Help! Someone stole my purse!" "May I buy an apricot?"). The phrases inside can serve as useful bits of language that you can learn starting in Chapter 5. At the end of most phrase books (certainly those made by Lonely Planet), you'll find a great little dictionary. This is an easy, convenient way to find good translations for the 625 words in Appendix 5.

PRONUNCIATION GUIDEBOOK

Books that walk you through the pronunciation and spelling system of your target language. They should come with CD recordings, and you should be able to listen to and mimic those recordings.

PRONUNCIATION TRAINERS

Software programs that are designed to rewire your brain to hear new sounds. They're the easiest and fastest way I'm aware of to learn the sound system of a new language.

Fluent-Forever.com/chapter3

PRONUNCIATION VIDEOS

Videos that explain in depth how you make sounds in your mouth. I've made a series of (free) YouTube videos that take you through a tour of the IPA and your mouth and have really helped out a lot of people. Check them out.

Fluent-Forever.com/videos

RECALL PRACTICE

Just another word for "testing." You're trying to remember something, and that effort is what makes a memory lodge itself into your long-term memory.

RHINOSPIKE

A free language exchange community, devoted to providing audio recordings. You submit a text in your target language and a native speaker will read that text aloud and send you an MP3. In exchange, you'll record someone else's English text. The service is lovely, but be aware that it can occasionally take several days to get a response.

Rhinospike.com

SELF-DIRECTED WRITING

See Output.

SKYPE

A computer program that facilitates free phone calls and video chats across the Internet. For the purposes of language learning, it's the program you'll use to connect with language exchange partners and private tutors on the Internet.

Skype.com

SPACED REPETITION

An extraordinarily efficient learning method whereby you learn something and then wait a few days to review it. If you still remember, then you wait even longer before your next review. By studying in this way, you push memories deeper and deeper into your long-term memory.

SPACED REPETITION SYSTEMS (SRSs)

Automated to-do lists for flash cards that monitor your progress and tell you which flash cards to study on which days to maximize efficiency. They come in two main forms: computerized systems, which create your daily to-do list based upon relatively sophisticated algorithms, and paper versions (known as Leitner boxes), which accomplish the same goal using a set of simple game rules, a flash card file box, and a calendar.

SPOT THE DIFFERENCES

A game you can play with Google Images, in which you look up a word in your target language and see whether the pictures are what you expect to see. The more differences you can spot between your expectations and what you see, the better you'll remember your word.

SUMMARIES OF TV SHOWS AND MOVIES

You can find target-language summaries of your favorite TV shows and films on Wikipedia.org. If you read them before you watch a film or TV show in your target language, you'll have a much easier time, since you won't have to try and figure out what's going on, and you'll already be exposed to much of the vocabulary that will show up in the dialogues.

TABOO / THE GAME OF TABOO

A party game by Milton Bradley that closely resembles the ideal type of practice for fluent speech in a foreign language. In the game, you have a list of forbidden words that you must talk around. In real life, you have a bunch of words that you simply don't know, and you have to talk around them, too.

TENSE-ASPECT-MODE

I don't specifically discuss tenses, aspects, or modes in this book, but I do hint at them in Chapter 5. These are all just ways of playing around with verbs. We can play with the *time* of a verb (tense: *I am eating / I was eating*) or play around with our sense of a verb's *progression through time* (aspect: *I am eating now / I eat regularly*). We can even play around with the *certainty* of a verb (mode: *I would eat / I could eat*). These three are often intermingled: *Tomorrow you will get me cookies* (future tense) / *You will get me Girl Scout cookies. Right. Now* (mode). You'll pick up on tense, aspect, and mode by reading the explanations in your grammar book and learning lots of example sentences.

THEMATIC VOCABULARY BOOK

A book of several thousand words (and their translations), arranged by theme: words about money, words about music, words about clothing, and so on. It's a handy tool for customizing your vocabulary to your individual needs once you've built a foundation using a frequency list.

TIP OF THE TONGUE

A phenomenon in which you can recall parts of a memory but not all of it. If you experience a tip-of-the-tongue event and successfully recall something, you'll double your chances of recalling it successfully in the future.

VERBLING

Verbling facilitates language exchanges in the form of speed dating. You tell it what language(s) you speak and what language(s) you're learning, and it connects you with a language exchange partner automatically, in five-minute bursts.

Verbling.com

VOCABULARY BOOK

See Thematic vocabulary book.

VOWEL

A phoneme made by allowing the air to come out of your lungs relatively unimpeded. You can make different vowels by changing the position of your tongue and lips.

VOWEL BACKNESS

One of the three components of any vowel. Your tongue can move forward ("eh") and back ("uh").

VOWEL HEIGHT

One of the three components of any vowel. Your tongue can move up ("ee") and down ("ah").

VOWEL ROUNDING

One of the three components of any vowel. Your lips can round into a circle ("oo") or flatten out ("ee").

WIKIPEDIA

A kind of magical dictionary. If you find an article in English, you can often find that same article in your target language by clicking on one of the links on the bottom left-hand side of your browser window (the links labeled "Languages"). This lets you find the translations of terms that won't show up in your dictionary—terms like *The Game of Thrones*, which may not be translated word for word when remarketed to a non-American audience. The *Game of Thrones* TV series, for example, is called *Le Thrône de Fer* (The Throne of Iron) in France. Wikipedia is the easiest way to find this information, and you can use it to help you search for DVDs, books, and so on.

Wikipedia.org

WIKIPEDIA, "IPA FOR [INSERT-LANGUAGE-HERE]" ARTICLES

Articles on IPA in various languages (e.g., "IPA for Spanish") that can show you all of the sounds in your target language, its IPA symbols, and a bunch of example words. If you know IPA, they can be really handy.

Google for "IPA for [Insert-Language-Here]." *But don't actually type* "[Insert-Language-Here]." *Type "French" or something.*

WIKTIONARY

A crowd-sourced dictionary, much like Wikipedia. Aside from the enormous English dictionary (which can show you translations of most words in the English language into most languages), Wiktionary contains a large number of excellent monolingual (French-French, Spanish-Spanish) dictionaries. Many of these also contain quality IPA transcriptions of most words.

Wiktionary.org

WUG

A fake word used by linguists to test children on their ability to internalize a language's sound rules. English-speaking kids learn to say "one wug, two wugz" automatically by the age of five, which is kind of neat, since they've clearly never heard of "wugz" before in their lives.

YOUTUBE

A source for pronunciation advice and information. While it can be somewhat unreliable, many of the tutorials you'll find there (if you search for, say, "How to trill an *r*" or "the Arabic A'yn") have been created by native speakers and can help you hear and produce new sounds. If you're going to start somewhere, start with my series (linked at *Fluent-Forever .com/videos*).

YouTube.com

APPENDICES

Books to Get and Websites to Visit

The Modern Language Association performs routine surveys of the languages that American college students are learning. Here are its results for fall 2009:

Language	Enrollments in Fall 2009
1. Spanish	864,986
2. French	216,419
3. German	96,349
4. American Sign Language	91,763
5. Italian	80,752
6. Japanese	73,434
7. Chinese	60,976
8. Arabic	35,083
9. Latin	32,606
10. Russian	26,883
11. Ancient Greek	20,695
12. Biblical Hebrew	13,807
13. Portuguese	11,371
14. Korean	8,511
15. Modern Hebrew	8,245

I'll give you resources here for every language on this list except for American Sign Language, Latin, Ancient Greek, and Biblical Hebrew. Those languages require some special modifications, since the first is not a spoken language at all and the last three have no native speakers.

For every language, I'll list a grammar book or two, a phrase book, and a pronunciation trainer. When available, I'll also point you toward a pronunciation book, a frequency dictionary, and a thematic vocabulary book. For links, additional book/website recommendations, and for less commonly learned languages, go to *Fluent-Forever.com/language-resources*.

Arabic Language Resources

FULL LIST AND LINKS: *Fluent-Forever.com/Arabic*

Grammar Book: Jane Whitewick et al., *Mastering Arabic (With 2 Audio CDs)*

Phrase Book: Siona Jenkins, *Lonely Planet Egyptian Arabic Phrasebook*

Pronunciation Trainer: Gabriel Wyner, *Arabic Pronunciation Trainer*

Frequency Dictionary: Tim Buckwalter et al., *A Frequency Dictionary of Arabic*

Chinese (Mandarin) Language Resources

FULL LIST AND LINKS: *Fluent-Forever.com/Chinese*

Grammar Book: Yuehua Liu et al., *Integrated Chinese*

Phrase Book: Anthony Garnaut et al., *Lonely Planet Mandarin Phrasebook*

Pronunciation Trainer: Gabriel Wyner, *Mandarin Chinese Pronunciation Trainer*

Pronunciation Book: Live ABC, *Chinese Pronunciation with CD-ROM*

Frequency Dictionary: Richard Xiao et al., *A Frequency Dictionary of Mandarin Chinese*

Thematic Vocabulary Book: Andrey Taranov, *Chinese Vocabulary for English Speakers*

French Language Resources

FULL LIST AND LINKS: *Fluent-Forever.com/French*

Grammar Book: Mary Crocker, *Schaum's Outline of French Grammar*

Phrase Book: Michael Janes et al., *Lonely Planet French Phrasebook*

Pronunciation Trainer: Gabriel Wyner, *French Pronunciation Trainer*

Pronunciation Book: Christopher Kendris et al., *Pronounce It Perfectly in French*

Frequency Dictionary: Lonsdale, Deryle, and Yvon Le Bras, *A Frequency Dictionary of French*

Thematic Vocabulary Book: Wolfgang Fischer et al., *Mastering French Vocabulary*

German Language Resources

FULL LIST AND LINKS: *Fluent-Forever.com/German*

Beginner Grammar Book: Joseph Rosenberg, *German: How to Speak and Write It*

Intermediate Grammar Book: Martin Durrel, *Hammer's German Grammar and Usage*

Phrase Book: Gunter Muehl et al., *Lonely Planet German Phrasebook*

Pronunciation Trainer: Gabriel Wyner, *German Pronunciation Trainer*

Frequency Dictionary: Randall Jones et al., *A Frequency Dictionary of German*

Thematic Vocabulary Book: Veronika Schnorr et al., *Mastering German Vocabulary*

Hebrew (Modern) Language Resources

FULL LIST AND LINKS: *Fluent-Forever.com/Hebrew*

Beginner Grammar Book: Zippi Lyttleton, *Colloquial Hebrew*

Intermediate Grammar Book: Luba Uveeler et al., *Ha-Yesod: Fundamentals of Hebrew*

Phrase Book: Justin Ben-Adam Rudelson et al., *Lonely Planet Hebrew Phrasebook*

Pronunciation Trainer: Gabriel Wyner, *Hebrew Pronunciation Trainer*

Italian Language Resources

FULL LIST AND LINKS: *Fluent-Forever.com/Italian*

Grammar Book: Marcel Danesi, *Practice Makes Perfect: Complete Italian Grammar*

Phrase Book: Pietro Iagnocco et al., *Lonely Planet Italian Phrasebook*

Pronunciation Trainer: Gabriel Wyner, *Italian Pronunciation Trainer*

Frequency Dictionary: Gianpaolo Intronati, *Italian Key Words*

Thematic Vocabulary Book: Luciana Feinler-Torriani et al., *Mastering Italian Vocabulary*

Japanese Language Resources

FULL LIST AND LINKS: *Fluent-Forever.com/Japanese*

Grammar Book: Eri Banno et al., *Genki: An Integrated Course in Elementary Japanese*

Phrase Book: Yoshi Abe et al., *Lonely Planet Japanese Phrasebook*

Pronunciation Trainer: Gabriel Wyner, *Japanese Pronunciation Trainer*

Frequency Dictionary: Yukio Tono et al., *A Frequency Dictionary of Japanese*

Thematic Vocabulary Book: Carol Akiyama et al., *Japanese Vocabulary*

Korean Language Resources

FULL LIST AND LINKS: *Fluent-Forever.com/Korean*

Grammar Book: Ross King et al., *Elementary Korean*

Phrase Book: Minkyoung Kim et al., *Lonely Planet Korean Phrasebook*

Pronunciation Trainer: Gabriel Wyner, *Korean Pronunciation Trainer*

Pronunciation Book: Miho Choo et al., *Sounds of Korean*

Frequency Dictionary: Jae-wook Lee, *Korean Essential Vocabulary 6000*

Portuguese Language Resources

FULL LIST AND LINKS: *Fluent-Forever.com/Portuguese*

Grammar Book: Fernanda Ferriera, *The Everything Learning Brazilian Portuguese Book* (with CD)

Phrase Book: Marcia Monje de Castro, *Lonely Planet Brazilian Portuguese Phrasebook*

Pronunciation Trainer: Gabriel Wyner, *Portuguese Pronunciation Trainer*

Frequency Dictionary: Mark Davies et al., *A Frequency Dictionary of Portuguese*

Thematic Vocabulary Book: Andrey Taranov, *Portuguese Vocabulary for English Speakers*

Russian Language Resources

FULL LIST AND LINKS: *Fluent-Forever.com/Russian*

Grammar Book: Nicholas Brown, *The New Penguin Russian Course*

Phrase Book: James Jenkin et al., *Lonely Planet Russian Phrasebook*

Pronunciation Trainer: Gabriel Wyner, *Russian Pronunciation Trainer*

Pronunciation Book: Thomas Beyer, *Pronounce It Perfectly in Russian* (see note)

Frequency Dictionary: Nicholas Brown, *Russian Learner's Dictionary*

Thematic Vocabulary Book: Eli Hinkel, *Russian Vocabulary*

Note: Thomas Beyer put his recordings for this book online. You'll find a link on my website.

Spanish Language Resources

FULL LIST AND LINKS: *Fluent-Forever.com/Spanish*

Grammar Book: Marcial Prado, *Practical Spanish Grammar*

Phrase Book: Marta Lopez et al., *Lonely Planet Spanish Phrasebook*; or Roberto Esposto, *Lonely Planet Latin American Spanish Phrasebook*

Pronunciation Trainer: Gabriel Wyner, *Spanish Pronunciation Trainer*

Pronunciation Book: Jean Yates, *Pronounce It Perfectly in Spanish*

Frequency Dictionary: Mark Davies, *A Frequency Dictionary of Spanish*

Thematic Vocabulary Book: Jose Maria Navarro et al., *Mastering Spanish Vocabulary*

For English Speakers

The Foreign Service Institute (FSI) is the US government's training center for diplomats, ambassadors, and James Bond–types. They've been in the language business since 1947 and have some of the best data on language difficulties for English speakers. Their students take on an intense workload: twenty-five hours of language classes per week and three to four hours of independent study per day. Not surprisingly, they reach advanced levels of fluency very quickly. Still, we'll be able to beat them in terms of total time spent, because our methods are more efficient. FSI courses are relatively traditional in format, although they do have a respectable emphasis on pronunciation that keeps them ahead of the curve. They may beat us in terms of total time to fluency, simply because you get a lot done when you make language learning your full-time job. However, our use of imagery, mnemonics, and spaced repetition will push us ahead in terms of overall efficiency.

The following estimates show the total amount of time FSI students spend in class for each language. Languages in parentheses aren't in their official list, but are so closely related to other languages in the same category that I stuck them in anyway. Languages with an asterisk are slightly harder than other languages in their category.

Level 1: Languages Closely Related to English
23–24 WEEKS (575–600 CLASS HOURS)

Afrikaans
(Catalan)
Danish
Dutch
French
Italian

Norwegian
Portuguese
Romanian
Spanish
Swedish

Level 1.5: Languages with Slight Linguistic and/or Cultural Differences from English
30–36 WEEKS (750–900 CLASS HOURS)

German (30 weeks / 750 hours)
(Ilocano) (36 weeks / 900 hours)
Indonesian (36 weeks / 900 hours)

(Javanese) (36 weeks / 900 hours)
Malay (36 weeks / 900 hours)
Swahili (36 weeks / 900 hours)

Level 2: Languages with Significant Linguistic and/or Cultural Differences from English
44 WEEKS (1,100 CLASS HOURS)

Albanian
Amharic
Armenian
Azerbaijani
Bengali
Bosnian
Bulgarian
Burmese
Croatian
Czech
*Estonian
*Finnish
*Georgian
Greek
(Gujarat)
Hebrew
Hindi
*Hungarian
Icelandic
(Kannada)
(Kazakh)
Khmer
(Kurdish)

(Kyrgyz)
Lao
Latvian
Lithuanian
Macedonian
(Marathi-Urdu)
*Mongolian
Nepali
Pashto
Persian (Dari, Farsi, Tajik)
Polish
(Punjabi)
Russian
Serbian
Sinhalese
Slovak
Slovenian
Tagalog
*Thai
Turkish
(Turkmen)
Ukrainian
Urdu

Uzbek
*Vietnamese

Xhosa
Zulu

Level 3: Languages Which Are Exceptionally
Difficult for Native English Speakers

88 WEEKS (SECOND YEAR OF STUDY IN-COUNTRY, 2200 CLASS HOURS)

Arabic
Cantonese
*Japanese
Korean

Mandarin
(Min Nan)
(Wu Chinese)

Computerized Spaced Repetition Systems: Anki

Anki's website is *Ankisrs.net*. There you'll find download links and installation instructions.

Once you've installed Anki, you'll need to learn how to use it. To make your job easier, refer to my series of video tutorials and demonstration decks, which you can find at *Fluent-Forever.com/chapter2*.

Making Cards by Hand: Leitner Boxes

If you prefer the feel and look of paper to the cold blue glow of a smartphone screen, then you can make an SRS by hand. It will take you longer than using a computer, but you'll learn a lot more while making your cards.

Keep in mind that many of the online resources I'm going to discuss are just as useful whether you use computerized or physical flash cards. Your copy/paste process is simply different: it takes longer, it's more flexible, and it might look a little sillier if you're not much of an artist. If you find a great example sentence on Google Images with a seemingly useless image (Google Images can provide sentences for every word, if you ask it nicely), you'll be in a better position than someone using a computerized SRS. If you're trying to make three hundred cards in an evening, or make a bunch of pairs of comprehension/production cards, you'll be working harder than someone who can cut-and-paste with a couple of keystrokes.

The Two Faces of Google Images

Google Images used to provide captions for every image, but in 2010, a new, flashier version was introduced that produces humongous walls of images without text. If you scroll *all* the way down to the bottom of any image search, you'll find "Switch to Basic Version." Click it, bookmark the link, and *voilà*—you now have access to the largest book of illustrated stories in the history of mankind. Enjoy!

Because you'll be using a physical box instead of a computer program, the intervals won't be the same for every card. Some cards' final intervals will wobble between two and four months. This doesn't turn out to be a big deal; if you have a problem remembering a card, it will return often enough to work its way into your long-term memory, and if not, then huzzah, you remembered it.

Here's what you'll need:
- A whole bunch of index cards (at least a couple thousand)
- A large index card box or file
- Eight index card dividers, labeled "New," "Level 1," "Level 2," and so on, up to "Level 7"
- A calendar
- A trusty set of pens and/or pencils (colors can help you make more memorable pictures)

Your index file will look like this:

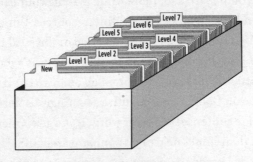

A LEITNER BOX

The Rules of the Game

Your Leitner box is a flash card game. You win the game when you get all of your new cards past level 7. To accomplish this, you'll need to successfully recall each of your cards seven times in a row, with increasing delays between each recall. If you win, you can expect to remember each of your cards for more than a year.

How do you get from level 1 to level 2? Every time you review a flash card, you'll look at the front side of the card and ask yourself a single question: "Do I remember what's on the back of this card?" Depending upon the type of flash card (vocabulary, grammar, pronunciation), this question may have multiple parts: "Do I remember the correct pronunciation of this word? Do I remember the word that goes along with this picture? Do I remember the proper spelling for the word that goes along with this picture?" In the Gallery, every time I introduce a new card type, I also discuss the questions associated with that card type.

If the answer to all of those questions is "Yes, I do remember!" then move that card to the next level (e.g., level 2 cards move to level 3). If you answer "No, I forgot something," then you'll move that card all the way back to level 1.

How do you know when to review your cards and which cards to review? The Leitner box game is designed for daily play. Each day, you'll follow the following two steps:

- Step 1: Move fifteen to thirty new cards into level 1.
- Step 2: Review your cards according to the Game Schedule.

The Game Schedule is a sixty-four-day repeating schedule that tells you how often to review your level 1/2/3/4/5/6/7 cards. Roughly, you'll review level 1 every day, level 2 every other day, level 3 every fourth day, all the way to level 7, which you'll review every 64 days. Since there aren't sixty-four days in a month, we'll need to add a sixty-four-day cycle to a calendar, like this:

May 2014

S	M	T	W	T	F	S
				1	2	3
4	5	6	7	8	9	10
	1	2	3	4	5	6
11	12	13	14	15	16	17
7	8	9	10	11	12	13
18	19	20	21	22	23	24
14	15	16	17	18	19	20
25	26	27	28	29	30	31
21	22	23	24	25	26	27

June 2014

S	M	T	W	T	F	S
1	2	3	4	5	6	7
28	29	30	31	32	33	34
8	9	10	11	12	13	14
35	36	37	38	39	40	41
15	16	17	18	19	20	21
42	43	44	45	46	47	48
22	23	24	25	26	27	28
49	50	51	52	53	54	55
29	30					
56	57					

July 2014

S	M	T	W	T	F	S
		1	2	3	4	5
		58	59	60	61	62
6	7	8	9	10	11	12
63	64	1	2	3	4	5
13	14	15	16	17	18	19
6	7	8	9	10	11	12
20	21	22	23	24	25	26
13	14	15	16	17	18	19
27	28	29	30	31		
20	21	22	23	24		

Once you've done that, you can simply refer to your calendar to figure out where you are in the sixty-four-day cycle of the Game Schedule (on page 273, May 5 and June 8 both correspond to day 1):

THE LEITNER GAME SCHEDULE

(You can print out a copy at Fluent-Forever.com/appendix3)

Day 1: Level 2, 1	Day 17: Level 2, 1	Day 33: Level 2, 1	Day 49: Level 2, 1
Day 2: Level 3, 1	Day 18: Level 3, 1	Day 34: Level 3, 1	Day 50: Level 3, 1
Day 3: Level 2, 1	Day 19: Level 2, 1	Day 35: Level 2, 1	Day 51: Level 2, 1
Day 4: Level 4, 1	Day 20: Level 4, 1	Day 36: Level 4, 1	Day 52: Level 4, 1
Day 5: Level 2, 1	Day 21: Level 2, 1	Day 37: Level 2, 1	Day 53: Level 2, 1
Day 6: Level 3, 1	Day 22: Level 3, 1	Day 38: Level 3, 1	Day 54: Level 3, 1
Day 7: Level 2, 1	Day 23: Level 2, 1	Day 39: Level 2, 1	Day 55: Level 2, 1
Day 8: Level 1	Day 24: Level 6, 1	Day 40: Level 1	Day 56: Level 7, 1
Day 9: Level 2, 1	Day 25: Level 2, 1	Day 41: Level 2, 1	Day 57: Level 2, 1
Day 10: Level 3, 1	Day 26: Level 3, 1	Day 42: Level 3, 1	Day 58: Level 3, 1
Day 11: Level 2, 1	Day 27: Level 2, 1	D ay 43: Level 2, 1	Day 59: Level 6, 2, 1
Day 12: Level 5, 1	Day 28: Level 5, 1	Day 44: Level 5, 1	Day 60: Level 5, 1
Day 13: Level 4, 2, 1	Day 29: Level 4, 2, 1	Day 45: Level 4, 2, 1	Day 61: Level 4, 2, 1
Day 14: Level 3, 1	Day 30: Level 3, 1	Day 46: Level 3, 1	Day 62: Level 3, 1
Day 15: Level 2, 1	Day 31: Level 2, 1	Day 47: Level 2, 1	Day 63: Level 2, 1
Day 16: Level 2, 1	Day 32: Level 1	Day 48: Level 1	Day 64: Level 1

When I play with my Leitner box on May 5 (day 1), I will follow the two main steps of the game. First, I'll move fifteen to thirty new cards into Level 1, and then I'll consult the Game Schedule. The schedule tells me that I should:

1. Begin with level 2.
2. Then proceed to level 1.

But I don't *have* any cards in level 2; I'm just starting out, after all. So I pat myself on the back for a job well done and proceed to level 1.

Level 1 is pretty simple today. I review my fifteen to thirty cards. Every time I remember a card, I move it into level 2. Every time I forget, I put it at the back of the pile of cards in level 1. With enough repetitions, I'll eventually move *every* card from level 1 up to level 2. Once I've done that, I'm done for the day.

May 6 (day 2) proceeds in much the same way. I'm supposed to review levels 3 and 1, but again, level 3 is empty, and level 1 only has my fifteen to thirty new cards for the day. By the end of the day, I have thirty to sixty cards waiting in level 2.

Now it gets interesting. On May 7 (day 3), I'm supposed to review levels 2 and 1. So I pull out those thirty to sixty level 2 cards. I review every card *once*. Every time I remember a card, I'll move that card up to level 3. Every time I forget a card, I'll move that card back down to level 1.

Next, I'll review my cards in level 1, which are now a mixture of the fifteen to thirty new cards I placed in it *and* the cards I had forgotten from level 2. Every time I remember a card, I'll move it into level 2. Every time I forget, I'll put it at the back of the pile of cards in level 1. Like I did on the previous two days, I'll keep going through the pile until all of my level 1 cards have moved into level 2. Then I'll pour myself a martini and call it a day.

A Winning Card

Let's track the progress of a winning card through the Game Schedule. On May 5 (day 1: levels 2, 1), one of my new cards looks like this ("*Macska* is the Hungarian word for *cat*"):

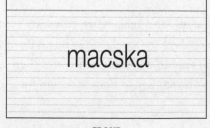

FRONT   **BACK**

I'll see it when I review level 1, and since I've spent *so* much time yammering away about cats in Chapter 2, I don't have trouble remembering what a *macska* is. I immediately move the card to level 2, finish the rest of my reviews, and put my Leitner box away.

On day 2 (levels 3, 1), I don't see *macska* because I'm not reviewing level 2 on that day. Instead, I see *macska* again on day 3 (levels 2, 1), at which point I still remember it, and put it into level 3.

Three days pass before I see it again, on day 6 (levels 3, 1). I've reviewed *macska* twice now, and so my memory is getting stronger, even though I'm waiting a longer and longer period of time between reviews. I remember it and bump it up to level 4.

Now I wait an entire week. On day 13 (levels 4, 2, 1), *macska* shows up a fourth time. A few days earlier, I learned *matrac* (mattress), and as a result, I have some trouble trying to remember whether *macska* is an animal or a piece of furniture. After a few seconds of gut-wrenching uncertainty, I remember. I move the card up to level 5.

We're getting close to the end of the game for *macska*. I wait more than two weeks before seeing it again on day 28 (levels 5, 1). After conquering my *macska/matrac* mix-up, I don't have a problem remembering, and I move *macska* to level 6.

Level 6 comes on day 59 (levels 5, 1), a full month since I saw it last. When I remember it and bump it into level 7, I can almost taste my victory over the word. I have a formidable task in front of me now: the only time I see level 7 is on day 56 (levels 7, 1). I have to wait for the cycle to repeat—two months—before seeing the card again. When it returns, I could lose everything. If I can't remember, *macska* will fall all the way back to level 1, and I'll need to repeat the cycle from the beginning. If I remember, I'll win, and *macska* will go into retirement, living out the rest of its days in the comfort of my long-term memory.

WHAT IF I MISS A DAY OR TWO?

Do all of your reviews from the missed days, and make sure you start with your *highest* level cards first. If you missed days 57 (levels 2, 1) and 58 (levels 3, 1), then on day 59 (levels 6, 2, 1), you should do levels 6, then 3, then 2, then 1. You can skip learning new cards on that day to help make up for the extra review time.

APPENDIX 4:
THE INTERNATIONAL
PHONETIC ALPHABET DECODER

You'll use this appendix for one thing: to discover how to make a new sound. If you're not using a Leitner box, you don't necessarily need to memorize every phonetic symbol in your new language (although I think it's a good use of your time, especially in the beginning). However, you're going to run into a few wacky sounds, and this appendix will tell you how to make them.

A caveat: this is intended as a reference. We're talking about things that move and make sounds in a book, a medium both static and silent. As such, I'd recommend the following: take a thirty-five-minute break from this book

---

Do You Really *Need the International Phonetic Alphabet?*

Nope! You don't. The IPA was invented a century ago, and people have been successfully learning languages for a wee bit longer than that. Like everything else in this book, the IPA is a tool. If you find it useful, then use it. If it fills you with dread, skip it. But do try this before you move on: In this section, I rarely stop yammering on about my YouTube series. Just watch the first few minutes. If you find it interesting, keep watching. If not, then stop. The IPA is not for you, and that's just fine. Go play around with some fun new words instead (and listen to recordings at *Forvo.com*!).

and watch my YouTube series on the IPA (*Fluent-Forever.com/videos*). Then you can come back at your leisure and refer to this section whenever you encounter a sound and have no idea how someone made it.

The IPA suffers from an infectious jargon disease—terms like *labio-velar voiced approximant* (also known as a *w*) can give you rashes and night sweats. I've designed this decoder to show you a path *around* the jargon—think of it like a biohazard suit. Still, we're entering into dangerous territory. There is a *lot* of information buried in the IPA, and you only need a small bit of it. Our goal is to go in, learn to make our new sound, and get out as quickly as possible, so don't try to stay any longer than you need to. You'll get a fever.

The Makeup of Consonants and Vowels

Almost every consonant is a combination of three pieces of information:
- Where's your tongue?
- What's your tongue doing there?
- Are your vocal cords doing anything?

Vowels are a combination of two:
- Where's your tongue?
- Are your lips in a circle?

That's it, for the most part. When we hear someone speak, we're hearing this information. I use this information to correct my students' accents; I hear where their tongues are and tell them how to correct.

You can do this for yourself, once you get attuned to it. Our ears and our mouths are deeply interconnected. No one ever told you how to say "k," yet you've learned how to raise the back of your tongue to hit your soft palate in

---

Regarding Resources

If your language uses some crazy stick-your-finger-in-your-mouth-and-crack-your-knuckle sort of consonant, then your textbook will describe it in great detail, and you'll be able to find YouTube tutorials on it. Don't worry about it. If, after reading this guide, you get really curious about other ways of making sounds, then have a romp around my website; there's quite a lot I've assembled there.

exactly the right way to make a "k" sound. To make new sounds, you only need to gain a bit of awareness about what you do automatically in English and then make a few small adjustments.

So let's gain some awareness, starting with consonants.

Consonants—Location—Where's Your Tongue (or Lip[s])?

Here's a talking head I found somewhere in the woods. His name is Frank.

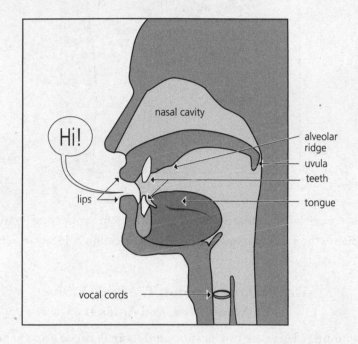

While you're looking at Frank, say this:

bee   fee   thee   see   she   ye   key   he

Notice that "bee" starts by your lips, "fee" touches your bottom lip to your upper teeth, and every successive word goes further back into your mouth, like this:

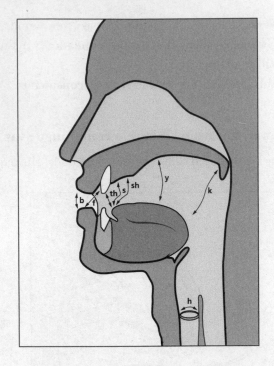

These are eight of the eleven possible locations for your tongue and lips. We'll refer to them by their letters (location B, location F, location S, etc.).

Three More Locations: The French ☞R, the Arabic A'yn, and Apu's D

What's missing? There are two locations hiding in between *k* and *h*: one that touches your uvula (the French *r* is here, along with the guttural *ch* as in *Chanukah*), and one that sits as far back as you can put your tongue (e.g., the Arabic A'yn, which can be [affectionately] described as "trying to choke yourself with your own throat").

The last missing location shows up regularly on *The Simpsons*. You know Apu, the Indian shopkeeper at the Kwik-E-Mart? His distinctive accent is largely due to the particular location of his *d*'s and *t*'s. Normally, a *d* or a *t* is articulated in the same place as *s*, with the tip of the tongue (Say "see," "dee," "tee"). Hank Azaria—the (not-Indian) voice actor for Chief Clancy Wiggum, Moe the bartender, and Apu—articulates Apu's *d*'s there, too, only instead of using the tip of his tongue, he's using the *underside* of his tongue. The *tip* of his tongue is curled back toward the roof of his mouth. This makes his *d*'s and *t*'s sound like a tom-tom, rather than like a snare drum, and it conveys an unmistakable sense of "This guy must be from India." You'll make sounds in this location if you learn Hindi, Chinese, or Swedish.

Consonants—Type of Sound—What Are You Doing There?

We have a lot more than eight consonants, so there must be a few options at each location. Try saying this group of words:

toe   no   so   low   row

They're all at the same location (location S). For each word, you're changing how and whether you allow air to pass around your tongue. You can mess with your tongue in eight ways, and you already use five of them frequently:

T TYPE (A SUDDEN POP OF AIR): Here you're preventing air from passing through until you've built up so much pressure that the air pops through in a sudden rush of sound and spittle. *T, d, p, b, k,* and *g* all fall in this group.

N TYPE (AIR THROUGH THE NOSE): These consonants come through your nose instead of your mouth. *N* and *m* are both in this group.

S TYPE (RUSTLING, HUSHING, BUZZING SOUNDS): There are a *lot* of sounds here, from sibilant *s* to buzzing *z* to hushing *sh*. You're allowing a *little bit of space* for air to pass over your tongue, which makes the air shoot off and make all sorts of angry noises—from the rustling, hushing sounds of *f, s, sh, h,* and *th* as in *thigh,* to the buzzing sounds of *v, z,* and *th* as in *thy*.

L TYPE (AIR MOVES OVER THE SIDES OF THE TONGUE): You're preventing air from escaping out the front, but you're allowing it to pass freely over the sides of your tongue. We only have one in English: *l*.

R TYPE (A SLIGHT OBSTRUCTION, ALMOST A VOWEL): The English *r* is a strange beast. It's one of the most difficult sounds to produce, which is why most children spend a fair portion of their childhood talking about "wascally wabbits." You're not obstructing the flow of air at all, but you're raising your tongue just enough to cause a change in the sound. We have three consonants that do this: *r, w,* and *y,* and they're more like vowels than consonants (*r* is basically the *ur* in *turkey, w* is basically the *oo* in *hoot,* and *y* is basically the *ee* in *see*).

The last three types show up in Spanish, Spanish (again), and Icelandic, respectively:

TRILLED TYPE (YOUR TONGUE/LIPS FLAP IN THE WIND): The Spanish double *r* resides here (as in *carro* [car]). Your tongue moves up to location S, but instead of allowing the air to hiss through, it flaps like mad against the roof of your mouth. If, instead, you let your uvula flap against the back of your tongue, you'll get the French *r*. Yay.

TAP TYPE (YOUR TONGUE/LIPS FLAP TOGETHER JUST ONCE): The *other* Spanish r (as in *caro* [dear]) resides here. You're doing the exact same thing as a trilled consonant, only instead of flapping your tongue a bunch of times, you're doing it once. It's *very* similar to an extremely short *d*. If you're trying to say Spanish's *caro* accurately, you can often get your tongue to behave properly by saying "*cado*" while *thinking* "*caro*."

CRAZY ICELANDIC L TYPE (CIL—A SLURPING, WET "L" SOUND): Unless you're learning Icelandic, Welsh, or a native American language, you can ignore this, but it's too neat to leave out. You know how L-type consonants allow air to flow freely over the sides of your tongue? Crazy Icelandic L-type consonants narrow that channel of air until you hear a loud, wet, rasping sound against your molars. It sounds something like "tttthhhhlpthshpthl."

Will you be able to produce a good French *r* merely by flapping your uvula against the back of your tongue? Probably not. Remember, this decoder is designed as a *supplement to your ears*. Your ears taught you all of these tongue positions in English, and they'll do most of the work in your new language, too. We're only discussing theory—flapping uvulas and all—in order to give your ears and tongue a helping hand when they need it. Sometimes a little "point your tongue toward your tonsils" is all the instruction you'll need to bridge the gap between what you can hear and what you can say.

Consonants—Vibration—Are Your Vocal Cords Doing Anything?

This last bit of consonant trivia is the simplest of the three. Put your finger on your throat, like this:

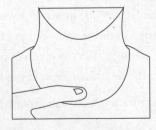

Now compare the sound "ssss" (like a snake) to "zzzz" (like a bee). Notice how you can't feel anything buzzing in your throat for "ssss," but you can for "zzzz." This buzzing is the sound of your vocal cords doing what they do best—

vibrate. Vibrating and nonvibrating consonants frequently show up in pairs: *b* and *p*, *v* and *f*, *d* and *t*, *g* and *k*, to name a few. Note that your vocal cords can be buzzing while you make a consonant that doesn't really sound like buzzing at all: "nnnnnnnn."

New Consonants and the International Phonetic Alphabet Decoder Chart

To make a new consonant, you'll mix and match all three features.

Without a specific sound in your ears to mimic, you may have some trouble creating a sound out of the blue, but we can certainly attempt a demonstration. The word for "Hungarian" (in Hungarian) sounds like a cross between "ma-jar" and "mag-yar." Not surprisingly, the real consonant is halfway between *j* ("ma-jar") and *g* ("mag-yar"), in the Y location:

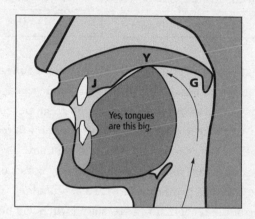

Keep the tip of your tongue down by your lower teeth and try to say "j." The middle of your tongue should raise up. If you succeed, you've just done a fairly complex new maneuver with your mouth—you've combined location Y, type T (a sudden pop of air), and vibrating vocal cords into a new consonant. Congratulations.

This is the basic method behind new consonants, and you should have an easier time doing it in your target language, because you've already listened to the sound you're trying to create (and because you've watched that video I told you to watch).

In a couple of pages, you'll find an annotated version of the standard IPA consonant chart. Here's how you use it:

1. Spend some time playing around with recordings of your language. Use any of the resources at the end of our sound chapter (your textbook, a

pronunciation book, one of my pronunciation trainers, *Forvo.com*, whatever). Try to copy all of the sounds you hear. Eventually, you're probably going to find a few consonants that cause you some trouble. Notice how those sounds are usually spelled. Now you're going to find those sounds in IPA, and the IPA will tell you what to do with your mouth.

2. Look up "IPA for [insert language here]" on Google. You'll find a Wikipedia article that looks like this (here I searched for "IPA for Spanish"):

Consonants		
IPA	**Examples**	**English approximation**
b	**b**estia; em**b**uste; **v**aca; en**v**idia	**b**est
β	be**b**é; o**b**tuso; vi**v**ir; cur**v**a	between ba**b**y and be**v**y
d	**d**edo; cuan**d**o; al**d**aba	**d**ead
ð	dá**d**iva; ar**d**er; a**d**mirar	thi**s**

Let's say that you've been plagued by the second sound in this list: β. Words like *bebé* and *vivir* sound like they contain some weird cross between a *b* and a *v*, and you want to know what on earth you're supposed to do with your mouth when you say these words. So let's figure out how to make a β.

3. First, let's make sure it's not a sound we know already from English. This can happen when your eye tricks your ear. For example, the Spanish word *envidia* (envy) is pronounced with a *b*: *"enbidia."* Even though you usually have no trouble recognizing a "b" sound when you hear it, you might second guess yourself when faced with such an unfamiliar spelling. So just in case, we'll look for our troublesome β in the sounds of English first.

You already know how to make twenty-five consonants, and you already know the *symbols* for fifteen of them, because they're just English letters:

IPA	Examples	IPA	Examples
p	**p**ond, s**p**oon, ro**p**e	b	**b**ut, we**b**
t	**t**wo, s**t**ing, be**t**	d	**d**o, o**dd**
k	**c**at, **k**ill, s**k**in, **q**ueen, thi**ck**	g	**g**o, **g**et, be**g**
f	**f**ool, enou**gh**, lea**f**	v	**v**oice, ha**v**e
s	**s**ee, **c**ity, pa**ss**	z	**z**oo, ro**s**e
h	**h**am	m	**m**an, ha**m**
l	**l**ow, ba**ll**	n	**n**o, ti**n**
w	**w**hy, s**w**ig		

Not surprisingly, β isn't here. Let's keep looking. You know ten more sounds from English, but they use weird symbols:

IPA	Examples	IPA	Examples
ɹ	ring, hairy	j	yes, yum
ʃ	she, sure, emotion	ʒ	pleasure, beige, emotion
tʃ	chip, catch	dʒ	Jack, badge
θ	thing, teeth	ð	this, breathe, father
ŋ	sing, sung	ʔ	Uh-Oh![21]

Alas, there's no β here either, so we'll take a deep breath and proceed to step 4.

4. You'll find almost every possible consonant in the big decoder chart on the next page. (It's missing the click sounds of eastern and southern Africa, but if you're learning those, I'll assume you know what you're doing or you have a good teacher!) You're going to go in, find your symbol, get your information, and leave before you get a headache. You're looking for answers to the following:

- Where's your tongue/lips? (listed on top)
- What's your tongue/lips doing? (listed on the left)
- Are your vocal cords vibrating? (Consonants with an asterisk [*] are vibrating.)

---

21. ʔ is the difference between "No, Pat" and "Nope at," as in "I entered the basement, saw it was full of spiders, noped at it, and left." It's an important consonant in Arabic (and German, to a lesser extent).

Location

Type of Sound	B — Both Lips	F — Bottom Lip / Upper Teeth	Th — Tongue Tip / Upper Teeth	T — Tongue Tip / Alveolar Ridge	Sh — Tongue Tip / Back of Ridge	Apu's D — Tongue Underside + Ridge	Y — Tongue Middle / Hard Palate	K — Back o' Tongue / Soft Palate	☞R — Back o' Tongue / Uvula	A'yn — "Choke yourself"	H — Vocal Cords
T — Sudden pop of air (!)	p b*			t d*		ʈ ɖ*	c ɟ*	k g*	q ɢ*		ʔ
N — Air through the nose.	m*	ɱ*		n		ɳ*	ɲ*	ŋ*	ɴ		
Trill — Tongue/Lips flap in the wind.	ʙ*			r*					ʀ*		
Tap — Tongue/Lips flap just once.		v̆*		ɾ*		ɽ*					
S — Rustling, Hushing, or Buzzing Sounds.	ɸ β*	f v*	θ ð*	s z*	ʃ ʒ	ʂ ʐ*	ç ʝ*	x ɣ*	χ ʁ*	ħ ʕ*	h ɦ*
C.I.L. — Slurping, wet L sound.				ɬ ɮ							
R — Slight obstruction, almost a vowel.		ʋ*		ɹ*		ɻ*	j*	ɰ*			
L — Over the sides of the tongue.				l*		ɭ*	ʎ*	ʟ*			

* Vocal cords vibrating (like "Zzz" or "Nnn").

THERE IT IS!

1. First, find your troublesome consonant.

2. Figure out its (secrets).

3. Get out of here!

How's your head? Here's what we know about β:
- Location: Both of your lips (your tongue isn't doing anything)
- Type of Sound: A rustling, hushing, or buzzing sound
- Vocal Cords: Yup, they're vibrating

To use this, start with your ears. As kids, we learned all the consonants from our native language(s) with our ears alone. You'll use them here, too. Go to *Forvo.com*, and get a recording of an example word. You can use *bebé* or *vivir*, from our "IPA for Spanish" article on Wikipedia. As I said in the beginning, it sounds like a cross between a *v* and a *b*.

Now you can use the information from the decoder chart. β requires you to put both of your lips together and let just enough air through to make a buzzing sound. Basically, you're making a *v*, but instead of putting your bottom lip against your teeth, you're putting both of your lips against each other.

Confused? I caught you! Go watch that video already. This will make a lot more sense once you have (although that decoder chart won't get any smaller!).

Vowels: Where's Your Tongue?

Vowels are simultaneously simpler and harder than consonants. You're not performing any complex motions when you say a vowel, but your tongue needs to be in a *very* precise position in order to sound right. Practically speaking, you'll have an easier time finding this position by relying upon your ears and imitating rather than trying to manually place your tongue in the right place. Still, knowing the basic tongue positions can help you out when some weird vowel causes you trouble.

Your tongue can go up, down, forward and back. Say "ee," "eh," "ah," and you'll feel your tongue move from high ("ee") to medium ("eh") to low ("ah") in your mouth. Forward and back are a little trickier to notice. Say "ee," "oo," "ee," "oo." Ignore the shenanigans going on with your lips for a moment and pay attention to your tongue. It moves forward on "ee" and back on "oo," like this:

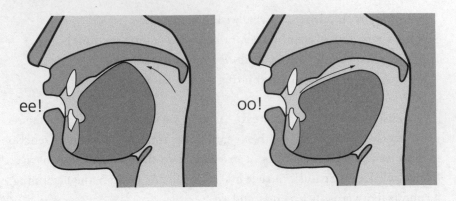

These movements are tiny; we're talking about a half inch, and that's as far away as any two vowels get. This is why your ears are so important in this equation. It's not that hard to benefit from a description of a consonant. ("Put your lips together and blow until they flap together and go 'bbbb.'") A vowel is a different animal. "Put your tongue in the position of 'ee,' and then go back an eighth of an inch and down a quarter of an inch" is of questionable practical use. You'll use this information in a different way, by comparing your new vowel to the vowels you *already* have (English has nine or more, depending upon how you count). Most new vowels you encounter will put your tongue right in between two vowels you already know, or they'll be the *same* as a vowel you know, only you'll do something different with your lips.

Vowels: Are Your Lips Rounded into a Circle?

You'll probably need to learn to separate your lips from your tongue.[22] We've already talked about the tongue positions in "ee" and "oo." Now we'll look at the lip shenanigans we ignored earlier. On page 289 are some lips. What vowels are they saying?

---

22. At least, you'll need to do it to learn French, German, Russian, Portuguese, Korean, Chinese, and Japanese. Out of the top eleven, you're safe in Spanish, Italian, Arabic, and Hebrew.

We can't know. What language are they speaking? You round your lips into a circle for "oo" and flatten them out for "ee," but those aren't the only possibilities. Korean features an "oo" with flat lips, and Chinese, French, and German all have a round "ee."

Try it. Just like you did before, say "oo," "ee," "oo," "ee" to get a feel for how your tongue moves back ("oo") and forward ("ee"), and then pick one of those tongue positions (we'll do "ee") and stick with it ("eeeeeeee"). Then, *without letting your tongue go back,* squeeze your lips into a circle. You'll hear the sound change into some weird hybrid of "oo" and "ee," which is exactly the sound we're looking for. Voilà! Now you can pronounce *fondue* correctly.

Making New Vowels and the International Phonetic Alphabet Decoder Chart

Let's play with the IPA Decoder Chart for Vowels.

1. As before, you'll spend some time mimicking words in your language until you figure out which ones cause you difficulties. Note how they're spelled.

2. Now Google "IPA for [insert language here]" and look up your vowels. Here's an excerpt of "IPA for French":

Vowels		
IPA	**Examples**	**English approximation**
o	sot, hôtel, haut, bureau	roughly like boat (Scottish English)
ɔ	sort, minimum	like not (British English)
u	coup	too
y	tu, sûr	roughly like few

These sorts of charts aren't designed to tell you *everything* about these example words. They don't tell you anything, for instance, about word stress (e.g., a **convert** vs. to con**vert**) or intonation (e.g., *what?* vs. *what!*). But that's not what we're using them for, and you can get that information from recordings or the pronunciation guides in your grammar book and dictionary.

We're just using these charts to help us find symbols for problematic sounds. Suppose you're learning French, and you run into a handful of words like *eau* (water), *beau* (beautiful), and *anneau* (ring). All three words sound *very* similar—they all seem to have the same vowel—but you can't seem to figure out how to actually *say* that vowel. You'll look up "IPA for French" and find similar spellings in one of the example words: *bureau*. According to the chart, the IPA for your troublesome vowel is o; now you just need to figure out what o sounds like.

The chart supplies English approximations but they won't help much. They're full of wacky accents and "roughly like *whatever*," and I'd suggest you take them with a great many grains of salt (assuming you even know how to pronounce "boat" in Scottish English).

Just for fun, let's look for all four vowels here: **o, ɔ, u,** and **y.**

3.   First, check to see if you know any of them from English. At your immediate disposal, you have:

IPA	Examples
ɑ	father, bra
æ	cat, sad
ɛ	head, dress
ɪ	sit, mill
i	heat, seed
ʌ	run, dull
ʊ	put, hood
u	boot, ruse

And probably (unless you're from California, in which case your "cot" and "caught" sound the same):

ɔ	thought, dawn

As is usually the case, a couple vowels are the same. The French **u** (as in *coup*, "a blow/strike") and **ɔ** (as in *sort*, "fate/destiny") turn out to be our familiar "oo" in "boot" and "aw" in "thought," respectively.

But you can scavenge a few more vowels from English. These vowels are stuck in pairs known as diphthongs; they start at one vowel and automatically move to a different vowel at the end (e.g., *high* sounds like "hah" + "ih"):

IPA	Examples
eɪ	**r**a**y**, the letter **"A"**
aɪ	h**igh**, the letter **"I"**
oʊ	s**o**, the letter **"O"**
ju	**u**se, the letter **"U"**
ɔɪ	b**oy**, c**oin**

These diphthongs are one of the hallmarks of an American accent (a British accent just uses *different* diphthongs). The French *o* (as in *pot de crème*) stays on *o*. An American *o* (as in *po'* de crème) dances all over the mouth. If you can learn to keep *o*'s feet still, you'll find your French **o**. You can learn to do this by saying "oh" for a long time—"oooooooohhhhhhhhh"—then stopping yourself before you move your tongue at the end. With practice, you'll find your **o**, and as a result, native speakers won't switch to English when they speak to you, in part because they can't figure out where you're from.

Now we just need to find **y**. The vowel decoder chart isn't quite as monstrous as the one for consonants, but you might want to take a deep breath before jumping in anyway.

4. Find your new vowel on the vowel chart (page 292). You're looking for two pieces of information:

- Where is your tongue? (Look at the closest vowel from English.)
- Are your lips in a circle? (Vowels with an asterisk [*] use round lips.)

Here's what you'll find:

The French **y** has the tongue position of "ee" and lips like "oo." Get recordings of French words with **y** (*tu*, *sûr*, *fondue*) from *Forvo.com* and let your ears guide you. Remember, the IPA is an *aid* to your greatest tool—your ears. If you've already learned how to *hear* some crazy new vowel, you'll have a much easier time producing it.

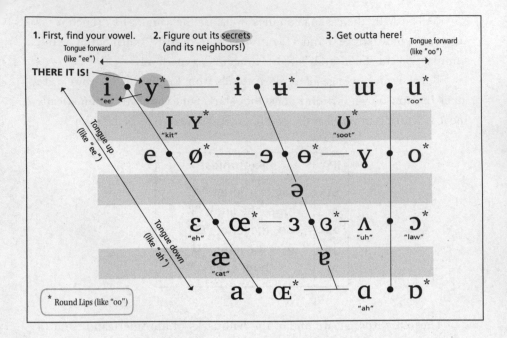

Welcome to the 625! These words will form the foundation of your language. They're some of the most frequent words you'll encounter in any language, and they're all relatively easy to learn with pictures. In general, you shouldn't have much trouble finding translations or pictures for these words, and they'll take you a month or two to memorize.

A Word of Warning

You won't be able to find a simple translation for every word on this list, because this is a list of *English* words. Your target language may have multiple words when you only have one—Russian, for example, has two separate words for blue (dark blue = *siny*, light blue = *goluboy*). Or the reverse may occur—Vietnamese, for example, has one word for both blue and green. Words don't always map easily from language to language.

We're only using this list as a time-saving device, so when you run into difficulties with a word, skip it. There are plenty of other words in the sea. There's no harm in spending a minute or two investigating a particularly elusive word on Google Images, but if none of the images make sense, then your time will be better spent elsewhere. Move on to the next word.

While you peruse your dictionary or phrase book, you may find a few interesting words that *aren't* in this list. Learn them, too. This is your vocabulary; learn whatever words you want as long as you can do it with pictures.

Which Word Form Should You Learn?

Most languages play around with their word forms; English's *to eat, eats, ate, eaten,* and *eating* all mean approximately the same food-in-mouth-related thing. Right now, don't worry about all of that; just learn whatever basic form is listed in your dictionary first. Most of the time, this means singular nouns, infinitive verb forms, and (for languages with gender) masculine adjectives. You'll learn to mess around with word forms in Chapter 5.

Formatting

I'm giving you this list in two different formats: a thematic list and an alphabetical list. The thematic list is much friendlier on the eyes: you'll see colors, foods, locations, occupations, the verbs, the adjectives, and so on. Skim through that list first. There I'll give you a few pointers about how to find the images you need (words like *December* take a bit of finesse). Then, when you're ready to make your flash cards, use the alphabetical list.

I prefer to use an alphabetical list for two reasons: it's easier to use with a dictionary, and it teaches you your words in the best possible order: randomly.

Order matters. In grammar books, we learn words in thematic order. We learn colors, articles of clothing, and numbers, one lesson at a time. This feels comfortable, but it makes words much harder to remember. They get mixed up. Is *sept* the word for "six" or "seven"? Was *jaune* the word for "green" or "yellow"? You can minimize this problem if you learn *green* and *seven* now and *yellow* and *six* later. You'll accomplish this automatically if you look up your words alphabetically, since the foreign language translations for an alphabetical list of English words aren't going to be in *any* recognizable order.

To save time, find your words in the glossary of your grammar book or in the little dictionary at the end of a pocket phrasebook. These are in alphabetical order, like a normal dictionary, but they're not full of synonyms or thousands of words you don't need. Just go through and mark off the 625 words as you find them. Any time a word is missing, skip it. Within a half hour, you'll have a giant list of useful words to learn. Then open up Google Images and get cracking.

A couple of tips:

First, there are three types of words that you'll find most easily in a *chapter* of your grammar book rather than the glossary: personal pronouns (e.g., *I, you, he, she, we*), numbers (e.g., *1, 2, 3, 1st, 2nd, 3rd*), and dates (e.g., *January, February, March, Monday, Tuesday, Wednesday*). You'll find reference to these in the table of contents or index of your book. When you want to learn these words, find these sections of your book, read through them and then make your flash cards.

Second, when you learn your words, keep in mind that you're not restricted to a single picture per word. You can use two or three pictures to help identify a word, and you can even add text. We're avoiding English, but that doesn't prevent you from adding names, numbers, and symbols to your cards. When learning the word for "friend," for example, you can write a friend's name under the picture. You can use numbers and symbols for many abstract words (e.g., 1 *minuto* = 60 *segundo*, parent = *papa/maman*). I've included suggestions of this sort when appropriate and marked off two special types of words (categories and easily confounded images), which I discuss in depth in the Four Special Scenarios section of the Second Gallery (page 199).

If you prefer to copy and paste your words into an online dictionary, you can download both of these lists online at *Fluent-Forever.com/appendix5*. In my experience, though, it's faster and easier to use a paper glossary or a little Lonely Planet Phrasebook.

Alternatively, I'm commissioning professional translations of this list in a bunch of common languages. You'll find those translations at the link above.

Your First 625 (in Thematic Order, with Notes)

KEY

Category words (e.g., animal) are designated with a little superscript c (^{c}). Learn these words by using two to three other pictures/words on your flash cards (e.g., animal = dog, cat, fish . . .). Check out the Four Special Scenarios section of the Second Gallery (page 199) to see an example.

Easily confounded images (e.g., "girl" looks just like "daughter") are designated with an asterisk (*). These are groups of words that will use very similar images (girl/daughter, marriage/wedding). Learn these words by adding a personal touch (e.g., the name of a daughter you might know) or an additional word or two in your target language (e.g., *daughter* might go with *mother/father*). Again, see the Four Special Scenarios section of the Second Gallery for examples.

ADJECTIVES: long, short (vs. long), tall, short (vs. tall), wide, narrow, big/large, small/little, slow, fast, hot, cold, warm, cool, new, old (new), young, old (young), good, bad, wet, dry, sick, healthy, loud, quiet, happy, sad, beautiful, ugly, deaf, blind, nice, mean, rich, poor, thick, thin, expensive, cheap, flat, curved, male, female, tight, loose, high, low, soft, hard, deep, shallow, clean, dirty, strong, weak, dead, alive, heavy, light (heavy), dark, light (dark), nuclear, famous

Note: For a few of these adjectives, you may need to learn your language's word for "adjective" and add it in cases of ambiguity (e.g., *to clean* vs. a *clean* room).

ANIMALS: dog, cat, fish, bird, cow, pig, mouse, horse, wing, animal[c]

ART: band, song, instrument (musical), music, movie, art

BEVERAGES: coffee, tea, wine, beer, juice, water, milk, beverage[c]

BODY: head, neck, face, beard, hair, eye, mouth*, lip*, nose, tooth, ear, tear (drop), tongue, back, toe, finger, foot, hand, leg, arm, shoulder, heart, blood, brain, knee, sweat, disease, bone, voice, skin, body

CLOTHING: hat, dress, suit, skirt, shirt, T-shirt, pants, shoes, pocket, coat, stain, clothing[c]

COLORS: red, green, blue (light/dark), yellow, brown, pink, orange, black, white, gray, color[c]

DAYS OF THE WEEK: Monday, Tuesday, Wednesday, Thursday, Friday, Saturday, Sunday

Note: You'll usually find pictures of people going to work on Mondays and partying on Fridays/Saturdays, and so on. To get more specific, use an image of a weekly calendar with weekends grayed out and indicate which day you want. I have an English-free one at *Fluent-Forever.com/appendix5*.

DIRECTIONS: top, bottom, side, front, back, outside, inside, up, down, left, right, straight, north, south, east, west, direction[c]

Note: You may not find all of these in your glossary, and you may have trouble finding pictures even if you do. That's fine. Skip them for now, or use my collection of images for directions and prepositions at *Fluent-Forever.com/appendix5.*

ELECTRONICS: clock, lamp, fan, cell phone, network, computer, program (computer), laptop, screen, camera, television, radio

FOODS: egg, cheese, bread, soup, cake, chicken, pork, beef, apple, banana, orange, lemon, corn, rice, oil, seed, knife, spoon, fork, plate, cup, breakfast, lunch, dinner, sugar, salt, bottle, food[c]

HOME: table, chair, bed, dream, window, door, bedroom, kitchen, bathroom, pencil, pen, photograph, soap, book, page, key, paint, letter, note, wall, paper, floor, ceiling, roof, pool, lock, telephone, garden, yard, needle, bag, box, gift, card, ring, tool

JOBS: Teacher, student, lawyer, doctor, patient, waiter, secretary, priest, police, army, soldier, artist, author, manager, reporter, actor, job[c]

LOCATIONS: city, house, apartment, street/road, airport, train station, bridge, hotel, restaurant, farm, court, school, office, room, town, university, club, bar, park, camp, store/shop, theater, library, hospital, church, market, country (United States, France, etc.), building, ground, space (outer space), bank, location[c]

MATERIALS: glass, metal, plastic, wood, stone, diamond, clay, dust, gold, copper, silver, material[c]

MATH/MEASUREMENTS: meter, centimeter, kilogram, inch, foot, pound, half, circle, square, temperature, date, weight, edge, corner

MISCELLANEOUS NOUNS: map, dot, consonant, vowel, light, sound, yes, no, piece, pain, injury, hole, image, pattern, noun[c], verb[c], adjective[c]

Note: Use these last three (noun, verb, adjective) as labels to help distinguish between very similar-looking words (e.g., *to die* [verb], *death* [noun], *dead* [adjective])

MONTHS: January, February, March, April, May, June, July, August, September, October, November, December

Note: You'll usually find pictures of holidays and weather. Add in the number of each month (1–12) to get more specific.

NATURE: sea*, ocean*, river, mountain, rain, snow, tree, sun, moon, world, Earth, forest, sky, plant, wind, soil/earth, flower, valley, root, lake, star, grass, leaf, air, sand, beach, wave, fire, ice, island, hill, heat, nature[c]

NUMBERS: 0, 1, 2, 3, 4, 5, 6, 7, 8, 9, 10, 11, 12, 13, 14, 15, 16, 17, 18, 19, 20, 21, 22, 30, 31, 32, 40, 41, 42, 50, 51, 52, 60, 61, 62, 70, 71, 72, 80, 81, 82, 90, 91, 92, 100, 101, 102, 110, 111, 1000, 1001, 10000, 100000, million, billion, 1st, 2nd, 3rd, 4th, 5th, number[c]

Note: If you search for a number (*uno* [one], *dos* [two], *tres* [three]), you'll find pictures of objects (1 apple, 2 monkeys, etc.). This usually works until ten. Then search for the digits (e.g., 10, 11, 12). You'll find colorful numerals, address signs, and so on. Use these images (picture of hotel room 33) instead of text (33); these pictures are easier to remember and they don't get mixed up as easily.

PEOPLE: son*, daughter*, mother, father, parent (= mother/father), baby, man, woman, brother*, sister*, family, grandfather, grandmother, husband*, wife*, king, queen, president, neighbor, boy, girl, child (= boy/girl), adult (= man/woman), human (≠ animal), friend (add a friend's name), victim, player, fan, crowd, person[c]

PRONOUNS: I, you (singular), he, she, it, we, you (plural, as in "y'all"), they

Note: Make sure you read about these in your grammar book before adding them. Languages divide their pronouns into many categories. Hungarian, for instance, has *six* words for "you" (singular informal, singular formal [for acquaintances], singular official [for teachers, policemen, bureaucrats], plural informal, etc.), and depending upon how you count, Japanese either has *no* pronouns or *tons* of pronouns. We'll need to have some pronouns *now* in order to deal with grammar *later*, so you'll want to find at least a few words to refer to yourself or someone else. You'll find a good explanation of pronouns (and a list of them) in the beginning of your grammar book. Note that you don't yet need *him*, *her*, *his*, *their*, and so on. We'll get them later, when we discuss grammar.

How do you learn these without translations? Use pictures of people pointing at themselves/each other. I have a collection of these at *Fluent-Forever.com/appendix5* if your Google Image searches don't turn up anything good. Use these images, and if your language, like Hungarian, has different sorts of pronouns for different sorts of relationships (e.g., to distinguish friends from acquaintances), then take a few minutes to think of some people you'd use these pronouns with. Use their names on your flash cards.

SEASONS: summer, spring, winter, fall, season[c]

SOCIETY: religion, heaven, hell, death, medicine, money, dollar, bill, marriage*, wedding*, team, race (ethnicity), sex (the act), sex (gender), murder, prison, technology, energy, war, peace, attack, election, magazine, newspaper, poison, gun, sport, race (sport), exercise, ball, game, price, contract, drug, sign, science, God

TIME: year, month, week, day, hour, minute, second, morning, afternoon, evening, night, time[c]

Note: You'll find pictures of clocks and calendars. If needed, define each time division in terms of another time division (e.g., 60 *minuto* = 1 ___ (*ora*), 1 *ora* = 60 ___ (*minuto*). Don't worry about plural forms (you don't need the word for "minutes" yet).

TRANSPORTATION: train, plane, car, truck, bicycle, bus, boat, ship, tire, gasoline, engine, (train) ticket, transportation[c]

VERBS: work, play, walk, run, drive, fly, swim, go[c], stop, follow, think, speak/say, eat, drink, kill, die, smile, laugh, cry, buy*, pay*, sell*, shoot (a gun), learn, jump, smell, hear* (a sound), listen* (music), taste, touch, see (a bird), watch (TV), kiss, burn, melt, dig, explode, sit, stand, love, pass by, cut, fight, lie down, dance, sleep, wake up, sing, count, marry, pray, win, lose, mix/stir, bend, wash, cook, open, close, write, call, turn, build, teach, grow, draw, feed, catch, throw, clean, find, fall, push, pull, carry, break, wear, hang, shake, sign, beat, lift

Note: For verbs, you'll probably need to learn your language's word for "verb" and add it to any verb that could masquerade as a noun (*to kiss* vs. *a kiss*). I give you guidelines for this in the Four Special Scenarios section of the Second Gallery (page 199).

Your First 625 (in Alphabetical Order)

The first entries for each letter are in bold.

actor	afternoon	alive	apple
adjective	air	animal	April
adult	airport	apartment	arm

army	bed	box (noun)	cat
art	bedroom	boy	catch (verb)
artist	beef	brain	ceiling
attack (noun)	beer	bread	cell phone
August	bend (verb)	break (verb)	centimeter
author (noun)	beverage	breakfast	chair (noun)
baby	bicycle	bridge (noun)	cheap
back (body)	big/large	brother	cheese
back (direction)	bill (noun)	brown	chicken
bad	billion	build (verb)	child
bag (noun)	bird	building	church
ball	black	burn (verb)	circle (noun)
banana	blind (adjective)	bus	city
band (music)	blood	buy (verb)	clay
bank	blue	**cake**	clean (adjective)
bar (location)	boat	call (verb)	clean (verb)
bathroom	body	camera	clock
beach	bone	camp (noun)	close (verb)
beard	book	car	clothing
beat (verb)	bottle	card	club (the location)
beautiful	bottom	carry (verb)	coat (noun)

coffee	dark	down	energy
cold	date (May 7)	draw (verb)	engine
color (noun)	daughter	dream (noun)	evening
computer	day	dress (noun)	exercise (noun)
consonant	dead	drink (verb)	expensive
contract (noun)	deaf	drive (verb)	explode (verb)
cook (verb)	death	drug (noun)	eye (noun)
cool (adjective)	December	dry	**face** (noun)
copper	deep	dust (noun)	fall (season)
corn	diamond	**ear**	fall (verb)
corner (noun)	die (verb)	Earth	family
count (verb)	dig (verb)	east	famous
country (United States, Spain)	dinner	eat (verb)	fan (electric)
court	direction	edge	fan (sport)
cow	dirty	egg	farm (noun)
crowd (noun)	disease	eight	fast
cry (verb)	doctor	eighteen	father
cup	dog	eighty	February
curved	dollar	election	feed (verb)
cut (verb)	door	electronics	female
dance (verb)	dot	eleven	fifteen

fifth (5th)	fourteen	grow (verb)	horse
fifty	fourth (4th)	gun	hospital
fight (verb)	Friday	**hair**	hot
find (verb)	friend	half	hotel
finger	front	hand	hour
fire (noun)	**game**	hang (verb)	house
first (1st)	garden	happy	human
fish (noun)	gasoline	hard	hundred
five	gift	hat	husband
flat (adjective)	girl	he	**I**
floor	glass	head	ice
flower	go (verb)	healthy	image
fly (verb)	God	hear (a sound)	inch
follow (verb)	gold	heart	injury
food	good	heat (noun)	inside
foot (body part)	grandfather	heaven	instrument (musical)
foot (measurement)	grandmother	heavy	island
forest	grass	hell	it
fork	gray	high	**January**
forty	green	hill	job
four	ground	hole	juice

July	library	March	mouse
jump (verb)	lie down (verb)	market	mouth
June	lift (verb)	marriage	movie
key	light (/dark)	marry (verb)	murder (noun)
kill (verb)	light (/heavy)	material	music
kilogram	light (noun)	May	**narrow**
king	lip	mean (/nice)	nature
kiss (verb)	listen (music) (verb)	medicine	neck
kitchen	location	melt (verb)	needle
knee	lock (noun)	metal	neighbor
knife	long	meter	network
lake	loose	milk	new
lamp	lose (verb)	million	newspaper
laptop	loud	minute	nice
laugh (verb)	love (verb)	mix/stir (verb)	night
lawyer	low	Monday	nine
leaf	lunch	money	nineteen
learn (verb)	**magazine**	month	ninety
left (direction)	male	moon	no
leg	man	morning	north
lemon	manager	mother	nose
letter	map	mountain	note (on paper)

November	pass (verb)	pool	restaurant
nuclear	patient (noun)	poor	rice
number	pattern	pork	rich
ocean	pay (verb)	pound (weight)	right (direction)
October	peace	pray (verb)	ring
office	pen	president	river
oil	pencil	price	roof
old (/new)	person	priest	room (in a house)
old (/young)	photograph	prison	root
one	piece	program (computer)	run (verb)
open (verb)	pig	pull (verb)	**sad**
orange (color)	pink	push (verb)	salt
orange (food)	plane	**queen**	sand
outside	plant (noun)	quiet	Saturday
page	plastic	**race (ethnicity)**	school
pain	plate	race (sport)	science
paint	play (verb)	radio	screen
pants	player	rain (noun)	sea
paper	pocket	red	season
parent	poison (noun)	religion	second (2nd)
park (location)	police	reporter	second (time)

secretary	side	soil/earth	strong
see (a bird)	sign (noun)	soldier	student
seed	sign (verb)	son	sugar
sell (verb)	silver	song	suit (noun)
September	sing (verb)	sound	summer
seven	sister	soup	sun
seventeen	sit (verb)	south	Sunday
seventy	six	space (outer space)	sweat (noun)
sex (gender)	sixteen	speak/say (verb)	swim (verb)
sex (the act)	sixty	spoon	**T-shirt**
shake (verb)	skin	sport	table
shallow	skirt	spring (season)	tall
she	sky	square	taste (verb)
ship	sleep (verb)	stain	tea
shirt	slow	stand (verb)	teach (verb)
shoes	small/little	star	teacher
shoot (a gun)	smell (verb)	stone	team
short (long)	smile (verb)	stop (verb)	tear (drop)
short (vs. tall)	snow (noun)	store/shop	technology
shoulder	soap	straight	telephone
sick	soft	street/road	television

temperature	tooth	voice (noun)	white
ten	top	vowel	wide
theater	touch (verb)	**waiter**	wife
they	town	wake up (verb)	win (verb)
thick	train (noun)	walk (verb)	wind (noun)
thin	train station	wall	window
think (verb)	transportation	war	wine
third (3rd)	tree	warm (adjective)	wing
thirteen	truck	wash (verb)	winter
thirty	Tuesday	watch (TV) (verb)	woman
thousand	turn (verb)	water (noun)	wood
three	twelve	wave (ocean)	work (verb)
throw (verb)	twenty	we	world
Thursday	twenty-one (etc.)	weak	write (verb)
ticket (train)	two	wear (verb)	**yard**
tight	**ugly**	wedding	year
time (noun)	university	Wednesday	yellow
tire (of a car)	up	week	yes
toe	**valley**	weight	you (singular/ plural)
tongue	verb	west	young
tool	victim	wet (adj.)	zero

My goal throughout this book is to show you how to learn a language on your own. But what if you're already enrolled in a language class? Many of my recommendations are at odds with standard classroom fare: I'm not a big fan of translation exercises, and I don't think that endless grammar drills are a great use of your time. So should you quit? Sit in the back and secretly make flash cards? Hand your teacher this book and demand that they redesign their class accordingly?

Or is there something to be gained from standard classroom language courses?

In the first chapter of this book, I made a claim: no one can give you a language; you have to take it for yourself. I stand by that claim. No language course will teach you a language on its own, nor will any grammar book, tutor, girlfriend, or computer program. Every language-learning resource is just that: a resource. In the end, *you* have to take those resources, wrap your brain around them, and turn them into a living language.

So, while I think that there are some things that can be *improved* in typical classroom courses, I think the exact same thing about typical grammar books and dictionaries and phrase books. Hell, there are a few things that could be improved in Google Images and Anki, for that matter.

What About "Bad" Classes?

If you *don't* particularly like your teacher or your class, then there's no reason to stay in it (unless it's required, in which case you can probably pass out of it on your own). Just keep one thing in mind: you may discover that you enjoy language classes *much* more once you start using flash cards to remember everything anyone says. Try that out, and if you still dislike your class, then drop it and study on your own.

But I've never told you to throw away your grammar book, and I'm not going to tell you to quit your language class.[23] Quite the opposite, in fact: as long as your teacher is any good and you're enjoying yourself, your class is a *wonderful* resource. Stay in it. It's like a walking, talking grammar book. Every time you show up, you're exposed to a bunch of new grammar rules and example sentences, you hear words and sentences spoken aloud and acted out, you get to try out new patterns in spoken and written exercises, and you even get corrected homework assignments and tests (both of which are *pure grammatical gold*, from my perspective).

When you're in a class, your primary goal should be to take the information you receive and stick it into your own head. Use illustrated flash cards. If you encounter a new grammar rule, get some example sentences (if need be, ask your teacher) and create flash cards accordingly, so that you never forget the rules. If you get corrections on your homework assignments, turn *those* into flash cards, so that you don't make the same mistakes ever again.

If you do this, and if you review those flash cards on a daily basis, you'll find that you progress *much* faster than your peers. Your class is going to get very easy, and as a result, you'll have more time to devote to your own, personal language goals—learning vocabulary, reading books, watching TV, and so on—while your language class continues to spoon feed you information.

Whenever I'm taking a class and there's a wireless Internet connection handy (for accessing Google Images), I'll often take my notes directly into

---

23. To be fair, I suppose I *did* tell you to throw away your grammar book, but only if it used *bawn-JURE*-style pronunciation entries.

Anki. I'll make flash cards for everything we discuss, and within a few weeks, I'll have memorized basically every word the teacher has ever said.

This strategy makes you feel *really, really* clever, and it's a great way to use your classroom time efficiently. When you know how to teach yourself a language, a good language class is a true luxury; savor every minute of it.

ONE LAST NOTE (ABOUT TECHNOLOGY)

The techniques described in this book take advantage of many Internet-based tools, all of which have a tendency to change, break, or improve from month to month. If you try to use one of these tools and find that it doesn't behave the way it should, go here: *Fluent-Forever.com/changes*.

I'll use that page to keep track of any drastic changes (and provide alternative tools if needed).

Chapter 1. Introduction: Stab, Stab, Stab

8   **English vocabulary is 28 percent French and 28 percent Latin:** How can I possibly separate French words from Latin words, when French comes from Latin? English picked up words from these languages in two big waves. Most of the French words came into English in the eleventh century during the Norman Conquest. The Latinate words came later, along with the Greek ones during the Renaissance. No matter what, if you're learning a romantic language like French, you'll recognize an enormous number of words from English.

Chapter 2. Upload: Five Principles to End Forgetting

20   **They were identified in the 1970s:** If you'd like to read more about Levels of Processing, there are two articles you should check out. The first provides a nice overview of the research in general, and the second delves a bit deeper into the mnemonic advantages of Personal Connection (also known as the Self-Reference Effect): Robert S. Lockhart and Fergus I. M. Craik, "Levels of Processing: A Retrospective Commentary on a Framework for Memory Research," *Canadian Journal of Psychology* 44, no. 1 (1990): 87–112; Cynthia S. Symons and Blair T. Johnson, "The Self-Reference Effect in Memory: A Meta-Analysis," *CHIP Documents* (1997): Paper 9.

25   **This effect even applies to totally unrelated images:** Note that a related image works better, so if you need to learn the word *apple*, you might as well grab a picture of an apple. Also note that if the image is the *opposite* of what you're learning (if you're learning *hot* with a picture of an ice cube), you're going to have a *harder* time remembering that combination. The best summary of this stuff comes from the following article: W. H. Levie and S. N. Hathaway, "Picture Recognition Memory: A Review of Research and Theory," *Journal of Visual/Verbal Languaging* 8 no. 1 (1988): 6–45.

27   **Hermann Ebbinghaus:** Ebbinghaus's 1885 study earned praise from contemporaries and modern psychology historians alike. William James—the father of American psychology—referred to Ebbinghaus's work as "really heroic" in his book *Principles of Psychology* (James, William. *The Principles of Psychology*. New York: Dover Publications, 1950). And the already quoted "single most important investigation" comes from Duane Schultz's textbook, *A History of Modern Psychology* (Schultz, Duane P., and Sydney Ellen Schultz, *A History of Modern Psychology*. Australia: Thomson/Wadsworth, 2012). If you'd like to read about Ebbinghaus's "exhaustion, headache and other symptoms" directly from the source, his study has been translated into English by Henry Ruger and Clara Bussenius (Ebbinghaus, Hermann. *Memory: A Contribution to Experimental Psychology*. Translated by Henry Alford Ruger and Clara E. Bussenius. New York City: Teachers College, Columbia University, 1913).

30   **Two different study schemes:** There is *so* much research on testing and studying that it's hard to point you in one particular direction. If I were you (and if I wanted to learn more), I'd start with Henry L. Roediger and Jeffrey D. Karpicke, "The Power of Testing Memory: Basic Research and Implications for Educational Practice," *Perspectives on Psychological Science* 1, no. 3 (2006): 181–210. Roediger and Karpicke summarize *most* of the research, and they do it in a (relatively) friendly way.

Chapter 3. Sound Play

58   **The best data we have on this process come from studies of Americans and the Japanese:** Patricia Kuhl is my favorite researcher in this field, and her TEDx talk "The Linguistic Genius of Babies" (see http://tinyurl.com/TEDKuhl) is a wonderful, accessible introduction to this line of research.

60   **The most promising research in this field comes from a collection of studies:** To read up on this, start with James L. McClelland, Julie A. Fiez, and Bruce D. McCandliss, "Teaching the /r/–/l/ Discrimination to Japanese Adults: Behavioral and Neural Aspects," *Physiology & Behavior* 77.4 (2002): 657–662. It's a fascinating study, and their results are really impressive. They brought Japanese adults from terrible (roughly 50 percent) accuracy all the way up to 70–80

percent accuracy in differentiating their locks from their rocks. The research subjects didn't hear the L-R distinction as accurately as a native speaker (and after interviewing the researchers, it became clear that they're pretty bummed about that), but from a language learning standpoint, it's a huge deal.

72 **English operates under (a large set of) dependable rules:** You can find a cool breakdown of the English spelling rules into fifty-six simple rules at *Zompist .com/spell.html*. If you blindly follow these rules, you can accurately predict the pronunciation of *any* English word with 85 percent accuracy. Not bad for a language with seven different ways to pronounce "ough" (tough, cough, plough, though, thought, through, and hiccough).

Chapter 4. Word Play and the Symphony of a Word

106 **When forming images, it helps to have a dirty mind:** Joshua Foer's book is a wonderfully written tour through the human mind, not to mention a *fabulous* story (Foer, Joshua. *Moonwalking with Einstein: The Art and Science of Remembering Everything.* New York: Penguin, 2011). Highly, highly recommended.

Chapter 5. Sentence Play

110 **There's a subtle grammar rule operating here:** You might note that "mouse-infested" doesn't sound terrible, and indeed, Google NGrams (*books.google .com/ngrams/*) shows roughly similar amounts of mice-infested and mouse-infested stories in English literature. Irregular plurals seem to sound fine either way. However, with regular plurals, the rules become totally rigid. "Rats-infested" just doesn't exist in English.

111 **If you ask linguists how kids do this, most of them will tell you about a language-learning machine hidden within the brain of every child:** The inventor of the language machine theory, Noam Chomsky, calls it a "language acquisition device." Chomsky's device explains two phenomena: why kids are so good at learning grammar and why the grammar of every language is so weirdly similar. All seven thousand documented languages, for example, seem to possess subjects, verbs, and objects. And if a language puts its objects *after* its verbs (He eats *fish*), then that language will use prepositions (*from* the sea). If, on the other hand, verbs come after their objects (He fish *eats*), then that language will use postpositions (the sea *from*). There are a few languages that break these rules, but they're rare—much too rare for mere chance. It's as if every language starts with the same overarching grammatical system and, with a few slight tweaks, turns that system into French, English, or Chinese.

If Chomsky is right, then kids can talk about *rat-eaters* because they're genetically preprogrammed with *every* language's grammar—they come into the world already knowing the overarching grammatical system behind every language. Then they just listen to their parents, flick a few switches on their language acquisition device ("Verb, then object?" "Object, then verb?"), and poof, they know which grammar they're supposed to use.

Other linguists will point out that *Europeans* have made most linguistic observations, and that they've overlooked the tremendous diversity of non-European languages. If only they looked closer, they'd find hundreds of languages that defy the standard grammatical patterns. To fit *all* of these languages, we'd need language acquisition devices preprogrammed with an *enormous* amount of information. Perhaps kids are just good at inferring patterns.

If you'd like to get a good feel for Chomsky's side of the story, check out Steven Pinker's wonderful book, *The Language Instinct: How the Mind Creates Language.* New York: HarperPerennial, 2010. If you'd like to check out the other side of the debate, read Nicholas Evans and Stephen C. Levinson, "The Myth of Language Universals: Language Diversity and Its Importance for Cognitive Science," *Behavioral and Brain Sciences* 32, no. 05 (2009): 429–448.

114   **No amount of drilling a particular grammar rule . . . will enable a student to skip a developmental stage:** Note that these developmental stages don't prevent you from memorizing and using a few phrases with relatively advanced grammar. You could learn a phrase like "Would you like some coffee?" within your first few weeks of studying English, even though it contains *would*, the (difficult) English conditional form. Still, that doesn't mean you'll correctly spit out "would" in any other contexts until you've reached the proper developmental stage.

114   **On average, adults learn languages** *faster* **than kids do:** This fact blew my mind. Check out Ortega, Lourdes. *Understanding Second Language Acquisition.* London: Hodder Education, 2009, for a lovely summary of the differences and similarities between child and adult language learning.

130   **There's one last tool at your disposal, and it's where everything comes together: output:** Lourdes Ortega does a good job of summarizing the research on output in her aforementioned book. Basically, research seems to indicate that input is necessary, but not sufficient for successful language learning. While you can learn to *comprehend* a language very well using input alone, you need output to learn how to *produce* it well. (You also need to *care* about the quality of your output; there's a fascinating case study in Ortega's book in which a Japanese man is perfectly happy speaking in broken English, so he never improves, even though he's hanging out with English native speakers all the time and speaking in English constantly.)

Chapter 6. The Language Game

152 **Practically speaking, we'll automatically learn an unknown word 10 percent of the time:** If you'd like to learn more about the benefits of reading (and how well we learn from context), check out W. E. Nagy, P. A. Herman, and R. C. Anderson, "Learning Words from Context," *Reading Research Quarterly* 20 (1985): 233–253.

Chapter 7. Epilogue: The Benefits and Pleasures of Learning a Language

171 **Recent studies show that you don't need to be bilingual from birth:** This is from a little article in the neuroscience journal *NeuroImage:* Johan Mårtensson, et al, "Growth of Language-Related Brain Areas After Foreign Language Learning," *Neuroimage* 63 (2012): 240–244. It's some of the very first confirmation that second language learning and bilingualism from birth look *very* similar from a physiological standpoint.

171 **They're more creative:** If you want to really jump into bilingual superpowers, start with the introduction to Reza Kormi-Nouri, et al, "The Effect of Childhood Bilingualism on Episodic and Semantic Memory Tasks," *Scandinavian Journal of Psychology* 49, no. 2 (2008): 93–109. It provides a nice, quick overview of all sorts of research on the problem solving and creative capabilities of bilinguals.

172 **On average, elderly bilinguals will show symptoms of dementia five years later:** There are all sorts of cool studies on this, but one of the most interesting ones is Gitit Kavé, et al, "Multilingualism and Cognitive State in the Oldest Old," *Psychology and Aging* 23, no. 1 (2008): 70–78. It looked at the number of languages each person knew, how well they knew them, and all sorts of neat things.

Appendix 4

280 **"Trying to choke yourself with your own throat":** This is a quote from a *delightful* YouTube video about A'yn (see *http://tinyurl.com/arabicayn*). The teacher, Maha, is a bit mistaken when it comes to the position of A'yn (it's even farther back in the throat than the uvula), but she does a *wonderful* job of teaching you how to make the sound, and her enthusiasm is infectious.

ACKNOWLEDGMENTS

There is only one name on the cover of this book, and I find that ridiculous. Yes, I wrote it. Yes, this book is a reflection of me and my experiences. But this is not *my* book. Every single word and every single step along this journey has been shaped by others. My family, my friends, my colleagues, my teachers, my community: you've made me what I am and this book what it is, and for that, you have my eternal gratitude. In particular, I'd like to thank Melanie Henley Heyn. This book is a testament to the adventures that she and I shared. It would not exist without her or be nearly as good without her courageous editing and support.

As for the others, I'll start at the beginning. In 2003, my friend Rob Istad casually recommended a German immersion program that would eventually start this whole journey. Thanks for that; it's been quite the ride.

This book was sold thanks to the support of Melanie Pinola and the Lifehacker team; the input of Brette Popper, Karen Schrock Simring, and Gretl Satorius on the proposal; and the torrent of passion, knowledge, and all-around kick-assery that continuously pours out of my agent, Lisa DiMona.

Rick Horgan, my editor, tore me and this book to pieces, and I cannot thank him enough for the experience. Without his brutal honesty, this book would be *terrible*. Seriously.

Andrea Henley Heyn is the best first reader I could have hoped for. Her patience and keen sense of structure made this book a *lot* more sensible to people who don't live inside of my head. Additional thanks to Colette Ballew and Meghen Miles Tuttle. Your input was invaluable.

Last but not least, to friend and video editor extraordinaire Nick Martin, and to my dear Kickstarter backers: I love you all. I'd like to especially thank Joel Mullins, Marc Levin, Mike Forster, Mike Wells, Nikhil Srinivasan, and Xavier Mercier for their extraordinary support.

Together, you've allowed me to take a book and a few ideas, and turn them into a system with all the bells and whistles I could have hoped for. Thank you.

INDEX

Bold numbers refer to a detailed description of a tool or concept.